ORIGIN AND GROWTH OF MODERN POLITICS:
A Study of Political Concepts

ORIGIN AND GROWTH OF MODERN POLITICS:

A STUDY OF POLITICAL CONCEPTS

Dr. L. K. Garg

SWASTIK

SWASTIK PUBLICATIONS

DELHI-110094 (INDIA)

SWASTIK PUBLICATIONS
31 Gali No. 1, A Block, Pocket 5, CRP Water Tank,
Sonia Vihar, Delhi-110094
Cell: 9968482939, 9899462604
e-mail: swastik_books@yahoo.com

ORIGIN AND GROWTH OF MODERN POLITICS:
A STUDY OF POLITICAL CONCEPTS

First Published 2012

ISBN:- 978-93-81084-13-7

PRINTED IN INDIA

Published by Indra Mani Pandey for Swastik Publications, Delhi and Printed at Deepak Offset Press, Delhi-32

PREFACE

Democracy has its origins in Ancient Greece. However other cultures have significantly contributed to the evolution of democracy such as Ancient Rome, Europe, and North and South America. The concept of representative democracy arose largely from ideas and institutions that developed during the European Middle Ages and the Age of Enlightenment and in the American and French Revolutions. Democracy has been called the "last form of government" and has spread considerably across the globe. The right to vote has been expanded in many Jurisdictions over time from relatively narrow groups such as wealthy men of a particular ethnic group, with New Zealand the first nation to grant universal suffrage for all its citizens in 1893.

20th century transitions to liberal democracy have come in successive "waves of democracy," variously resulting from wars, revolutions, decolonization, religious and economic circumstances. World War I and the dissolution of the Ottoman and Austro-Hungarian empires resulted in the creation of new nation-states from Europe, most of them at least nominally democratic.

However, most of Eastern Europe, including the Soviet sector of Germany was forced into the non-democratic Soviet bloc. The war was followed by decolonization, and again most of the new independent states had nominally democratic constitutions. India emerged as the world's largest democracy and continues to be so. By 1960, the vast majority of country-states were nominally democracies, although the majority of the world's populations lived in nations that experienced sham elections, and other forms of subterfuge (particularly in Communist nations and the former colonies.)

A subsequent wave of democratization brought substantial gains towards true liberal democracy for many nations. Spain, Portugal (1974), and several of the military dictatorships in South America returned to civilian rule in the late 1970s and early 1980s (Argentina in

1983, Bolivia, Uruguay in 1984, Brazil in 1985, and Chile in the early 1990s). This was followed by nations in East and South Asia by the mid-to-late 1980s.

Economic malaise in the 1980s, along with resentment of communist oppression, contributed to the collapse of the Soviet Union, the associated end of the Cold War, and the democratization and liberalization of the former Eastern bloc countries. The most successful of the new democracies were those geographically and culturally closest to western Europe, and they are now members or candidate members of the European Union. Some researchers consider that in contemporary Russia there is no real democracy and one of forms of dictatorship takes place. The liberal trend spread to some nations in Africa in the 1990s, most prominently in South Africa. Some recent examples of attempts of liberalization include the Indonesian Revolution of 1998, the Bulldozer Revolution in Yugoslavia, the Rose Revolution in Georgia, the Orange Revolution in Ukraine, the Cedar Revolution in Lebanon, and the Tulip Revolution in Kyrgyzstan.

Currently, there are 123 countries that are democratic (up from 40 in 1972). As such, it has been speculated that this trend may continue in the future to the point where liberal democratic nation-states become the universal standard form of human society. This prediction forms the core of Francis Fukayama's "End of History" controversial theory. These theories are criticized by those who fear an evolution of liberal democracies to post-democracy, and other who points out the high number of illiberal democracies.

This book is a comprehensive study of modern democratic developments and concepts that has emerged with the requirement of time. Extremely useful for the students and academicians of political science this is a huge source of reference.

Author

CONTENTS

1

The Origin, Development, and Possible Decline of the Modern State

A political system is a system of politics and government. It is usually compared to the legal system, economic system, cultural system, and other social systems. It is different from them, and can be generally defined on a spectrum from left, *e.g.* communism, to the right, *e.g.* fascism.

However, this is a very simplified view of a much more complex system of categories involving the views: who should have authority, how religious questions should be handled, and what the government's influence on its people and economy should be.

There are several definitions of "political system":

- A political system is a complete set of institutions, interest groups (such as political parties, trade unions, lobby groups), the relationships between those institutions and the political norms and rules that govern their functions (constitution, election law).
- A political system is composed of the members of a social organisation (group) who are in power.
- A political system is a system that necessarily has two properties: a set of interdependent components and boundaries toward the environment with which it interacts.
- A political system is a concept in which theoretically regarded as a way of the government makes a policy and also to make them more organised in their administration.
- A political system is one that ensures the maintaining of order and sanity in the society and at the same time makes it possible

for some other institutions to also have their grievances and complaints put across in the course of social existence.

Commonalities between political systems:

- Interdependent parts
  - o Citizens Culture
  - o Government
- Boundaries
  - o Citizenship
  - o Territory
  - o Property

Basic forms of Political Systems

The following are examples of political systems, some of which are typically mutually exclusive (*e.g.* Monarchy and Republic), while others may (or may not) overlap in various combinations (*e.g.* Democracy and Westminster system, Democracy and Socialism).

- Anarchism (Rule by all/no one)
- Democracy (Rule by majority)
- Monarchy. (Rule by monarch) Monarchies are one of the oldest political systems known, developing from tribal structure with one person the absolute ruler.
- Meritocracy (Rule by best)
- Technocracy (Rule by scientist/intellectuals)
- Republic. (Rule by law) The first recorded republic was in India in the 6th century BC.
- Sultanates. (Rule by Allah) an Islamic political structure combining aspects of Monarchy and Theocracy.
- Islamic Democracy. (Rule by majority in Islamic context) an Islamic and democratic political structure, which combines aspects of Theocracy (as the framework) and Democracy (as the decision making method under Islam's ethical system). Iran's constitution is based on such a system.
- Theocracy (Rule by alleged representative of God)

- Westminster system (rule by republic and representative democracy through parliament)
- Feudalism (Rule by lord/king)

Anthropological Forms of Political Systems

Anthropologists generally recognize four kinds of political systems, two of which are uncentralised and two of which are centralised.

- Uncentralised systems
  - o Band
  - o Tribe
- Centralised systems
  - o Chiefdom
  - o State

Main Differences

- Uncentralised systems
  - o Band
    - i. Small kin group, no larger than an extended family or clan; it has been defined as consisting of no more than 30 to 50 individuals.
    - ii. A band can cease to exist if only a small group walks out.
  - o Tribe
    - i Generally larger, consisting of many families. Tribes have more social institutions, such as a chief, big man, or elders.
    - ii. More permanent than bands; a band can cease to exist if only a small group walks out. Many tribes are sub-divided into bands.
- Centralised systems
  - o Chiefdom

i. More complex than a tribe or a band society, and less complex than a state or a civilisation

ii. Characterised by pervasive inequality and centralisation of authority.

iii. A single lineage/family of the elite class becomes the ruling elite of the chiefdom

- o Complex chiefdoms have two or even three tiers of political hierarchy.
- o "An autonomous political unit comprising a number of villages or communities under the permanent control of a paramount chief"

o State

i. A sovereign state is a state with a permanent population, a defined territory, a government and the capacity to enter into relations with other sovereign states.

Recent scholarship in political science has returned with vigor to examining the origins and development of the modern state. On the one hand, this revival of interest has been due to expectations that the state might have reached its high water mark. Such supranational entities as the European Union, and the increasing powers of such multinational entities as the World Trade Organisation, seem to foreshadow an end to the ultimate authority of national governments. From that perspective, state sovereignty appears to be shifting, albeit imperfectly, to multilateral and supranational levels of authority (Rosenau 1989, Rosenau and Czempiel 1992).

On the other hand, we are daily confronted with states fractionating into multiple entities. Some polities, which once appeared to be coherent territorial units, have broken apart, sometimes with remarkable speed. And these centrifugal tendencies have not been limited to developing states, where one might presuppose that ethnic tensions would have a rich feeding ground in artificial borders imposed by former colonial powers, and in feeble economies. Advanced capitalist and socialist states have not been immune. Few foresaw the demise of the Soviet Union as a federal entity. The Quebecois only narrowly lost a referendum that would have brought Canadian territorial integrity into doubt.

Aggregational dynamics and centrifugal forces seem to uneasily coexist in the post–Cold War world. Some scholars have thus turned to tracing the historical origins and subsequent evolution of the state in the hope that this may shed light on the future of the state and the process through which new logics of organisation may be emerging. Examining the modes of previous transitions might lead to insights concerning current transitions.

Other paradoxes come to mind as well. Some modern states excel in their ability to regulate many spheres of social activity and in their capacity to affect economic outcomes. Many such states are located in regions that have been blessed by a period of "Long Peace." Other states have lacked such abilities, and they have been unable to provide welfare and security to their citizens in regions fraught with peril. Nominally juridically equivalent with other states in the system, they in fact differ markedly from developed countries in their capacity and functions.

Jackson (1987) has aptly described these entities as "quasi-states." Here, a study of different historical trajectories might clarify why such states exist as international legal entities but lack the positive trappings of modern states.

For many years, the study of the state and its origins has been relegated to secondary status. Neo-Marxist arguments, world systems theory, and structural functionalist perspectives accounted for the rise of the state as a response to macro structural changes. Linear and teleological in nature, such theories pictured the modern state as the logical endpoint in the evolutionary development of polities. International relations scholarship too found little reason to examine how states evolved, since structural realism argued that structure fully determined state behavior. Different types of states engaged in similar patterns of behavior. Macro-level patterns and deductive arguments obfuscated a far more complex and diverse pattern of state formation and made closer inspection of state development superfluous.

Such macro-structural accounts have been found wanting. Empirically, they fail to recognize the multiplicity of institutional types that often coexist in any period. Theoretically, they neglect agency, the variant choices that individuals make to pursue their interests given existing constraints and opportunities. Recent scholarship has addressed these deficiencies. It has at once opened up the empirical universe by examining often neglected and alternative institutional arrangements, and it has interjected a micro-level perspective to complement macro-level analyses.

Before entering these discussions, however, modern states must be differentiated from their predecessors. I highlight two features in particular: the capacity of modern states to intervene in their societies, and the principle of international legal sovereignty based on the recognition of domestic sovereignty and the juridical equivalence of states. Both features, though first appearing in the Late Middle Ages, took many centuries to come to fruition. Indeed, the full extension of international legal sovereignty across the globe only came in the wake of World War II.

We then then turn to a discussion of various accounts for the emergence of the modern state and links them to insights about contemporary statehood. Admittedly, this chapter concentrates on materialist accounts, leaving culturalist explanations aside despite their relevance (Ruggie 1993). I do, however, examine the constructivist insights on the origins of the state and the implications of the constructivist challenge for state theory and the study of international relations. Accounts of the origins of the state can be divided into three categories: scholarship that stresses changes in the military environment; economic perspectives that highlight the growth of trade and production; and institutionalist views that accentuate the particular features of territorial sovereignty.

The key argument of this chapter is that although the first two perspectives contain many insights, a micro-level institutionalist perspective forms a necessary complement to macro-level accounts that focus on military and economic functions. Macro-level explanations must take human agency into account. The institutional framework, however, mediates individual choices. I argue for a three-tiered perspective incorporating macro-level variations, institutional constraints and opportunities, and individual preferences and choices given the conditions at the first two levels.

I then examine why contemporary debates in political science have returned to the study of the origins and development of the state. Scholars of comparative politics have turned to such analysis in order to elucidate the various patterns of state formation in developing areas. Students of transition economies have also found value in examining how early modern states constructed market economies, created institutional frameworks that tied rulers' hands, and formalised bureaucratic administration. In international relations, with the waning of structural realist primacy, scholars have started to realize that the nature of the polities in the system, and, hence, the nature of the state, fundamentally affects the structural properties of the system.

DIFFERENTIATING EARLY AND MODERN STATES

Premodern States

Discussing the origins of the state has widely divergent meanings across the various social sciences. For anthropologists, sociologists, and historians, the origins of the state lie in the earliest transitions from tribal or kin-based societies to stratified forms of organisation. Indeed, accounts of state formation become virtually synonymous with accounts of agricultural settlement, civilisation, and recorded history (Mair, 1962). The ability to govern corresponded closely to the ability to keep records, to issue orders, to organize large-scale forces, and to exercise legal authority. Thus, such accounts of state formation might—by examining the Egyptian dynasties, the Mesopotamian region, China, or early Greece (Runciman, 1982)—stress the ability to issue laws and administrative decrees and to create a bureaucracy and army.

At a second level of generalisation, accounts of early state formation tend to emphasize how formal authority structures replaced personalistic rule. The ability to command individuals who were not blood relatives enabled rulers to expand their domains over much larger population bases and territories. This required, however, alternative modes of legitimation. Blood ties of the clan, tribe, or kin group were relatively obvious. But how could one bind others to one's rule? Rulers needed to expand conceptions of tribal affinity and grant others the means to join. The ascriptive markers used to delineate membership and authority had to be replaced with associational criteria if the polity wished to transcend its temporal boundaries (legitimate rule would then attach to roles rather than individuals) and to expand its geographical frontiers (the polity could then incorporate more potential members).

As Doyle (1986) suggests, the Roman willingness to expand its basis of rule from tribal affinity to associational citizenship, and to extend that citizenship to all parts of the empire, greatly aided the long-term viability of Roman imperial rule. One might similarly explore the earliest formations of polities in the Middle East and East Asia (Mann 1986).

This separation of personal connections between ruler and ruled, however, requires a second transformation before rule becomes fully formalised and abstract. In early states, even when rulers and ruled were not personally related, rulers still governed people. Clovis the Merovingian, who ruled the Frankish empire in the late fifth century, ruled as "King of the Franks." Less than a millennium later, however, the Capetians were considered "Kings of France," that is, rulers of a fixed and defined territory (Claesen 1985). In the Early Middle Ages, one spoke of Rex Anglorum (King of the English), but by the Late Middle Ages, he had become Rex Anglie (King of England). Similarly, the systems of law that emerged in the wake of the Roman Empire specified the group for whom that law was meant. The "Lex Burgundium" applied to Burgundians, wherever they might be. Authority attached to people, not to a defined geographical area. But by the Late Middle Ages, systems of law started to emerge that were demarcated by territorial parameters.

Thus, a variety of key features distinguish early states from the variants that we knowtoday (Claesen 1985, p. 212). Most forms of early statehood revolved around some form of kingship and the relationship between the king and his retinue. Kings and aristocracy acted within a reciprocal set of obligations: The king's retinue remained loyal as long as he succeeded in war and could distribute booty. The exercise of authority flowed from loyalty to the king as a person, rather than to the kingship as a public function. Such early states had only weakly defined market economies and property rights. Formal administration through salaried officials, legislative frameworks, and taxation hardly existed. The interactions between such polities also looked markedly different from the state system of today. Given the personalistic nature of rule and the lack of any conception that rule affixed to territory (the analog of property rights), such polities were neither territorially defined nor exclusive in character (Kratochwil 1986).

Universal empires recognised only material frontiers, not mutually acknowledged borders. Such borders entail juridical equivalence, which such universal empires as the Roman or the Chinese did not recognize. Multiple authority structures also coexisted side by side. Such contemporary distinctions as secular and religious authority blurred in early state practice. For example, medieval European emperors claimed sacral status and the right to appoint members of the clergy, while the papacy claimed the authority to levy taxes, raise armies, and depose secular rulers, including the emperor himself (Tierney, 1964).

The personalistic aspects of rule permeated Europe until the Late Middle Ages and arguably even later. The feudal state revolved around personal ties of obedience and loyalty. Kings and dukes commanded those lords who had sworn fealty to them. Those lords in turn commanded lesser vassals. Only through this command of men did one control territory. Thus, the control of a lord over his vassals resembled social networks and bundles of rights rather than the exclusive control over a fixed territory. Individuals might be subject to multiple patterns of rule from various lords, from the ecclesiastical authorities, and occasionally from urban authorities that had their own distinct modes of governance (Strayer, 1965, 1970; Cheyette 1975).

Finally, early states only tangentially affected their societies. Premodern states constituted capstone governments (Gellner, 1983, Mann, 1986, Crone, 1989, Hobsbawn 1990). Ruling elites were often integrated and dispersed throughout the area of control, but society remained relatively untouched. Society consisted of multiple divided communities, differentiated along ethnic, religious, and linguistic lines. Horizontal elites (the capstone government) overlaid vertically segregated societies. In short, the capacity of early states remained relatively limited. Their abilities to tax, to raise troops, and to forge any sense of national identity remained weak. Early states ran wide but not deep.

The Transition to Modern Statehood

Modern statehood first took form in late medieval Europe. Although early states in many regions of the world showed similar traits, the modern European state evolved in a unique manner. Here governments developed institutional capacities far beyond the capstone polities of the premodern age, and here states became synonymous with sovereign territorial rule. That model was subsequently transplanted from Europe to other areas. On such empirical grounds, and following the methodological maxim that the explication of a specific case or several cases can demonstrate more generalizable logics of organisation, this account focuses on developments in Europe during the past millenium, beginning at the end of the feudal era, to shed light on the contemporary world-wide system of states.

In the course of the fourth century and culminating in the fifth century, the Roman Empire came under increasing pressure of internal power struggles and external enemies. By the middle of the fifth century, only the East Roman Empire (the Byzantine empire) survived while a variety of tribes from beyond the imperial border overran the western empire. Church leaders took on some of the imperial administration (indeed the dioceses overlaid the previous provincial borders), while local chieftains provided a measure of security. Economic transactions and public security thus became highly localised with a large degree of barter exchange, and the use of coin declined greatly. The Carolingian empire momentarily brought greater unity, particularly under Charlemagne (crowned emperor in 800), but without primogeniture, the empire soon fell apart in smaller kingdoms.

Once again, foreign invasions (the Maygar, Viking, and Muslim intrusions) advantaged localised defense, thus empowering local barons over any centralised rule. Feudal rule dominated with serfs who were tied to the land and local lords, and local lords who in turn were enfeoffed to higher aristocrats through personalistic, reciprocal ties. Kingship and centralised authority remained contested and weak. Such was the fate of Western Europe until the middle of the eleventh century.

By the late eleventh century, however, the situation in Western Europe started to change, and here we find the beginnings of the modern state. Shifts in climate, advances in military and agricultural technology, declining levels of external threat, and expanding trade placed ever-increasing pressure on the feudal order. Aspiring monarchs started to assert themselves against local rulers.

Capstone governments gave way to far more intrusive authority. Taxation, administration, and the subsequent policing of society increased the ability of the state to intervene in all aspects of social life. The increasing economic productivity allowed rulers to raise more revenues. By giving lesser lords a stake in central rule through pensions and tax sharing, royal authority gradually extended the royal domain. Higher revenues in turn allowed kings to eventually raise standing armies to replace the ad-hoc feudal service, which often amounted to no more than 40 days a year. Thus, by the mid fifteenth century, the French monarchy could finally raise a standing army of almost 15,000 troops.

Homogeneous governance and formalised legal codes, evinced by the reappearance of Roman law from the thirteenth century on, replaced the previous juridical segmentation of society based largely on informal customs and traditions. This enhanced the formal legitimation of royal authority as the rule over subjects rather than the personalistic ties of the feudal period. Monarchy became a public office rather than a private possession. Roman law also aided the rise of a market economy: Private property replaced possession (*seisin*); written contract supplanted oral agreement; formal courts took the place of trial by ordeal and combat (Berman, 1983).

These trends would continue in subsequent centuries. Advances in military technology, production techniques, and transportation enabled mercantilist states to consolidate their rule. Externally, they began to project force at ever-greater distances and to incorporate even non-European territories into the European economy.The process came to full fruition in the wake of the French Revolution of 1789.

Napoleonic rule extended formal legal codes over much of continental Europe, extinguished the last vestiges of aristocratic particularism and clerical privilege, and standardised weights, measures, and administration. Democratic ideals gave rise to increasing levels of integration and identification of subjects and rulers. Indeed, subjects became citizens. In the course of the nineteenth century, public education and conscript service led to linguistic homogeneity and uniformity (Weber, 1976). Territorial states thus became nation-states. Whereas the term nation originally referred only to the linguistic background of university students, it later came to denote the aggregation of individuals that had come to consider itself a coherent political entity. State building (the attempt to enhance the capacity to rule) and nation building (the attempt to construct a shared political identity among the subjects of that particular territorial state) thus went hand in hand. States became increasingly homogeneous entities, with governments that had the loyalty of their citizens and thus the commensurate ability to deploy those citizens in service of the state on an unprecedented scale.

But the European state evolved not only in terms of capacity. The institutional logic of state organisation changed. First, the state became coterminous with territorial sovereignty. Sovereignty, as a claim to final jurisdiction, had originated in Roman law. The emperor was deemed sovereign in the sense of being the ultimate source of law. Hence, he himself could not be bound by any other authority.

Following the defeat of the Roman Empire in the West, the Roman legal tradition continued in the East Roman, Byzantine empire. Here again the emperor remained superior to any other authority including the church. In the West, however, imperial authority had faded, and the church had usurped many previously imperial functions. Thus, when the German emperors tried to revive the empire in the West, designating it the Holy Roman Empire, clashes between imperial and papal authority became unavoidable.

In the twelfth century, therefore, the German emperor Frederick Barbarossa returned to Roman sources of law to claim superiority vis-a-vis the rival claims of the papacy. This conflict should not be interpreted in the contemporary context of secular and ecclesiastical contests. Both sides advanced secular and transcendental claims. The issue revolved around ultimate hierarchy. Who had the authority to appoint bishops? Could a pope depose an emperor and vice versa? Importantly, because authority claims were both secular and sacerdotal, these claims to rule were not territorially restricted. Both emperor and pope invoked their rights to rule over all the faithful. Both, at least nominally, could judge kings (even though the emperor seldom pressed the issue).

Emperor and pope both sought allies in their contest. Nominally lesser rulers, kings and powerful dukes, were solicited for support. But aspiring monarchs, who wished to free themselves from either imperial or theocratic oversight, soon advanced their own claims to sovereignty. Less than a century after the emperor had claimed sovereignty, the kings of France and England argued that they were emperors in their own kingdoms (rex imperator est in regno suo). Hence, they could not be held subject to any higher authority within their domain. The papacy, desperate for allies, supported such monarchical ideas to gain royal aid against German imperial pretensions. Besides, the kings initially did not seem to advance claims against ecclesiastical authority. In contrast to the universalistic claims of empire and papacy, the kings laid no claim to rule outside their realms. They merely claimed sovereignty within their territorial domains.

For centuries thereafter, sovereignty remained contested. Dynastic linkages and remnants of feudal rule continued to litter the European political landscape arguably until the Napoleonic era. Empire and papacy retained considerable authority for centuries after the beginning of the conflict, thus constraining the latitude for territorial states, but neither emperor nor pope escaped unscathed from the imperial battles. German imperial pretensions met opposition from lords and towns, thus limiting any hierarchy within German borders. The failure of the imperial project gave rise to city-leagues in the North and powerful city-states in the South. In the West, assertive kings soon curtailed papal universalist pretensions. Territorial sovereignty remained imperfect but started to make inroads into the political landscape of Europe.

Many scholars have argued that the Treaty of Augsburg (1555), which delimited religious claims by territorial borders, and particularly the Peace of Westphalia (1648), firmly established the principle of sovereign, territorial rule. Mutually recognised borders circumscribed the extension of political authority. Within such borders, authority would be exclusive (Gross 1968). So strongly has Westphalia been identified with these principles that scholars sometimes denote the contemporary system as the Westphalia system. As said, however, the early articulation of such principles started well before Westphalia and took many years thereafter to complete. Indeed, according to Krasner

(1993, 1999), sovereignty was not even uniformly extended by the nineteenth century. Indeed, sovereign equality was not fully extended to other parts of the globe until decolonisation in the post–World War II period.

Whatever the exact periodisation, it remains clear that the principle of territorial sovereignty is now a constitutive feature of the modern state. Rule is territorially demarcated. Rulers have no legal claims to ultimate authority beyond their own borders. Conversely, within their borders, their authority is absolute. Sovereignty is mutually constitutive. Only if leaders have voluntarily signed away some of their states' prerogatives may another state claim authority over those states. The sovereignty principle has become a keystone of international law, at once regulating juridical autonomy and the means through which societal interests can be pursued at the international level. The logic of state organisation thus changed internal government and external relations.

THEORETICAL EXPLANATIONS OF THE EMERGENCE OF THE MODERN STATE

Recent scholarship on the origins of the state and its subsequent development differs in three respects from its predecessors. The older literature tended to focus on the macro historical transformations that swept through Europe from the Late Middle Ages through the Renaissance to the present. By starting from the modern state, and by retracing the process through which the state had evolved, such accounts provided a linear, teleological explanation for the observed outcome. More recent scholarship, however, has criticised such unilinear evolutionary accounts and drawn attention to the myriad forms of polities that emerged in response to the macro historical contextual variations.

In contrast to such macro-level, unilinear accounts, modern scholarship tends to analyze the variation in institutional types and looks for explanations of such variations at the micro level. While recognising the impact of broad environmental shifts, the attention has shifted to the particularities of individual calculations, coalitional bargaining, and contractual relations. Methodological individualism has augmented macro accounts.

Traditional explanations for the rise of the modern state also focused on the capacity of the state rather than on the particular institutional logic of state sovereignty. Such accounts thus highlighted two features in particular: the ability of the modern state to wage war at an unprecedented scale and the ability of governments to directly intervene in and mobilize their economies. Without denying these functions of the state, the more recent institutionalist scholarship has drawn attention to states' ability to facilitate collective action at the domestic level and to stabilize relations at the international level.

War as the Catalyst for State Formation

One prominent explanation for the emergence of the modern state emphasizes the effects of war making on state capacity. Starting roughly around the end of the fourteenth century, the nature of military technology changed dramatically. Massed infantry of archers and pikemen started to displace the mounted heavy cavalry that had typified feudal warfare for several centuries.

This had several repercussions. Most obviously, the privileged position of the mounted knight declined. Under feudal obligations, vassals were responsible for their own equipment of horse, armor, and retinue. This private possession of armed force in turn gave vassals and lower lords the opportunity to resist hierarchical obligations without reciprocal privileges. Service (usually no more than 40 days) corresponded with considerable autonomy and jurisdiction in one's own feudal domain. Lords thus retained considerable political and economic rights.

The changes in the mode of warfare now led to changes in the composition of the armed forces. Kings and dukes desired larger armies of individually cheap, although collectively more expensive, manpower. The leverage of lower lords on their superiors thus declined. Since armored cavalry declined in importance, monarchs and dukes were not obliged to make concessions to counts, barons, and lesser lords. Indeed, the army might be used against such lesser lords themselves. Mercenary armies could be turned with equal ease on foreign enemies or internal foes.

The increasing scope of warfare gradually led to the emergence of standing armies and the advent of large mercenary contingents.

These changes required rulers to raise ever larger sums of capital to fund such forces. Money is the sinews of power, argued Machiavelli succinctly, observing the winds of military change in his day. This transformation in warfare led to a greatly expanded royal administration and a rise in the levels of taxation.

Changes in the fifteenth and sixteenth centuries exacerbated these trends. The advent of artillery and eventually hand-held firearms reduced the role of the mounted knight even further. Simple fortifications no longer sufficed. Elabourate, and thus far more expensive, fortifications such as the *trace italienne* required ever larger sums of money. Efficiencies of scale, both in terms of manpower resources and tax base, gave bigger units an advantage. Whereas the army of France at the end of the Hundred Years War amounted to no more than 15,000 troops, by the late 1600s France had more than 300,000 men under arms. These developments continued unabated because of the high frequency of warfare. Some of the great powers of the sixteenth and seventeenth centuries, such as Spain and France (and, to a slightly lesser extent, England and the Netherlands), were constantly at war for those two centuries.

The French Revolution and the *levee en masse* raised warfare yet one step higher. Rather than rely on vast mercenary contingents, governments now managed to mobilize their own populations on a heretofore unknown scale. The Napoleonic armies could bring hundreds of thousands of troops to bear, as they did in the Russian campaign. In reaction to these challenges, France's rivals, Prussia, Austria, Russia, and Britain, altered their army structures and manpower levels. Ratchet effects permeated all of Europe.

Such earlier accounts that stress the changes in warfare as the primary causal mechanism behind the emergence of the modern state tend to emphasize macro pressures at the systemic level. The long revolution in military affairs and the incessant struggle for hegemony and counter hegemony forged the high-capacity states of Europe.

More recently, scholars have turned to micro-level analyses of how the military context provided new opportunities for individuals to reshape existing political organisations. Macro-level accounts focus primarily on the selective aspects of warfare. Given that defeated powers would fall by the wayside, the remaining polities would all have roughly similar abilities to wage war and would all have the administrative and economic capacity to support such a war effort. Micro-level accounts, by contrast, concentrate on the changing balances of power within the state that favoured individual monarchs over lesser lords and created new incentives for such rulers to forge alliances with heretofore excluded groups.

Sophisticated scholarship in this vein blends both macro and micro-level perspectives. For instance, Tilly uses systemic selective explanations. States that could not wage modern warfare were simply weeded out (Tilly, 1990). Simultaneously, he also wields a micro-level account. Comparing states to organised crime syndicates, he suggests that rulers operate similarly to protection rackets. They contract with their subjects to exchange protection for taxes. The ability of rulers to offer subjects a more reliable protection racket favoured centralised rule over feudal lordship. The strengthening of central authority over decentralised rule, in turn, increased the state's capacity to wage external war. International conflicts then fed back on the rulers' demands on society.

Economic Explanations for the Rise of the State

Like military accounts, economic explanations for the emergence of the modern state may operate at a variety of levels. At the macro level, neo-Marxists tend to emphasize the inherent weakness of economic arrangements that required subsequent adjustment. Other economic accounts might emphasize selective mechanisms. Those rulers who failed to create states that facilitated trade and production lost out to rival modes of organisation that succeeded. And here, too, some offer micro-level accounts that concentrate on the changing incentive structures for individuals to alter the older arrangements.

At the macro level, the neo-Marxist variant of this school emphasises the connections between the rise of capitalism and the emergence of modern states, particularly of absolutist states. Anderson submits that the inherent flaws of feudal production necessitated state intervention, as occurred in France and Eastern Europe. Waller stein (1974) too suggests that capitalism emerged simultaneously with the rise of strong states in Europe, which then incorporated peripheral states into the world economy.

Macro-level accounts that focus on the selection of fit and unfit states sometimes note the close ties between military state development and the emergence of early capitalism. If money did indeed constitute the sinews of power, then military competition between states meant that political rulers had vested interests in stimulating their respective economies. It is no surprise, therefore, that the earliest state ventures in capitalism took place in military enterprises. The production of Venetian galleys, for example, in the eleventh century, arguably constituted one of the first capitalist firms (McNeill, 1974). Similarly, governments matched mercantilist economic ambition with intervention in such key military sectors as gunpowder production. States that lacked the means to modernize their economies beyond elementary feudal agricultural modes of production were at a disadvantage.

Hence, maritime powers such as Britain and the Netherlands, with more advanced economies (because of trading skills, financial techniques, and the protection of private property), displaced less advanced powers such as Spain and Portugal. Like new perspectives on the effects of military changes that blend macroand micro-level narratives, new perspectives on the economic changes permeating late medieval Europe blend macro-level with micro-level accounts that emphasize changes in economic incentive structures. These incentive structures changed in a variety of ways. First, the dispersion of political authority over multiple states (Europe around 1500 included about 500 of them) prevented the blatant exploitation of trade by capricious rulers. Unlike imperial rulers in the Middle East and the Orient, rulers in Europe needed to take mercantile interests into account. Should the level of public protection decline or should the tax burden on traders become too heavy, such merchants could take their business elsewhere. Random predation by rulers was thus checked by the ever-present exit option open to the merchants.

Second, with changing demographic patterns and with dispersed political authority, labour could seek less repressive means of production. The worst cases of lordly repression would lead to labour flight; thus, the possessor of labour, land, and capital made compromises, which prevented the autocratic forms of rule seen in non-European imperial polities. These contractual relations at once gave a measure of protection to trade and early industrial interests, and in so doing brought private profit incentives in line with public welfare maximisation.

Third, because rulers had a vested interest in enhancing their economies, they also had a stake in defending private wealth. The more rulers recognised this link between public and private welfare, the greater the likelihood of economic success. Rulers and the possessors of capital (merchants and early industry) came to be mutually dependent.

The Institutionalist View of the Modern State

New institutionalism sees institutions as means to resolve cooperation and coordination problems. Squarely based in rational choice theory and its attention to individual preferences, new institutionalism examines transaction costs, information asymmetries, and principal-agent problems to explain the choice of particular institutional arrangements. In this sense, institutions are the dependent variables. The choice of territorial sovereignty thus has micro-level origins, and we should explain the rise of the state as an institutional solution to cooperation and coordination problems and as a provider of information and reducer of transaction costs.

At the same time, however, other versions of institutionalist analysis, particularly the historical institutionalist school, convincingly demonstrate that choices are constrained by prior institutional arrangements. Institutions are only moderately amenable to dramatic change. More often than not, they following the footsteps of long-gone historical predecessors. Institutions form the independent variables to explain agent behavior.

Thus, between the macro-structural context and agency, institutions act as conduits of choice and constraint. The institutionalist explanation makes little effort to place primacy on either the military or economic aspects of state formation. And indeed, empirically, for early modern rulers the pursuit of powerwas synonymous with the pursuit of plenty. Mercantilist doctrine formalised the sentiments. Even England and the Netherlands, often considered proponents of laissez-faire relative to France and Spain, practiced mercantilism to a considerable degree. The aims of English navigation acts and Dutch attempts to protect key economic sectors differed little from those of absolutist rulers elsewhere.

Also, as seen, the earliest large-scale enterprises often blended economic and military functions. Although it is true that the larger part of public revenues (until the late-nineteenth-and early-twentieth-century nascence of a welfare state) went to warfare (Brewer 1989), this is not evidence that the state had no economic effects. The state's protection of private property, its enforcement of legal codes, and its creation of institutions (such as the Bank of England) that remained untouched by the whims of the government might have taken up little of the overall revenue, but they clearly had profound effects on the subsequent development of the economy and the state.

Thus, institutionalists do not try to disentangle whether military or economic explanations are the more powerful. They do not focus on the growing capacity of the state but on the particular institutional logic of state organisation. Here institutionalist accounts provide insights into why the particular mode of territorial sovereign state organisation has become predominant. Seen from a new institutionalist perspective, the modern state provided more efficient solutions to cooperation and coordination problems than its predecessors did. Internally, sovereign state institutions formalised relations between subjects and rulers, and between subjects themselves. By justifying rule as the public and exclusive provision of collective goods (defense, legal frameworks), sovereignty also created homogeneity in governance and greater stability in social interactions.

Contrary to the multiple and overlapping feudal jurisdictions, sovereignty created hierarchical authority structures. Roman law not only facilitated the extension of royal authority, it also created a legal system that would form the basis of legal codes to this very day. Rather than be subject to multiple and competing taxation, central authority standardised the type and level of exactions. Monarchs also worked to regulate their economies through standardisation of coinage, weights, and measures.

In short, internally, sovereignty proved a more efficient form of organisation than feudal arrangements. It reduced cooperation and coordination problems between rulers and ruled, as well as between subjects themselves. Social and economic life became regularised, and transaction and information costs were reduced. Sovereign territorial states even proved better than the fragmented citystates or the loose confederal town-leagues at organising their own subjects.

But the sovereign territorial state also operates as a gatekeeper to the external environment. Internationally, the organisation of the state represents domestic society to the outside. Here as well, states resolved cooperation and coordination problems more successfully than rival forms of organisation. Externally, territorial sovereignty delimited claims to rule by fixed borders, in contrast to universal claims to empire or theocratic organisation. In this sense, sovereignty geographically delimited a domestic sphere of jurisdiction (subject to the ruler of that area) and an international sphere of jurisdiction with all actors nominally (but not de facto) equal. Indeed, it created the distinction of domestic and international politics (Holzgrefe, 1989).Within the international arena, agreements between the sovereigns would regulate the interactions of private actors of their respective realms that went beyond the geographic extension of the territorial state.

Consequently, rulers who could credibly commit their realms and their subjects were more attractive to other rulers in such international negotiations. Polities with less formal geographic boundaries and less hierarchical authority, such as the city-leagues of the late medieval and Renaissance eras, proved less reliable and thus less attractive as partners (Lloyd, 1991). This demand for convergence further aided the spread of territorial sovereignty as the dominant form of state organisation through Europe and ultimately across the globe. Institutionalists have also shed new light on the consequences of variations among modern states.

North suggests that states with limited coercive abilities, such as Britain and the Netherlands, fared better in relative terms than more absolutist governments. State institutions that curtailed the ability of rulers to intervene in society created incentives at the micro level for individuals to pursue innovation and profit. Conversely, this incentive at the individual level enhanced the capacity of the state to compete at the international level. Britain and the Netherlands were able to raise larger funds than their absolutist competitors. Not only were sovereign states superior to no sovereign entities, but within the group of sovereign states, less coercive institutions had a decisive advantage.

THE CONTEMPORARY RELEVANCE OF DISCUSSIONS ON THE ORIGINS OF THE STATE

Recent scholarship has emphasised the need to blend both comparative perspectives and views from international relations in order to elucidate the various trajectories of state formation. External, macro-historical processes propel individuals to seek new political arrangements, but internal conditions provide the constraints and opportunities through which such choices are mediated. Studying the historical nuances of state formation in the past clarifies the current predicament and future of the modern state. Whereas European states concurrently developed state capacity and international legal sovereignty, the non-European states often had the latter imposed on them. Juridically sovereign entities, their governments lack the institutional and economic features of advanced capitalist polities. Herbst's analyses of African states compares the European historical trajectory to African experiences.

Taking the militarist view of the origins of the state, he notes that Africa lacked Europe's long periods of high-intensity warfare. If war made the European states, the lack of technologically advanced large-scale warfare in Africa implies that African states will remain weak. Incentives may thus exist for political entrepreneurs in that continent to engage in risky external relations in order to build their own state capacity.

Those emphasising economic or institutionalist functions of the state, however, might suggest that the African experience need not mimic the European. Instead, one might argue that judiciously interventionist states, governments that create incentives for private wealth maximisation that translate into overall welfare gains as well, might be an alternative outcome. As with early European states, the question would not be whether states have the capacity to compete in external war but whether they have the institutional arrangements to bring private welfare maximisation in line with public welfare gains. Some late-developing countries, such as Korea, have apparently managed to build state capacity and provide public rather than private goods. Others, such as some African countries, have seen the state cater to narrower clienteles.

Students of recent transitions in formerly communist countries have similarly returned to examining the origins of states in the West. The questions faced by reformers in Eastern Europe resemble those of early state development. How does one create an efficient market? How does one create a formal institutional network that ties the ruler's hands?

In international relations, the predominance of the structural realist perspective precluded any careful examination of the emergence of the state. International relations showed a strong continuity across historical periods. Anarchy constituted the key structural feature of the international system, which explained the behavior of units, be they states or other forms of organisation (Waltz, 1979, 1986).

But, as critics pointed out, this presumes that domestic politics (organised hierarchically) and international politics (where anarchy reigned) could clearly be distinguished. That presupposition has been criticised across a range of epistemological vantage points. One set of critiques has focused on the particular logic of organisation invoked by the principle of territorial sovereignty. The feudal order, for example, revealed heteronomous and cross-cutting jurisdictions, as argued above. In the same spirit, one can criticize structural realism for neglecting the variety of modalities between anarchy and hierarchy.

The emergence of territorial sovereignty, with the separation of jurisdictional power into discrete territorial units—what has been described as the Westphalia system—creates anarchy. Anarchy is not a transhistorical given. Neoliberal institutionalists as well criticize the strict demarcation of domestic hierarchy and international anarchy (Milner, 1991). Neoliberal institutionalists also suggest that the Hobbesian anarchy of structural realism fails to recognize how states may create institutions to mitigate the consequences of anarchy. Indeed, some institutional arrangements, such as the European Union, might even create a measure of supranational organisation, thus bringing international legal sovereign units under higher multilateral bodies (Sbragia, 1992).

Even some realists themselves suggest that different types of polities conducted different international interactions. They have also started to pay attention to the various modalities between anarchy and hierarchy. While still acknowledging material interests and relative distributions of power as the primary factors driving international relations, they suggest that territorial sovereignty with juridically equivalent units has often been denied to less powerful states. Studying why certain types of units predominate an international system (states, informal empires, formal empires) and examining how the set of predominant units may change over time sheds light on the patterns of international relations one should expect.

The same conclusion emerges from a radically different epistemological perspective. Constructivists have argued that international relations needs an account of the state, because the particular nature of the state, its moral purpose and identity, profoundly affect the type of international system that states create. Stressing cultural and ideational factors rather than materialist variables, constructivists suggest that the state's perspective regarding its internal function and its external role will determine how it acts toward other states. This identity is partially self-constructed and partially determined by the role configurations developed by previous exchanges with others. Social networks and mutual expectations inform and are in turn determined by state identity. Thus, even if the separation of states may be described as a condition of anarchy (the absence of hierarchical authority), polities may create a variety of institutional arrangements that transform the condition from potential conflict to a more benign environment. States may interact as predators, as in Hobbesian anarchy, or they may create Lockean societies or Kantian cosmopolitanism.

WITHER THE STATE?

The discussion of the origins of the state has gained further relevance because of questions regarding the future of the state. However, some debates regarding the origins, role, and future of the state in contemporary political science confuse changes in the autonomy of the state with changes in the institutional logic of territorial sovereignty. Whereas the autonomy of the state has undergone a transformation in some respects, the principle of territorial sovereignty remains robust. Recent changes in the international environment have led some to suggest that the state and the state system have been undergoing fundamental changes in the past decades. Accounts that stress the state's military, economic, or institutionalist dimensions generate divergent expectations regarding the future of the Westphalian system. Within each of these approaches there remains considerable variation as well.

An examination of the security environment does not lead to uniform conclusions regarding the future of the state. On the one hand, some argue that nuclear weapons technology has made the state obsolete. If the state's primary function is to protect its populace from foreign attack, the state today can no longer serve that function, as it cannot guarantee the safety of its citizens. Similarly, other scholars argue that nuclear weapons have turned the analogy between states in the international system and colliding billiard balls into fiction.

The hard shells of the nation-states have been breached, and catastrophic conflict might be avoided in the long run only by mutual binding mechanisms, for which Deudney deploys the term macro-republicanism. One might also infer from other developments in weapons technology that the scale of the political unit matters less than it once did. Previous centuries rewarded efficiencies of scale. The transition from feudal warfare to large-scale infantry combat had advantaged larger units, or units that had other means of raising the revenue necessary for the new mode of war. Thus, scale (either of geographical size or economic wealth) was vital to the survival of the state. Twentieth-century warfare, however, has diminished territorial size as a key measure of military standing. Territory has not become altogether irrelevant, but the ability to project force rapidly over great distance has diminished the use value of large numbers of troops and buffer zones. Even if one were to disregard the independent effects of nuclear-weapons technology, the third revolution in military technology (in precision-guided munitions, stealth technology, and advanced communications) has expanded the zone of immediate military action.

On the other hand, one might argue that the state still reigns supreme. If the key feature of the modern state is its monopoly on the use of force, as Max Weber argued, then states are still the primary possessors of military might. Despite some attempts to forge supranational or multilateral forces, most force structures still resemble traditional alliances, with individual states reluctant to yield their sovereign control. Realist views of international relations remain valid. Such debates between state-centric realists and state declinists deservedly receive much attention, particularly when one examines the implications of weapons of mass destruction, such as missiles and nuclear weapons, for conventional interstate relations. But such debates neglect the transnational actors who deploy means of violence below the level of the state.

The dispersal of such means to terrorist groups, drug cartels, and rogue military units of imploded states has created a new "security problematique" necessitating unexplored types of responses. This has led to greater transnational cooperation in some areas, such as international policing, as states attempt to reassert their authority over such actions. But it has also led to the emergence of shadow states within legitimate states. The latter problem poses unique questions of accountability, which the juridical notion of territorial sovereignty had sought to resolve. As Thomson shows (1990, 1994), the introduction of sovereign authority over transnational possessors of violence (mercenaries, pirates) by means of international agreements enhanced the violence monopoly of states, but it also made sovereigns accountable. Whether the same mechanism might apply to contemporary problems is open to debate.

Economic factors as well have led some to question whether the state in its current form will survive. The most prevalent argument has focused on the effects of globalisation. Increasing trade and financial flows are said to put pressure on national economies. This has led to a loss of governments' autonomy to set their own economic policy. Given the spread of international trade and commensurate organisations, and given the disciplining effect of financial markets, governments must heed external demands. An inward-looking mercantilist strategy runs the risk of international confrontation (through dispute panels or state retaliation) and capital flight. For example, some have argued that international pressures on the French interventionist economy in the late 1980s led to a retreat from dirigisme and to a greater willingness to accept liberal perspectives and further regionalisation of the European economy. The economic theory of clubs further elucidates why states must conform to international dictates. As the group of liberal trading states increases, the opportunity costs of not joining the club increase. Since liberal trade leads to net efficiency gains, and restrictions lead to deadweight losses, the gains for the group of free traders increase not only by the addition of new members but also by the growth in overall welfare efficiency. Conversely, the losses of mercantilists include both the loss of members and the increasing deadweight losses due to trade distortions.

This logic holds true even for non-market economies. In the absence of real price mechanisms, the difference between world market prices and the assigned prices will increase. In short, the movement of some states to regional organisations and greater liberalisation precipitates domino effects. Pressures to join regional and multilateral organisations will thus mount. Even prior to formal accession, governments will adopt institutions and standards that should make them viable partners. States seeking to join the European Union will start to amend their institutions to make them compatible with current members. Similarly, states seeking International Monetary Fund orWorld Bank support will conform to their institutional expectations (such as their demands for an independent central bank). In this sense, state autonomy has decreased.

On the one hand, then, states have incentives to pursue welfare gains by joining regional and multilateral institutions. Some regional organisations, particularly in the case of the European Union, will in fact take on tasks that were previously handled by sovereign governments. Indeed, although the European Union does not yet fulfill all conditions of Mundel's optimal currency area, the liberalisation of trade in goods and services and the advent of the Euro currency have greatly integrated the European economies.

On the other hand, liberalism reduces the costs of secessionism. In a mercantilist world with barriers to the free exchange of goods and services, scale becomes a decisive asset. Small states simply lack the domestic markets required for the efficient production of goods (hence, small states tend to rely far more on trade as a percentage of gross national product than large states). But if few barriers exist, size becomes a less important prerequisite. Some scholars have argued that progress on the North American Free Trade Agreement (NAFTA) in fact assisted secessionist sentiments in Quebec. Although institutionalists recognize that dramatic changes have taken place in the security and economic environment, they see greater durability in the existing state system. Institutions are often the end result of long historical processes and of individual choices mixed with serendipitous and unintended outcomes. Agents no doubt seek to design institutions to best serve their interests (to increase their chances at reelection, to achieve cherished policy goals, or to enhance welfare gains), but their choices are constrained by the available options. Thus, although external changes provide an impetus for change, the modalities of response are determined by previous choices. The timing of industrialisation and the security position of the state have often determined the degree of state intervention and the degree of liberal democracy. In this sense, institutions are often path-dependent. Once chosen, they subsequently structure a range of other choices around themselves. Lock-in will result.

Institutionalists further argue that external economic and military challenges can be met in a variety of ways. The particular response is determined by strategic choices on the part of politicians and economic actors and by previous historical legacies. Thus, at certain points, some models might seem to have an advantage over others, but these findings remain inconclusive.

The East Asian development model had great currency during the 1980s and early 1990s. However, with the crisis of the late 1990s, the model has lost favour, and less interventionist strategies gained credence. In light of the downturn in some of the less interventionist states, the latter model too seems to have its flaws. The drive toward convergence might thus be overstated. Empirically, at the level of the firm, evidence of convergence seems ambiguous. In short, institutionalists see less convergence and less pressure on the state.

Most arguments regarding the future of the state pertain to the capacity of states to act autonomously, or they pertain to state dissolution and secession. They do not have a direct bearing on whether territorial sovereignty as a constitutive principle of international relations is diminishing. Contrary to Krasner (1999), I would argue that international legal sovereignty remains robust, although I agree that domestic sovereignty in the past has often been infringed. Even by his own account, international legal sovereignty has been violated less often. Moreover, voluntary association in international or even supranational organisations, which he takes as evidence that sovereignty has not been respected, hardly constitutes a violation of the principle.

On the contrary, the very notion that governments are the primary contracting parties validates their supremacy as the key actors in international relations (over, say, nongovernmental organisations or intersocietal networks). Giddens (1987) argues that international organisations in fact reaffirm territorial states as the key actors. Finally, as Zacher shows (2001), the forceful imposition of rule over other polities has declined, particularly in the post-1945 period. The most egregious breaches of sovereignty have vanished with the end of colonialism.

The juridical notion of territorial sovereignty as a regulative device in international relations retains its influence. This is true even for regions where trans-state claims to affinity, such as Pan-Arabism, have vied with national statehood for individual loyalties. Thus, although interdependence and globalisation have diminished the capacity of governments to act autonomously, the principle that states have governments that are supreme within their borders, and that international relations are conducted between juridical equals, remains the key feature of the state and international relations today.

2

The Political Demography of the World System, 2000–2050

By the end of the twentieth century the bipolar competition of the Cold War had ended and the market economy model was triumphant. Economic globalisation—greatly expanded international trade and capital movements, and even, to a limited extent, cross-border mobility of labour—had spread beyond the developed countries and East Asia, although very unevenly. Thus the developing world, by then four-fifths of mankind, had become far less homogeneous in both its demographic dynamics and its income per capita than it had been at midcentury. It included many middle-income countries and several emergent economic giants, all of them intent on rapid economic growth and eventual emulation of the highconsumption economies of the West and Japan.

The giants—China, India, and Brazil—additionally displayed nascent ambitions for regional and even global projection of influence in political, military, and cultural as well as economic domains. But the developing world also contained large regions of persistent economic backwardness and a few even of retrogression, conditions aggravated by still-rapid demographic growth. At the same time the forces of globalisation had begun to create social and economic strains in the affluent countries that, in combination with aging populations, aging workforces, and incipient population decline, seemed to put in doubt the sustainability of their own gains in economic welfare and called into question the applicability of their economic success as a model for the rest of the world. The social sciences offer no means of forecasting the evolution of this global economic and political system over the next half-century—not even of distinguishing, among the plausible drivers of change, those that will in retrospect be judged the most significant. Recall how little of the world of 2000 was foreseen in 1950. But while steering clear of prediction, we can at least lay out some of the trends that are underway and explore their implications. Moreover, in comparison to some other efforts at future-gazing, we can call on the relatively robust structural frame that demography supplies. Compared to the rate of turnover and obsolescence in physical capital and technology, people are long lived. Some 40 per cent of the population of 2050 (and probably about the same proportion of the labour force) is already alive in 2005—whereas much of the technology and a large part of the capital stock of the economy in use in 2050 have yet to be created. Moreover, mortality and fertility also tend to change in fairly predictable ways with industrialisation and urbanisation, giving some assurance to population forecasts at least over the next several decades. (Based on past experience, uncertainties mount up rapidly thereafter.)

POPULATION AND ECONOMY: FORECASTS TO 2050

The near-worldwide decline of fertility over the second half of the twentieth century has taken the "population problem" off the agenda of international relations. That relegation is unfortunate. It misconstrues the likely role of the demographic factor in the world system during the coming decades.

The United Nations estimates for 2000–05 put the average total fertility rate (TFR) for the more developed countries at 1.6 children per woman, and for the less developed world at 2.9. There are large contrasts in age distributions between regions—still relatively youthful in the less developed regions, exhibiting advanced population aging in the developed world—reflecting the timing and pattern of past fertility and mortality declines. The medium UN projections envisage gradual convergence in demographic behavior and eventually also in age distributions. Over the coming decades, however, this convergence will not prevent continuing large shifts in relative population sizes between regions and among major countries.

The same UN projections foresee global population growth between 2005 and 2050 of 2.6 billion—a net increase larger than the total world population in 1950. That increase is distributed highly unevenly across world regions. Holding constant the categories of "more" and "less" developed (admittedly, labels that have become increasingly vacuous), the population of the more developed regions is projected to grow by only 25 million. This is despite the assumption that net immigration into those regions will amount to 98 million during the 45-year period. Thus, 99 per cent of the global growth is expected to occur in the less developed regions.

Among major regions, Europe (including Russia) shows the most pronounced loss in terms of relative size. Its population was 22 per cent of the world's total in 1950. By 2005 that figure had fallen to 11 per cent. In 2050 it is expected to be 7 per cent. In absolute terms, Europe's population is estimated to be 728 million in 2005. Despite an assumed net immigration of 32 million persons during the next 45 years, a further improvement in its mortality, and a recovery of its fertility from the current TFR of 1.4 to 1.85 by midcentury, the continent's population would fall to 653 million in 2050—that is, 75 million below its present level.

At the other regional extreme, Africa's population is projected to continue its rapid growth. Africa's share of global population was 9 per cent in 1950, increasing to 14 per cent in 2005. It will be 21 per cent in 2050. Its projected absolute population growth during the next 45 years is more than 1 billion. The anticipated growth in the first half of the twenty-first century against the previous half-century for major countries and regions. Africa and Western Asia are reconfigured into sub-Saharan Africa (as the UN defines it) and a group of countries termed the "Muslim tier".

This differentiated pattern of demographic expansion yields a new clutch of heavyweight countries in the world. Arbitrarily identifying these as countries with populations above 100 million, the picture given by the UN estimates for 2005 and medium-variant projections for 2050. Some rearranging of the list takes place over this period, with India overtaking China, and Pakistan and Nigeria moving up in the size ranking. No country is forecast to drop out of the list in this period, but Japan and Russia are not far from doing so. Emerging demographic heavyweights are Congo, Ethiopia, Philippines, Uganda, Egypt, Viet Nam, Iran, and Turkey. (Astonishingly—and implausibly—these projections place Afghanistan barely lower, reaching 97 million by 2050.)

However, if the EU with its current composition (EU-25) is taken as constituting a state-like entity, it would appear with a population of 460 million in 2005—third, after India and ahead of the US—and 450 million in 2050—still third, but by then some 20 million below its peak and within range of a still-growing United States. Of course, the EU may have expanded further by mid-century: accession of Turkey, should it occur, would alone raise its 2050 population by nearly one-quarter.

Such population figures take on a fuller meaning in combination with current economic conditions and their plausible future evolution. If so considered, they suggest a major gain in the coming decades in the economic weight and thence the geopolitical importance of the Asia-Pacific region and of South Asia, in comparison to the North Atlantic—the region which, at least for the last two centuries, has held a preeminent position in the global hierarchy of economic and military power, scientific and technological prowess, and cultural influence. China, and at a farther distance also India, may soon rival the United States in gross domestic product. For example, in recent forecasts by Goldman Sachs, China's GDP exceeds that of the United States around 2040, India's a few decades later. At purchasing power parity, by 2001 China's economy was already three-fifths the size of that of the United States, India's one-quarter. (In comparison, in that year by the same measure, Latin America's economy was 39 per cent of that of the United States, Africa's 15 per cent.)

Major per capita income differentials between currently rich and poor countries will, however, persist. Continued faster economic growth in per capita terms in the less developed world in comparison to the rich countries—the broad experience of recent decades, though with important exceptions—must eventually close that income gap, but even under the most daring assumptions in most instances this process will be far from completed by mid-century.

In the Goldman Sachs forecasts just cited, China in 2050 would have a per capita income roughly equal to the average of the developed world around the turn of the millennium. In the early phases of the catch-up process, of course, it is virtually an arithmetic certainty that absolute per capita income differentials between countries will further widen. Finally, the staggered pacing of demographic transition among world regions is reflected in a remarkable variation in the forecast levels and rates of increase in the proportions of youth and the elderly. Provision of old-age support, private or public, has mainly entailed pay-as-you-go transfers from workers or taxpayers to retirees. The increasing fragility of that mechanism as the proportions of the young and the old move in opposite directions. The order shown in the table corresponds to the comparative stage in the aging process: Japan and the EU in the vanguard, Africa bringing up the rear. China, with its precipitous fertility decline in the 1970s and 1980s, is two or three decades ahead of India.

Long-range forecasts of dependency ratios—as defined in demographic terms—are sensitive to assumptions about fertility and longevity (especially life expectancy at older ages), both of which are straddled by substantial confidence intervals. (Levels of immigration also affect dependency, but, as noted below, not by much at the ranges that are likely to be politically acceptable to countries of immigration.) A fertility recovery that yielded family sizes nearer two than one is not impossible in Europe and Japan, albeit unlikely in the view of many observers. The course of mortality at older ages in the developed world is even more uncertain—a further consequential matter for the financial condition of pension funds. The nearing approach of high old-age dependency combined with these uncertainties pushes governments toward adoption of retirement schemes involving individual retirement accounts, in which savings and later dissavings take place over each person's life cycle.

MIGRATION AND IDENTITY

Income differentials, in combination with relative population sizes and rates of increase, clearly point to the continuation and the likely intensification of migratory pressures, with the potential to generate massive population movements from poor to rich countries. To what extent such movements actually materialize is a different matter. Migrant receiving countries seldom plan the number of migrants to be admitted beyond the next few years—and where plans do exist, they can be and are revised at will or altered by circumstance.

The migration assumptions incorporated in the UN projections, such as those cited above, are arbitrary, hence purely illustrative. They typically assume, country-by-country, continuation of the volume of the migrant stream estimated for the most recent past, or at a somewhat reduced level. The actual number of migrants may turn out to be far greater than this. Mexican migration into the United States in the 1950s and 1960s, for example, poorly signaled the massive influx from Mexico in more recent decades.

Migration may also turn out to be smaller than simple extrapolations suggest. Public opinion in the main receiving countries, especially in Europe and more specifically in the European Union, has, on balance, increasingly favoured less migration—a sentiment reinforced by recently heightened tensions surrounding Europe's Muslim minority and by the volume of unskilled migration into the United States. Strict enforcement of the rules adopted in this sphere could greatly restrict migration flows, both legal and clandestine. Yet enforcement is costly in economic terms and infringes on other values and preferences of the native population.

Moreover, in every immigrant-receiving country there are numerous persons and interest groups strongly favouring relaxation of rules in particular cases or for particular types of immigrants: their wishes often prevail over the weakly expressed preferences of the greater number of those favouring tighter restrictions.

Such differences in attitude are typically strongly correlated with position in the income or class hierarchy. Whether in their private capacity or as entrepreneurs, more affluent segments of the population disproportionately benefit from greater access to low-wage domestic service workers or to wage labourers willing to work for wages below the rates that native workers would demand. At the same time, wealthier persons are apt to have less exposure to situations that may be seen by many as discomforting, such as the changing ethnic make-up in residential areas or in the schools their children attend. Persons in lower income classes bear the brunt of such exposure.

An often-repeated argument favouring immigration invokes the economic and social problems associated with population aging and the "needs" of the labour force. The influx of migrants, it is held, rejuvenates the age structure and fills jobs that otherwise would go unfilled. Migrants, if employed, thus ease labour force adjustments and prop up the pension and health care systems of the receiving country. But as demographers know, this, at best, is a temporary remedy for population aging. Immigrants also age; they eventually cease to be workers and taxpayers and become claimants on pensions and other entitlements. To maintain the rejuvenating effect would require sustained immigration on a scale that over time would radically change the numerical balance between natives and immigrants—a transformation unlikely to be welcomed by most persons in the receiving country. That transformation —David Coleman calls it the third demographic transition—is accentuated where native–immigrant cultural differences are large and migrant acculturation to the mainstream is slow. Cases in point are European cities like Rotterdam and Birmingham.

Within broad limits, modern industrial societies should be able to cope with the economic and social problems caused by population aging without recourse to immigration. The institutional changes required for that purpose are well known. The availability of an apparently "easier" solution for those problems, through immigration, allows societies to avoid the needed reforms—as well as to avoid thinking seriously about policies to encourage higher birth rates.

In filling labour force needs, the advantages and disadvantages of immigration would have to be compared to alternative means of adjustment, whether policy-induced or arising in response to market signals: mobilising labour reserves from the native population; developing and adopting technologies that substitute for labour; upgrading wage rates to elicit labour supply responses; and, not least, eliminating activities that could only be sustained with low-wage labour. Each of these adjustments, whether applied separately or in combination, has its costs. Over time these costs may, however, prove to be lower than those entailed in the reflexive reliance on immigration.

The migration solution looks easy because of the magnitude of the supply pool of potential migrants—a function of income differentials and relative population sizes. Although geographic proximity now has less influence on migration decisions than in the past, when transportation and communication costs were higher, the point may be illustrated by comparing migrant-receiving countries with potential sender countries in the same general geographic neighborhood. The European Union provides the principal case in point. (The North American case is similar in many respects, apart from its higher native-born fertility levels and its more flexible labour market.) Consider the three EU countries with the largest net immigration—Germany, Britain, and Italy—and the three largest potential migrant suppliers in the EU's "southern neighborhood"—Egypt, Turkey, and Iran. In 2005, the comparative population sizes of each group are almost the same: 204 million in the three EU countries, 217 million in the three countries of the southern neighborhood. For the next 45 years, the UN assumes net immigration of 9 million into Germany, 6 million into Britain, and over 5 million into Italy and substantial, although less massive, emigration from Egypt, Turkey, and Iran. Nonetheless, the medium projections for 2050 show a major shift in comparative population size: a slight decline, to 197 million, in the three EU countries, but a 50 per cent rise, to 329 million, in the southern three.7 Per capita income (2002 estimates in purchasing power parity terms) was above US$25,000 in each of the three EU countries; it was about $6,000 in Turkey and Iran and less than $4,000 in Egypt.

Vastly greater pools of would-be EU migrants exist in other parts of Africa and West Asia. Indeed this whole region might, somewhat provocatively, be called Europe's "southern hinterland." Its relative size contrasted with the EU itself, past and projected. Clearly, there is the potential for immigration into the EU on a much larger scale than is assumed in the UN projections. The same is true for other high-income areas, not only the traditional immigration countries—United States, Canada, and Australia—but also Japan and other prosperous East Asian countries and perhaps some emerging Latin American countries such as Brazil.

More to the point, the potential flows are larger too than envisaged by any of the migrant-receiving countries. Should such flows materialize, they would amount to only a modest downward correction to population growth trends in the sending countries but could radically change the demographic make-up of the receiving countries. Both historical experience and present-day indications suggest that such changes can have unwelcome consequences—cultural, economic, and political—whenever assimilation of migrants proves to be difficult, whether because of attitudes prevailing in the receiving society or attitudes of the migrants themselves.

The right to determine who is admitted as a migrant is fundamental to the modern state system. In practice, as suggested above, the complex mixture of gains and losses that are entailed and the interplay of interest groups with stakes in the outcome make the decision-making process inherently difficult. Moreover, sending countries may also claim a stake—through their concern for relieving domestic unemployment, for the well-being of their expatriate citizens, and, more tangibly, for the remittance flows that may be generated. This spread of claims has suggested to some a case for international regulation of migration. In the 1920s, Albert Thomas, then director of the International Labour Office, asked whether the time had come "for considering the possibility of establishing some sort of supreme supranational authority which would regulate the distribution of population on rational and impartial lines, by controlling and directing migration movements and deciding on the opening-up or closing of countries to particular streams of immigration" (Thomas 1927).

Such ideas resurface in contemporary policy discussions in the international arena—for instance, Kofi Annan's remark in a 2004 speech that "migration is an issue that demands greater international cooperation—norms and policies to manage migration in the interest of all." While any move toward sharing policymaking responsibility with sending states would no doubt be resisted by the receiving states, the issue introduces an additional level of uncertainty in forecasting the volume and direction of international migration in the coming decades.

For *temporary* labour migration, joint decision-making is certainly to be expected. Such schemes, bringing in migrants on work contracts for a fixed period, could be established to the mutual benefit of the receiving and the sending countries (justifying a quid-pro-quo in the form of material compensation for the sender), and, of course, of the migrants themselves. Although there are successful models for such guest-worker arrangements, their potentials have not been much explored. An expansion of temporary migration, skilled and unskilled, has been under consideration in the United States in response to employer pressures and, in the unskilled case, as an offset to more stringent border controls. Such schemes should be of particular interest to countries in which popular sentiment is unequivocally against permanent immigration, such as Japan. Short of draconian administration, full enforcement of the return provision for guest-workers (presumably to be replaced by new recruits) is not to be expected, but that goal is not necessarily a condition for success provided return rates can be kept high. A side benefit of such a scheme could be its use in selecting participants to be offered permanent residence.

Migration within the countries of the European Union presents a special case of international migration. The label "international" is warranted, as EU countries retain major elements of national sovereignty. Treaties guarantee citizens of member countries the right to free movement, for whatever purpose, within the Union. (Labour migration from countries that joined most recently is subject to temporary restrictions by some members of the EU-15.) Through the Schengen agreement, involving a large subset of the continental EU countries, the right to free movement and settlement is also guaranteed to persons to whom any Schengen member country has granted permanent immigrant status.

When differentials in income are minor, as in the case of the EU-15 countries, labour migration is likely to be small, an outcome reinforced by cultural and linguistic barriers. Few persons from Munich wish to take up work in Lyon, and vice versa. Labour migration from the rest of what is now the EU-25 has greater potential, evidenced by the labour inflow to Britain and Ireland (especially from Poland). But the most important migration type within the EU in the coming decades may turn out to be retirement migration—retirees attracted to parts of Spain, for example, in a pattern similar to that observed in Florida or Arizona in the United States.

Outside the EU, while free trade agreements have proliferated, the more radical integration involving common markets for labour has been rare. Australia and New Zealand have such an arrangement. Some regional groupings—notably ASEAN—have at times contemplated doing so. The North American Free Trade Agreement, in contrast, has deliberately refrained from promotion of cross-border labour mobility—indeed NAFTA was originally seen by some as a kind of bulwark against unregulated inflows to the United States and Canada. A fortiori that would be true of any extension further southward, as in the Central American Free Trade Agreement or the bruited Free Trade Agreement of the Americas (FTAA). In practice, as noted earlier, regulatory efforts to curtail migration reflect the diversity of economic and political interests in the matter, typically combining fairly strong if less than effective border controls with lax enforcement of employer sanctions.

This discussion is necessarily inconclusive, but it clearly suggests that migration flows from less developed countries to the rich countries during the next half-century—especially to North America and the European Union—will be at least as large as and possibly significantly larger than those observed in recent decades. At the same time, it seems probable that receiving countries will raise their expectations of migrant cultural assimilation and adopt more stringent control and surveillance measures (border security and registration or ID requirements), in part in response to xenophobic and nativist reactions by their citizenries. These measures notwithstanding, by midcentury both of these continent-size areas are likely to have populations far more varied by ethnic and cultural background and by geographic origin than they were at the turn of the millennium.

FRAYING SOVEREIGNTY: FISSION AND COALESCENCE

Countries are creations of history: their continuity over time is not carved in stone. They can split into smaller units or merge to form larger entities. The post–World War II period brought a proliferation of national units. This was largely the result of the dismantling of the colonial empires, the last phase of which was completed with the gaining of independence by the 15 former republics of the Soviet Union. Disintegration of some artificial national constructs contributed to the process, such as the separation of Bangladesh from Pakistan, Singapore from the Malay Federation, Eritrea from Ethiopia, and the split of the former Czechoslovakia and Yugoslavia into their major constituent units. The division of Korea into two separate states solidified after the 1953 armistice. Southern Sudan is promised a future opportunity to break from the country's Arab north.

It is possible to see this pattern as the triumph of atavistic nationalist hatreds over the economic logic of market size, but closer examination tends to reveal the continued relevance of economic motives. Often the impulse to secede comes from an economically successful or fortuitously resource-rich subregion of a country, seeking to preserve or enhance its position by erecting barriers to entry. The lessons of the economics of German reunification are read as proving the merits of disunity in rich South Korea; the economic success of Hong Kong holds a lesson for Shanghai as well as for China's several eastern provinces.

Subnational devolution of political power, short of national independence, is also in evidence, potentially offering the devolved entity greater economic returns (perhaps concealed in nationalistic rhetoric) while remaining under the security umbrella of the state. Quebec is an example, as are, in Europe, Scotland, Wales, Catalonia, Corsica, Wallonia, and Flanders. Far-reaching regional autonomy was built into the postwar reconstruction of Germany as a federal republic, and devolution by legislative reform gave greater powers to regions in France and Italy. Striving for movement in similar directions has been evident in many other countries as well, illustrated by the examples of Nigeria, Indonesia, Philippines, and Sri Lanka.

Is the present configuration of states approaching some near-permanent form or will the process of fission continue indefinitely? Working against further change is the entrenchment of the principle of national sovereignty in the United Nations Charter and in the everyday workings of international institutions. Efforts to override it by acknowledging a right to self-determination for some aspiring national entity (self-determination is also a UN principle)—or even to protect human rights in the face of egregious government violations—have been rare. A few states—perhaps Iraq included—may yet hive off separate nations; Russia could shed some troublesome Muslim territories along its southern borders. Ascendant powers, however, encounter few challenges in dealing as they please with minor would be states on their fringes, such as Sikkim or Tibet.

The reverse phenomenon to fission—the consolidation of multiple political units into one—has seen few examples in the past 60 years. The most notable is the merger of the former East Germany into the Federal Republic. And of signal importance, although not classifiable under the traditional category of independent statehood, is the creation of the European Union. Starting with the six-country association under the 1957 Treaty of Rome, by 2004 the EU encompassed 25 states, with a population of 457 million, pledged to form "an ever closer union."

Member states preserve essential elements of sovereignty but cede by treaty many former state functions to a common, non-territorial, political machinery headquartered in Brussels. Whether it should espouse more thoroughgoing federalist ambitions or settle for the less radical "Anglo-Saxon" confederate model remains a matter of disagreement among the member states, with far from predictable resolution.

East Asia has a number of efforts at regional integration. ASEAN, now including all Southeast Asian states except East Timor, is well established, seen by some as eventually growing into an EU-style entity. Institutional thickening can be measured in the continual invention of new ties among member governments, the progressive easing of bureaucratic barriers, and the profusion of meetings, dialogues, and working groups. There is no Brussels in view, however, let alone a regional parliament. It remains more an intergovernmental organisation than a superstate manque.

Integration across East Asia as a whole has not progressed as far but may have greater prospects. A Japan-centered East Asian economic system seemed in the cards in the 1970s and 1980s, with massive Japanese investments in the region creating a set of burgeoning economies following in Japan's train. (Lingering memories of Japan's colonial and wartime interventions precluded such relationships extending much beyond the economic.) But then came the dramatic slowing of Japan's economy in the 1990s, coinciding with China's economic take-off fueled by the rapid strengthening of the investment and production networks of "greater China" (China, Taiwan, and Hong Kong). By the end of the century it was apparent that any emerging East Asia–wide economic system would be centered on China, not

Japan. A plausible institutional framework for an East Asian community is the grouping known as ASEAN Plus Three (APT), adding China, Japan, and South Korea to the ten ASEAN states.

Moves toward regional coalescence, at least in the economic sphere, are also seen in the other major world regions. SAARC (South Asian Association for Regional Cooperation) formally brings together all South Asian states, though it could also be seen as defining India's hegemonic reach—aside from Pakistan's sometimes awkward inclusion and potential role as spoiler. But India's rapidly increasing economic strength and place as an emerging world power arguably gain little from that grouping.

Latin America south of Mexico, once to be accommodated by NAFTA's transformation into the Americas-wide FTAA, is now more often seen as an emerging region in itself, building on its two main existing trade pacts, Mercosur and the Andean Community. An envisaged continent-wide South American Community of Nations (CSN) would be explicitly modeled on the EU—even to a common passport and currency. Brazil is set to remain the region's heavyweight power: its GDP in 2004 was four times the size of Argentina's, the next largest economy (though not yet surpassing Mexico's). In the Goldman Sachs forecasts, it would be closing on Japan's GDP by 2050.

The Middle East and North Africa, from the Maghreb to the Gulf, has a loose political identity in the 22-country Arab League and has displayed sporadic aspirations to unity. There is substantial labour migration within this region but little basis for a strong regional economy. Finally, the African Union—successor to the Organisation for African Unity—has a broad integrative ambition, if as yet with scant accomplishment. In the words of the African Union Commission (2004: 16), "Africa must form vast and viable internal markets to…pave the way for inter-African division of labour according to relative domestic and external advantages, and confer on these huge collective entities a genuine power of negotiation with the markets already constituted on other continents."

The present and projected population sizes of the main regional groupings are shown in Table. Together these now make up 88 per cent of the world population, a proportion that would be maintained in 2050 under the assumption of unchanged country composition. Market size, of course, would yield a different ranking, with the EU and NAFTA currently well ahead but ASEAN Plus Three rapidly catching up and SAARC also becoming a major market force.

The more general change that permits moves toward "ever closer union" in regional groupings, but that extends beyond regionalism, is a shift in the meaning of national sovereignty itself. Such a change is signaled by the popularity of adjectives like virtual or postmodern to describe certain countries. The "virtual state," analogous to the virtual corporation —a company "with a head but no body"—supplants the older trading state that was obsessed with territory and resources and worried about locating production within its borders. Japan, Korea, and Singapore are in the vanguard of virtuality; China and Russia remain "territorial fetishists" (ibid.).

Post-modernity as a political characterisation appears in the work of international relations theorists like Buzan (1998) and Cooper (2003), who divide countries into premodern, modern, and postmodern. The modern group is made up of the conventionally-sovereign states that first emerged in seventeenth-century Europe and gradually became a universal model of statehood, spreading worldwide with the ending of the colonial empires. The premodern countries are the Somalias, Afghanistans, Sudans, and Liberias—characterised by "low levels of sociopolitical cohesion and poorly developed structures of government" (Buzan 1998: 223), whether not yet having reached modernity or having degenerated into political disorder and ungovernability. And the postmodern are those that have begun to relax their sovereignty. "Postmodern states have a much more open and tolerant attitude toward cultural, economic, and political interaction, and define a much narrower range of things as threats to national sovereignty" (ibid.: 221–222).

The postmodern world is the one taking shape in Europe, envisaged in the treaties underpinning the European Union ("a highly developed system for mutual interference in each other's domestic affairs, right down to beer and sausages"—Cooper 2003: 27), the Council of Europe, and the Organisation for Security and Co-operation in Europe, with glimmers of a wider application indicated by a slew of international treaties on matters such as security, justice, and the environment. America, in this classification, is in many respects still a "modern" state, its concessions to internationalism (principally the WTO) often reluctant and subordinated, when deemed necessary, to national interests. In East Asia, China is modern, Japan postmodern.

Is post-modernity, in this political sense, the all-but-inevitable path for the world as a whole as globalisation proceeds, or a fairly special outcome among a few groups of likeminded states? Consideration of demographic realities, undertaken below, would suggest the latter is the more likely.

DEMOGRAPHY AND GLOBALISATION

The large income differences that drive contemporary international migration are the results of a long process of uneven development. In a stylised depiction of economic history, each country journeys from a position of poverty along a path toward greater material comfort. Some countries progress rapidly, others lag behind. The speed of advance is not uniform: overtaking and backsliding occur, gaps between countries narrow or widen. At least since the industrial revolution, however, Europe and its overseas offshoots, notably the United States, along with Japan, have led the pack. Their lead increased considerably over the last century.

The factors explaining the economic ranking at any moment are complex, intertwined, and often deeply rooted in the past. Among them are differences in acquisitiveness and in aptitude in seeking material advancement; ability to develop institutions conducive to thrift, trust, and cooperation beyond kin groups; interest in science and in its practical applications; favourable geographic location, climate, and access to natural resources; military prowess and skills in making and maintaining peace; and willingness to take risks and luck in having them pay off. A host of others could be added.

One of these factors, again in interaction with others, is demographic behavior. During their modern history, the presently rich countries benefited from the economic stimulus of spurts in population growth, yet they avoided the kind of expansion that, by natural increase alone, can multiply a population eightfold or more during a single century. Europe, in particular, could have built up a population that today would be a numerical match to China or India, or that could even have surpassed those countries in size. But, under the guidance of fortuitous institutional structures, Europe's aggregate population growth was kept in check during its modern history. By the late twentieth century, under circumstances of unparalleled prosperity, Europe was approaching zero population growth. Its countries developed elabourate welfare states, promising, and to a large extent providing, material comforts and security to every citizen. Europe seemed prepared to settle down to enjoy the pleasures of a stationary state.

Europe's offshoots in North America and Oceania retained much the same demographic pattern of moderate to low natural increase (births minus deaths). Their distinctiveness lay in tolerating and even promoting a large migrant influx, accommodated initially by an open land frontier and subsequently by similarly open labour markets—and, in the US case especially, more modest provision of an economic safety net.

Being born in one of these rich, stable societies in effect automatically imparts a gift—an unearned rent traceable to the wise demographic choices, individually or in their aggregate result, made by ancestors in a parade of generations reaching back into the deep past. Those seeking entry into these lucky countries by immigration can be thought of as trying to capture that same rent by the only other available route.

Threats to the European Social Model

Ironically, even before being fully able to realize its promises, this "European social model"—both in Europe and in its counterparts elsewhere—is now under threat. It is menaced from two developments, each of which has a key demographic component.

The first of these threats is overshoot in the reduction of fertility. Bringing fertility to a long-run replacement level is a historical imperative. Falling somewhat under replacement need not be differently characterised: fertility cannot be fine-tuned to 2.06 children per woman. For a long period, affluent industrial societies could certainly live with a slow decline in their populations and adjust to the economically less advantageous age structure associated with it, without suffering grim economic and social consequences.

But should fertility settle at a level deeply below replacement, the rapid fall-off in population numbers together with the associated age structure—resembling, if plotted as an age pyramid, a pear stood on its stem—cannot be accommodated. Short of a policy-engineered revival of fertility, which, of course, has a long (20 years plus) lead time, mass immigration then becomes the only possible remedy. The scale of migration called for, however, elicits the kinds of responses discussed earlier in this chapter. Not least among them would be the erosion of political support for the redistributive measures of the welfare state.

The second population-linked threat is external: it arises from the processes of globalisation, which draw mature postindustrial, post-demographic transition societies into economic interaction with materially much poorer societies—societies that have a different demographic past, different current demographic configurations, and different demographic prospects. Economic theory supplies a convincing demonstration of the advantages of extending the scope of economic interactions from the narrowly local to the national and, beyond that, to the global level. Although the demonstration is studded with massive ceteris paribus assumptions that dictate caution, it is evident that larger markets permit greater division of labour, stimulate competition, specialisation, innovation, and higher productivity, and provide their participants with access to a greater variety of goods. In so doing, the enlarged market delivers higher incomes and promotes economic growth: it makes individuals and countries richer.

Historical experience bears out the thesis. The first great epoch of globalisation, the late nineteenth and early twentieth century, brought rapid economic growth in the leading industrial countries and sparked the beginning of industrialism throughout the rest of the world. The drastic curtailment of international trade by protectionist policies in the interwar years was associated with low growth and eventually with the misery of the Great Depression. After World War II, renewed efforts at international liberalisation resulted in a vast expansion of international trade and unprecedented prosperity.

But that postwar success story was, in fact, geographically quite limited, and hence is a less than compelling argument for the merits of globalisation. Much of the expansion of trade took place among the rich countries. These countries possessed similar or fast-converging levels of income, rendering them natural partners in trade. The second world—the Soviet Empire, with China nominally also included—was not part of the emerging free trade zone. Neither was India, an official admirer and would-be imitator of the Soviet prewar ambition of "socialism in one country." The countries of Africa mostly espoused and in part practiced "African socialism," and those of the Middle East similarly experimented with local varieties of the socialist model. Ideology also kept much of Latin America out-side the revived world market: interaction with the "center" was seen as perpetuating peripheral status and solidifying economic dependency.

The conspicuous exceptions to these stand-apart regions were the market-oriented countries of East Asia. Guided by the visible but skillful hand of their governments, these "tiger economies" seised the opportunity for rapid industrialisation offered by trade with, and unimpeded flow of capital investment from, the leading capitalist countries. Strategic considerations in the context of the Cold War helped to make the West a willing partner in these exchanges. But relative demographic size clearly facilitated that willingness. Even if Japan is included among the newly industrialising trading partners—and, of course, by the 1970s Japan was solidly positioned within the core of the capitalist world—their combined population, or, more relevantly, the combined size of their potential labour resources, represented a small fraction of the labour force of the leading capitalist countries. Any pain from losing industrial jobs to the East Asian tigers was clearly overshadowed by the economic gains generated by increased trade.

Not surprisingly, the lessons of success are eventually absorbed by others, and the recipes are adopted. The big turnaround came in China, marked by the Dengist reforms of the early 1980s that freed trade between China and the outside world and opened the Chinese market to foreign investment. The ranks of imitators thereafter grew rapidly. The latest major convert to the advantages of exploiting the global marketplace has been the formerly autarky-seeking, reform-socialist India. Today, despite the loud protests voiced at successive World Social Forums, ostensibly speaking on behalf of the world's poor, there are hardly any less developed countries that wish to shut themselves off from globalisation.

For the industrialised countries, however, this new globalisation of globalisation presents an unprecedented challenge. It places them in competition with newly emerging industrial countries that possess labour forces, actual and potential, vastly greater in size than their own and does so under circumstances in which the former advantages that favoured them in such competition are rapidly disappearing. The problem is highlighted in warnings insistently issued to the citizenry in the EU and, with less justification, in the United States: "You must work harder and longer than before; you must give up privileges to which you have grown accustomed; and even if you do so, your job may evaporate tomorrow." Why? "Because of globalisation! You are in competition with countless millions of workers in faraway lands who are eager and able to do what you do and do it just as well, and are willing to do it for wages that are a fraction of yours."

Such rhetoric in part simply draws attention away from problems that have nothing to do with globalisation but derive from features in the existing design of systems of social protection that are becoming unsustainable because of population aging. These problems require domestic reforms, regardless of the extent of exposure to foreign competition. But the element of truth the warnings contain, when considered alongside the demographic realities alluded to, warrants further examination. What is at issue is the viability of the WTO trade regime from the standpoint of the developed world over the lengthy period—perhaps decades—during which technological differences between the demographic giants largely vanish but substantial wage differentials persist.

Off Shoring and the Demographic Overhang

In the past, the relatively high wages (and high non-wage costs) prevailing in the rich countries were routinely explained and justified by the higher productivity of their workers. That competitive edge derived from advantages that developing countries were once unable to replicate—a well-educated labour force that has privileged access to the best technology and to superior complementary factors of production such as management and marketing skills, organisational prowess, modern communication and transportation infrastructure, and a secure and healthy environment.

These advantages have fast been eroding as transnational corporations increasingly recreate them in locations where labour costs are much lower. Transferring industrial production to other countries then becomes an option favoured by an elementary economic calculus. The wage differentials are initially seen in the "rubber shoes, bicycles, and umbrellas" type manufactures. In the West, many one-time worriers about Japan's postwar economic predicament thought such products would be Japan's future way of earning a (modest) living through exports. Today no observer could miss the ability of China or India to produce a vast range of consumer and capital goods using the most advanced technologies, and their ability to sell such goods more cheaply than those manufactured in the high-wage industrial countries.

China's Minister of Commerce, Bo Xilai, sought to defuse European objections to high levels of textile imports by remarking that China would need to sell 800 million shirts to afford one Airbus A380 (*China Daily*, 5 May 2005). A more significant calculation he did not essay was how long it would be before there was a Chinese-built A380. Services are similarly prone to "offshoring" from high-income countries, and, as with manufacturing, skills in themselves offer no necessary protection. The criterion, as Blinder (2006) has noted, is whether the output of a job can be delivered electronically: "Janitors and crane operators are probably immune to foreign competition; accountants and computer programmers are not."

Many jobs in the personal care industry—a growth sector in any country with an aging population—cannot be exported. And at least for a while, headquarters of transnational enterprises may remain in the centers from which much of the capital and most of the technology driving the new industrialisation still originate. In this last case, however, even if such geographic specialisation could be seen as permanent, favouring a well-compensated elite, not everybody in the former seats of manufacturing can be a banker, a lawyer, an advertising and public relations executive, marketing strategist, systems analyst, or management consultant. Moreover, research and development activities —the labouratories that power innovation and raise productivity—are among the strongest current candidates for outsourcing to China and India. The "symbolic analysts" who were to maintain the technical edge of the West's postindustrial economies are then as likely to be found in Shanghai and Bangalore as in Silicon Valley or the two Cambridges.

A more promising and steady jobs-assuring and export-earning large industry in the advanced stage of international specialisation could be tourism—say, between the EU and the emerging modern Asia. In essence, Europe could be transformed into a huge theme park, geared for the entertainment of curious visitors, increasingly comprising the newly rich of Asia. In the ensuing equilibrium position, general material affluence might reign.

But such a future, even on aesthetic grounds, would not appeal to countries with the memory of a quite different history. Enthusiasts for globalisation, whether seeing it as accelerating world development or as improving returns to capital, do of course recognize the major adjustment problems that off shoring imposes on developed-country workforces—even after taking account of the lower prices of the foreign-sourced goods and services and, partly in consequence, lower inflation. But they argue that any disadvantage is temporary: currencies will adjust to correct some of the trade imbalance, and industrial wages will quickly rise in the new locations.

The problem with this expectation lies in the sheer demographic scale of the emerging economies. China and India, and many countries coming behind them, have large labour reserves in the traditional sectors of their economies that will not be exhausted for decades to come and will keep wages down. (That expectation is not belied by signs of upward pressure on wages, as observed recently in urban China. More probable explanations would point to temporary labour market frictions and educational bottlenecks.) For the West, moreover, a shift in manufacturing locations from China or India to Vietnam or Bangladesh would be no gain: the bottom line is the still-massive rural and fringe-urban populations in emerging manufacturing economies, providing several decades of something approaching an "unlimited" labour supply. As long as these populations exist and can be mobilised, permitting wage equalisation upward would retard full modernisation of the countries that possess them.

The absolute numbers of potential entrants to the modern economy are sobering. UN projections of urban growth extend only to the next 25 years, but they show proportions rural in 2030 still at 40 per cent in China and nearly 60 per cent in India. In China, admittedly, that population will by then be aging rapidly; but elsewhere, notably in India, the cohort of entrants to the labour force shows only modest fall-off— under the UN's most optimistic scenario of fertility decline. The overall demographic contrast over time with the United States and the European Union, the two main components of the West.

This line of argument is set out in only the sketchiest terms, and may seem overdrawn. But its consideration in the ongoing debate about the merits of globalisation is likely to be unavoidable. The weight of academic opinion, especially among economists (for example, see Lal 2006), is on the side of pushing ahead along the track we are on. But popular opinion disagrees, and its potential for exploitation by populist demagogues is all too real. Are there alternative models for the organisation of the international system over the next few decades that might lessen the opportunity for and appeal of demagoguery?

One that is worth fuller consideration (it is discounted by Lal) might be described as "regional quasi-autarky." What this entails is not a return to inward-looking protectionism at the country level: that has no attraction—if indeed it were even feasible. But a regional grouping of countries of comparable income levels, together offering a substantial productive base and internal market, could make good sense. A European Union is large enough, with nearly half a billion people, to exploit almost all conceivable economies of scale (perhaps only the Airbus actually requires a global market) and to provide a competitive environment assuring innovation and steadily improving product quality. Within its boundaries its rules already forbid protectionism. And it is large enough to provide balance—a diversity of industries and activities allowing for complementarities and unplanned synergies.

How much more advantage can be squeesed out of extra diversity, in a region where Finns rub shoulders with Portuguese and Irish with Greeks? In short, as a region in itself the EU could flourish with a fair degree of autarky (energy excepted), working primarily to satisfy its internal market. The same recipe could fit North America or a larger Western Hemisphere grouping. And something similar could be fashioned from what some already call China's co-prosperity sphere, or an analogous region for India. These regions could live in peace with each other—a supposed attribute of democracies—and also trade. The EU needs some exotic spices; its citizens want to visit the Great Wall, the Grand Canyon, and the Taj Mahal. Mutatis mutandis, each of the other regions has comparable needs and desires. As with the EU and the United States today, there would be no objection to crafting special trade relationships in support of particularly backward economies. In a more remote future, setting aside all that may go wrong, population pyramids around the world will even out—and, we can hope, will not have converged to the inverted pear-shaped structure. Worldwide economic prosperity of a sort will have been attained. In such a world, true globalisation is likely to emerge as a real option. That future, however, not least for solid demographic reasons, is not within our grasp in the next 50 years.

AN UNDERCLASS OF STATES?

The "global" in globalisation and the global economy thus far and perhaps well into the future is less than all-encompassing. A significant number of countries have fairly negligible links with the major trading economies aside from the trickle of imports financed by foreign aid; others have substantial exports but deriving from extractive-industry enclaves with revenues diverted to a narrow elite in the society. For whatever reason—there are many candidates—these countries have not managed to find or hold to the development path taken by the successful emerging economies. Disproportionately they are located in sub-Saharan Africa.

Per capita GDP in sub-Saharan Africa, based on Maddison's (2003) calculations, has hardly moved since the 1970s. The two vaunted regional high-flyers, Botswana and Mauritius, are impressive exceptions but their combined populations amount to less than 0.5 per cent of the regional total. The past ten years have seen an improvement in this dismal record, which some observers believe may presage a larger turnaround under which Africa would slowly regain the economic promise that it possessed in the immediate aftermath of decolonisation in the 1960s. That, at least, is the vision promulgated by the Commission for Africa, whose 2005 report was endorsed by the G-8 and by major foreign-aid donor agencies.

It is implicit in the rhetoric of the African Union and its NEPAD (New Partnership for Africa's Development) initiative. The factors militating against such a turnaround, though, are formidable. The AIDS epidemic is one such factor. The bleak future for sub-Saharan Africa portrayed by Christopher Clapham (2006) has much to do with AIDS. The extraordinary fall in life expectancy at birth beginning in the 1990s in South Africa, Botswana, and Zimbabwe—by 20 years or more, to numbers not seen at a country level for many decades—presents huge development problems in addition to the tragedy it represents for individuals, families, and communities. Predictions of the future course of the AIDS epidemic vary widely—indeed, even estimates of current HIV prevalence rates are often questioned—but many analysts have retreated from earlier dire predictions of a continent-wide pandemic.

Some countries that had experienced high rates of HIV prevalence and AIDS mortality in the early years of the epidemic have managed to reduce both; others, against expectations, seem to have largely avoided epidemic rates of infection.

These outcomes apparently stem from some combination of health education, modifications in sexual behavior, interventions to prevent mother-to-child HIV transmission, and the fortuity of particular cultural practices (such as male circumcision, which apparently lowers infection risk). It is not wholly implausible that even without wide access to effective medical treatment—still a distant prospect for much of the region—the impact of the disease will gradually subside to a level that, while still serious, is more comparable to that of other health risks.

Heavy AIDS mortality over coming years but a less-than-dire scenario for the duration and spread of the epidemic are the assumptions made in the current UN population projections for Africa. As statistics shows, the medium projections for 2050 foresee a Uganda of 127 million, an Ethiopia of 170 million, a Congo of 177 million, and a Nigeria of 258 million. Overall, sub-Saharan Africa is expected to grow from 0.75 billion in 2005 to 1.69 billion in 2050; at mid-century, even though average fertility is assumed to have halved from its current level, the absolute annual increase in population would still be growing. This added weight of numbers will be a burden on development efforts and intensify already severe problems of governability. Glib assertions about economy-boosting demographic bonuses provided by favourable youth-dependency ratios—the potential reallocations from consumption and capital-widening expenditures to growth-enhancing investments—presuppose just those conditions of social order and administrative capacity that rapid population growth threatens.

A sanguine prognosis for the region would see some countries doing well (South Africa is the main hope among the larger economies) and many others, in one way or another, advancing at a pace sufficient to allow substantial improvement in social and economic conditions. Even under such a favourable outcome it is all but certain there will also be laggards and backsliders.

States that combine poverty, economic retrogression, and pervasive domestic insecurity can be described as failing or, where these conditions have been longstanding, as "failed." African examples include Angola, Burundi, DR Congo, Guinea, Ivory Coast, Liberia, Sierra Leone, Sudan, and Zimbabwe. The category is far from clearcut and by no means precludes a state so described eventually regaining a foothold on the development path—though it may be starting from a much lower position.

Failing or failed states are not found only in Africa. Afghanistan, East Timor, Haiti, Iraq, Nepal, North Korea, Papua New Guinea, and Yemen are among others that also fit the description. Few are populous: only in sub-Saharan Africa and perhaps the south-western Pacific do such states amount to a significant fraction of their respective regional populations.

By some assessments, however, states "at risk" include Nigeria, Bangladesh, and Pakistan. That would lend the problem a truly ominous global dimension. But even a lack of significance in economic and demographic terms does not mean that failed states have no bearing on the evolution of the global economy and polity. The energy exporters among them obviously remain important in a tight suppliers' market for fossil fuels. Others figure disproportionately as sources of refugees and, through criminal and terrorist activity, as regional destabilisers or even threats to more distant states. And without functioning civil administrations, they are ill-equipped to combat infectious disease or environmental destruction, both with potential for damaging spillover effects beyond their borders.

UNCERTAINTIES AND SURPRISES

The varying assumptions underlying population forecasts like those of the United Nations concern the pace of fertility transition, 17 which in turn reflects the course of economic growth and cultural change. As was discussed above, such forecasts can go seriously awry over a span of half a century even without effects that would count as surprises. Interestingly, however, most of the dramatic events that are thereby ignored—wars, famines, floods, plagues—are barely visible at the broad regional scale and not at all at the global level. Thus the 1959–61 Great Leap Forward famine in China, perhaps the largest in history, killing some 30 million, can hardly be discerned in an East Asian population series. AIDS deaths in the tens of millions in sub-Saharan Africa go with a projected net addition of one billion persons in that region (150 per cent) over the half-century to 2050.

In his assessment of the risks of other such "fatal discontinuities" in this period, from asteroid collisions to microbes and nanobots, the geographer (and polymath) Vaclav Smil (2005a) finds most of the usual candidates for worldwide catastrophe comfortably distant or improbable. Influenza and war are the main exceptions—with broadly similar risk fatality profiles. A worldwide influenza epidemic is seen as unavoidable in the next few decades—the unknown being whether its fatalities can be kept down to a few tens of millions.

Precisely because its effects would be so widespread, however, a flu pandemic is not likely to be a destabilising force in the global political economy. That is not true for war, which ample historical precedent shows can be genuinely transformational. While encouragement can be taken from the declining trend in major conflicts over the twentieth century, what in the past have turned out to be transformational wars have sometimes been wholly unforeseen.

Discontinuities in the evolution of the global system can come about without mass fatalities. Environmental change offers several such scenarios, and doubtless many others that have not been imagined. The gradual atmospheric warming over the twenty-first century, predicted by general circulation models of the climate system, is the best known of these scenarios—its most severe effects coming later in the century but likely to be clearly visible well before. There are potentially large implications for the regional distribution of agricultural zones, for the prevalence ranges of particular infectious and parasitic diseases, and for coastal erosion and flooding from a rise in sea levels, in addition to drastic effects on the nonhuman biota. Rising fossil-fuel use and resultant greenhouse gas emissions, the main anthropogenic factor in global warming, owe more to economic than demographic expansion. But per capita emissions, bound to rise fast in China, India, and the other main emerging economies even under optimistic assumptions about abatement technologies, are multiplied by these countries' huge population numbers.

Wealth brings improved means to adapt to change, so global inequalities will be accentuated by these environmental effects. Many poor countries are particularly vulnerable. New food-deficit regions will probably emerge—and new areas of surplus—calling for major adjustments in the international trade in cereals. Coastal settlement will be affected: in more alarmist scenarios, "environmental refugees" would be created in great numbers. Responsibility for damage, once assigned, elicits demand for compensation. In the international arena such claims are sometimes recognised—for wartime occupation, for instance—typically through ad hoc bilateral negotiations. The possibilities of broad-scale damage to particular groups of countries through climate change may elicit claims of an altogether greater magnitude. The guilty parties—guilty of a kind of aggression, from one perspective—would be the industrialised countries, many of them not only current large emitters but the main contributors to the build-up of greenhouse gases over decades past.

Adjudication of such claims may well devolve into more rounds of debate like those that have taken place in follow-up meetings on the 1992 Climate Convention (one of which produced the Kyoto Protocol), yielding treaties notably lacking in enforceable sanctions for nonperformance and with few repercussions on other spheres of international relations. Or, it may be that these distributional issues originating in environmental change will become a dominant concern for the international system.

Climate modeling of the kind that underpins the projections of the Intergovernmental Panel on Climate Change yields smooth output trajectories—a warming, say, of a few degrees Centigrade by the end of this century. But sudden climatic shifts, beyond the predictive ability of current models, also seem possible. A widely publicised scenario of this sort is for ocean warming to disrupt heat circulation by ocean currents in the North Atlantic, and in particular to halt the moderating effect of the Gulf Stream on the climate of Western Europe. (Edinburgh and Copenhagen are on the same latitude as Moscow.) Research on the fine detail of climate history has uncovered many instances in the distant past of abrupt regime change—major rises or falls in mean temperatures in a region, sometimes taking place in a period as short as a decade but lasting perhaps for centuries. What can set off such events is unknown, but their existence adds to the range of uncertainty surrounding the effects of present trends in atmospheric composition.

Climate change aside, environmentalists also point to looming problems of degradation of ecological services—the often unpriced benefits humans receive from the various ecological systems they are part of. Examples of ecosystem services are crop pollination, fresh water supply from streams and aquifers, natural processes of soil formation and erosion control, nutrient cycling, and photosynthesis. Mounting evidence indicates that many such services are being degraded or drawn on at unsustainable rates, as a consequence of population growth, economic expansion, and poor management practices. Here too there are many possibilities for repercussions for human well-being and for economic and political systems beyond national borders.

A particular class of ecosystem service has to do with the aesthetic values humans derive from the natural environment. Those amenity values can in some measure be price rationed like ordinary goods and services, thereby limiting adverse congestion effects for users. Population growth itself has been a factor in the enclosure or privatisation of many common-access resources. But given the choice, most people would likely resist that privatisation route beyond modest limits, preferring to retain open access. Unless other kinds of rationing can be devised, degradation through overuse becomes a serious risk. David Victor (2006) addresses these issues in relation to wilderness areas. The international spillovers implicated in wilderness preservation or wilderness destruction are mostly intangible —the satisfaction many people find in knowing of their existence, and the pain over their loss—

but not a negligible element of welfare. Some conservation efforts attempt to translate those sentiments into monetary terms.

FUTURES FOR THE DEMOGRAPHIC FORERUNNERS

In the very long term, beyond the time-horizon of this essay, full or near-full global convergence in demographic patterns might be achieved, along with—most would no doubt hope—a fairly stationary population or one trending slowly downward to a preferred global optimum. That is the future that the cosmologist Fred Hoyle (1963), in a brief foray into demography, called dull (his less-dull alternative was a time-series of population explosions and collapses), although a vision of human continuity is hard to reconcile with large departures from demographic stationarity. Dullness is not a risk over the next 50 years. The coming half-century is likely to see the ending of massive global population expansion—at least, if the UN medium-variant projections are borne out. The demographic marginalisation of the countries currently classified as "more developed" vis-a-vis those classified as "less developed" will proceed apace, with a ratio of 1:10 in births virtually unchanged over the period. The striking contrasts in age structures across countries and regions will also persist, although lessening by mid-century. These differentials and trends have ramifying effects on the international political economy. For the more developed countries, they pose dilemmas for public policy, the chosen resolution of which will have profound implications for the societies and cultures that emerge.

Low fertility was discussed above as one of the main threats to the European social model, as it is to Japan's also. Continuation of the ultra-low fertility now experienced in Japan, Russia, and parts of the EU leads to a rapid and hard-to-reverse downward trend in population. Under the UN low-variant assumptions, for instance, Japan's and Italy's populations would both diminish by nearly one-quarter by 2050, Russia's by more than one-third. Future levels of fertility stuck below 1.5 children per woman are quite plausible—even as a Europe-wide average—implying, if maintained, generational population declines (aside from migration) of more than 25 per cent. Accompanying those declines would be burgeoning proportions of the old and very old, requiring costly medical care (and invidious rationing).

As a long-run prognosis offered as an option in a policy debate, this demographic outlook might well be judged unacceptable. Its presence in the background sets the stage for consideration of expanded immigration on the one hand and pronatalist measures on the other. Mere numbers, of course, are only the simplest of the issues that migration policy needs to be concerned with, but they are a convenient starting point. Low or moderate rates of immigration, combined with expectations of (and supporting measures for) integration, are unexceptionable responses to below-replacement fertility. Migration at rates that would be needed to significantly offset very low fertility, however, is a different matter. Integration then becomes far more problematic, and there is a likelihood of generating or further exacerbating serious cultural tensions. Even moderate inflows can yield high urban or fringe urban concentrations of immigrants, impeding assimilation—and, in the subsequent generation, producing alienation and anomie among persons with cultural roots in neither their parents' society nor the one surrounding them.

Heavy reliance on migration, as earlier remarked, is in some sense an easy option for public policy, assuming that ethnic and cultural tensions can be kept in check. But in avoiding the institutional reforms that would be called for in adapting to a low-fertility, aging society, political leaders and their constituents are setting the stage for a deeper societal transformation. Historically, of course, that has happened often enough, but it entails a potentially huge loss of cultural patrimony. Such a calculation may no longer have much force in affluent, late-capitalist societies—with individualism triumphant and self-fulfillment acknowledged by many as a principal goal. But realisation of impending transformation can also be a potent generator of populist reaction.

Maintaining fertility at a level that does not fall much below a two-child average—say, around 1.7–1.8—would largely avert this problem. Such levels (arguably creditable to some extent to supportive population policies) are found in some countries of Western and Northern Europe and in Australia and New Zealand; in the United States, fertility is even higher. But for those many countries in Europe—and for Japan—where levels are well below 1.5, that prospect is dim. There are narrow limits to welfare-state generosity in bribing would be parents, especially when the state is already overburdened with pension and health-care costs. There is a reluctance to make family allowances disproportionately high for third or later children—or for higher-income parents. There is lingering ideological resistance to the state trying to override personal preferences about childbearing. There is a strong economic interest in increasing female labour force participation, which, policy efforts notwithstanding, is a discouragement to childbearing.

And the state is powerless to counter cultural and value changes that favour low fertility or even childlessness. It is possible to imagine a spontaneous recovery in birth rates, like the prosperity-linked baby boom in the years after World War II or, more speculatively, through some radical cultural shift—a millenarian movement?—as yet unforeseen. The role for social policy in engineering an upturn, however, seems fairly marginal. Even if an upturn were to happen, moreover, it would take a quarter-century before the new homegrown labour force began to be felt in the economy; the migration alternative is at hand and has no delay.

As this discussion makes clear, the post-transition demographic predicament of the low-fertility West—the European Union and Japan most notably—is both serious and intractable. That appreciation should argue for concentrated deliberation over what kinds of societies and economies these countries should be trying to construct for themselves and about how they might protect them through the remaining decades of the global demographic transition. Over most of that time they must expect to be continually challenged by low-wage but high-skilled competitors in the world's populous dynamic economies over the whole range of tradable goods and services; at the same time, they will face continued clamoring for entry to their societies by a stream of would-be economic migrants and refugees from fragile or failing economies. Against these formidable pressures they must seek to maintain the levels of social protection and leisure and the other components of the quality of life that affluence has won for them, in the face of further population aging and steadily diminishing numbers of native-born labour force entrants. If nothing more, the deliberation called for might begin a process of strategic thinking about these issues, helping to avert a day-by-day caving in of policy to narrowly based interests and recourse to least effort political remedies. In the long run, if environmental and other dangers can be held in check, most human societies will have to find their way through the same demographic landscape, hence the experience of the forerunners should have much to teach.

In the United States, fertility has remained close to a two-child average, well above European and Japanese levels, and immigrants—even unskilled immigrants, provided they carry the requisite documents—are broadly welcomed. (The main caveat on migration applies to the large inflow from Mexico, seen by some as the making of a cultural—even political—*reconquista*.) Hence, there is no prospect of population growth ceasing in the foreseeable future. Medium Census Bureau projections show the 2050 US population at 420 million, almost 50 per cent above the 2000 census count; decadal increases are undiminished, in the range of 25–30 million. The words of the 1972 Commission on Population and the American Future ("recognising that our population cannot grow indefinitely," and recommending "that the nation welcome and plan for a stabilised population" —the population was then 210 million) have been decisively sidelined if not altogether rejected.

In its absence of a sense of national population *scale* or interest in stabilisation, the United States is something of an oddity in the developed world. What might eventually change that situation is unclear: localised congestion does not seem to. The contrast with other rich societies may extend to views of economic growth as well—albeit with elements of caricature on both sides. The vision Keynes spelled out in 1930, echoing John Stuart Mill a century earlier, plausibly resonates more in Europe and Japan than in the United States. The struggle for material goods, said Keynes (1963: 365–366), should not be "the permanent problem of the human race." He looked for a time when both material and demographic growth will have ceased, with attention turned to intellectual and aesthetic endeavors.

For the first time since his creation man will be faced with his real, his permanent problem—how to use his freedom from pressing economic cares, how to occupy the leisure, which science and compound interest will have won for him, to live wisely and agreeably and well. A contrasting vision of the pursuit of happiness is that described by Richard Easterlin (1996: 153–154)—a perspective with a distinctly American flavor: The future, then, to which the epoch of modern economic growth is leading is one of never ending economic growth, a world in which ever growing abundance is matched by ever rising aspirations, a world in which cultural differences are leveled in the constant race to achieve the good life of material plenty.

The world in which either of these futures might be near to realisation will also contain plenty of economic laggards. Some will be on an upward path—eased, no doubt, by flows of investment funds from the developed world, seeking economic returns wherever they can be found. But others might be more in the position of wards of the international community —though exposed to an ever-present risk of default on the part of that community and with their prospects worsened to the degree that any exceptional human talent they produce is siphoned off. Foreign assistance will still have a role, both in covering troughs in food production and in promoting development and demographic transition. Whether it can do so without repeating the many fruitless efforts of the past—by drawing on mature reflection on what should have been done in the last half-century—is far from certain.

3

EVOLUTION OF THE MODERN STATE SYSTEM

The modern state system emerged in Europe between the start of the 12th century and the end of the 17th. States began to replace existing forms of political organisation in the late Middle Ages in Europe when key actors, responding to a diverse set of political and economic incentives, formed coalitions that undermined one set of political arrangements, feudalism, and gradually replaced it with another, the sovereign state. The state was not the only available alternative to feudalism; and it took centuries for the state to emerge as the winning alternative.

The political arrangements in feudalism were very different from the modern state system. Feudal arrangements were personal commitments by individual lords and vassals. Public power and authority – including the military – were held by private individuals. Because feudal arrangements were not based on territorially defined political boundaries, the modern distinction between domestic and international politics has little meaning in a feudal context. During the Middle Ages most of the key actors in Europe thought of themselves as part of a single society defined by their allegiance to the Catholic Church and a shared heritage dating back to the Roman Empire. The close connections between the Church and the secular nobility further increased the cross-territorial nature of political institutions in the Middle Ages and greatly complicated the structure of medieval linkage politics.

Two internal sources of pressure destabilised the feudal system. The first was a centuries-long conflict between the pope and the Holy Roman Emperor, which exhausted the only two claimants to universal authority in medieval Europe. The second was a large and sustained increase in trade, which led to an increase in the number of new actors: the merchants and craftsmen who made up the burghers. They had both the ability and the desire to seek coalition partners who could help them challenge existing political and economic arrangements.

The large territorial state won as the successor to feudalism because it was better than the two other principal alternatives to feudalism – city leagues and city states – at organising the economy, mobilising internal resources in support of preferred policy outcomes, and creating a set of mutually acceptable, long-term relationships that could manage how the political units in Europe interacted with each other.

The first European states emerged during the Renaissance. Initially there were no agreed-upon norms that could legitimize either their domestic political arrangements or the relationships among states. The conflicts produced by the Reformation (the Protestant challenge to the hegemony of the Catholic Church) and the Counter-Reformation (the Catholic attempt to reassert the Church's dominant position) greatly worsened this problem, producing a century of war from the mid-1500s to the mid-1600s.

In 1648, the Peace of Westphalia, which ended the Thirty Years' War, created a set of agreed-upon principles for legitimate rule that provided the first normative basis for the modern state system. War would continue, but (with one major exception) it was war for incremental advantage within a system, not war about the system. As a result, wars were usually fought for limited aims, and treaties were negotiated with an eye toward compromise and jointly acceptable outcomes that would last over a long period of time.

The classical balance of power system (c.1648-c.1789) had a simple goal: to preserve the independence of the key states by preventing any one state from becoming so powerful militarily that it could dominate all the others. Wars of containment were a central mechanism for achieving that goal. Classical balance of power principles called for defeated states to be rehabilitated, not destroyed, so that they would be available as potential alliance partners against any new threats in the future. There were supposed to be no permanent friends or enemies; all the major powers had to be availabie as potential alliance partners for one another. The small states, including especially the many principalities in central Europe, were considered expendable.

All of the prerequisites for an effective balance-of-power system that existed between the Peace of Westphalia in 1648 and the French Revolution of 1789 gradually disappeared under the combined pressures of the Industrial Revolution, the growth of nationalism, and the demand for democratic governments. The French Revolution signaled the beginning of the end of the classical balance of power system. The Westphalian norm that sanctioned dynastic rule was directly threatened not only by the demand for democratic representation that was at the center of the French Revolution but also by the nationalism it unleashed. The French Revolution also generated a drive for preponderance, thereby directly attacking one of the most cherished goals of classical balance of power.

The Concert of Europe, the diplomatic coalition of major powers established after the Napoleonic wars, was an effort to restore the old order and the balance-of-power system. It was simultaneously innovative and profoundly conservative. The innovations were in the international arena, where the major powers (with the exception of Great Britain) replaced the decentralised approach of classical balance of power with a standing alliance designed to enable them to act in concert. The conservative dimensions of the Concert were in the domestic arena, where monarchs tried to save the legitimising principles of the old order by suppressing domestic coalitions that supported social and political change.

The efforts by the states in the Concert of Europe to restore the old order failed, largely because the legitimising principles established at Westphalia – and the goals and methods of the classical balance of power – were incompatible with fundamental economic, political, and social changes. Between 1863 and 1890, Bismarck demolished what remained of the balance-of-power system. After exploiting German nationalism to unify the German states in a series of three wars, he scrapped the idea in the Westphalian system that a regime's legitimacy was based on interstate agreements ratified by treaty. He then built a network of alliances that were qualitatively different from those in the balance-of-power system. The Bismarckian security system was a complex web of alliances designed to deter the strong and restrain the weak. It was also designed to prevent the creation of reinforcing grievances and antagonistic blocs while simultaneously isolating France and preserving German preeminence on the European continent.

Bismarck's post-unification alliance system was designed to preserve the status quo. After 1890, his successors' decision to use power politics to demand a global role for Germany led to the collapse of Bismarck's intricate web of alliances and the diplomatic encirclement of Germany by Britain, France, and Russia. In response, German policy makers developed a defense strategy – called the Schlieffen Plan – that was designed to win a two-front war. Unfortunately, the only way they could see to do that required starting a war as soon as any of their neighbors mobilised their armies. That put the German military on a hair trigger in any crisis.

The Rise of the Sovereign Territorial State

Feudalism and the Manorial System

The modern state claims final and exclusive authority over a defined territory. As part of that claim, the state refuses to recognize any external claims to authority as legitimate. The political arrangements in *feudalism* were very different: they were built on personal ties among the nobility that were often overlapping and crosscutting (in the sense that they frequently tugged actors in different directions).

Because feudal arrangements were not based on territorially defined political boundaries, the modern distinction between domestic and international politics has little meaning in a feudal context. Moreover, as Joseph Strayer, one of the most eminent 20th century historians of the feudal period, stressed, public power and authority—including the military—were held by private individuals: "the basic characteristics of feudalism in Western Europe are a fragmentation of political authority, public power in private hands, and a military system in which an essential part of the armed forces is secured through private contracts."

Significantly, the feudal arrangements of the High Middle Ages (c. 1000–c. 1300) were themselves the product of a long period of selection that had followed the fall of the Roman Empire in about A.D. 476. Whatever the atrocities committed in its name—and its many other limitations from a modern perspective—the Roman Empire had created a system of law and education throughout much of Europe. When a combination of internal decay and external attack led to the empire's collapse, Europe entered a long period (the Early Middle Ages) of barbarism and military conflict. As a result of this centuries-long conflict, regional trade virtually ground to a halt, cities emptied as people fled to the countryside in an effort to raise enough food to survive, and the Roman system of laws and education crumbled. In those areas that did not depend on pillage to survive, economic activity came to focus on the *manorial system. Manors* were large, private holdings of agricultural land that formed self-sufficient economic systems in which the nobility (who owned all the land and buildings by virtue of birth and inheritance) and the peasants (who were in many ways as much the property of the lord as the land and buildings) survived off what the land would produce.

In the midst of this disintegration, one institution grew significantly stronger during the Early Middle Ages—the Catholic Church. The Church had been brutally suppressed during the Roman Empire. In the aftermath of the fall of Rome, the Church became the most important source of education, moral law, and social services in most of Europe. These functions were supported by the Church's ability to mobilize resources. The Church owned more land than any other institution or actor in Europe in this period. It also was the recipient of religious taxes (the tithe, imposed on all Christians, was set at 10 per cent of gross income). In addition, a variety of subsidies and payments from political and economic actors around Europe enriched the Church.

By the eighth century, the combination of its extensive resources and its dominant religious role made the Church the most pervasive political actor in Europe. It was, however, vulnerable to growing military assaults being made by Muslims on the periphery of Europe and to challenges by secular rulers within Europe who wished to gain access to the Church's resources by controlling the choice of the pope. Consequently, the Church needed a secular ally with significant military resources. These strategic needs were met by Charlemagne, the most important of a series of kings in the Carolingian family, who controlled much of the area in what is now France. On Christmas Day of 800 in

Rome, the pope personally crowned Charlemagne "emperor of the Romans," with the responsibility to protect all Christians. This arrangement gave each coalition partner something of value: the pope got military support against his enemies; Charlemagne was able to claim, on the best earthly authority available in Christian Europe, the right to rule and expand. As we discuss below, this deal later became a recipe for long-term conflict between the pope and the Holy Roman Empire, which claimed that it was the legitimate heir to Charlemagne's mantle.

By the beginning of the High Middle Ages, most of the key actors in Europe thought of themselves as part of a single society defined by their allegiance to the Catholic Church and a shared heritage dating back to the Roman Empire. The assumption that Christendom created a common society was reinforced by a widely shared set of laws woven around three strands of legal principles. Perhaps the most important of these was *canon law*, which was enforced by hierarchically organised Church courts.

Canon law claimed both exclusive jurisdiction over the clergy and concurrent jurisdiction over lay actors in all matters involving religious law. Much more decentralised, but still quite widespread throughout Europe, was a shared framework that had evolved from Roman *civil law* and a growing body of *customary law*. These shared legal principles were not, however, backed by an overarching set of legal institutions. Instead, the compatibility of customary and civil law across Europe simply reflected the similarity of the beliefs and values built into Catholic culture. Indeed, confidence in these shared norms was high enough that it was taken for granted that ambassadors and other diplomats would be subject to the courts of the princes to which they were posted.

The result of all these factors was a distinctive form of linkage politics. For instance, the Count of Luxemburg was simultaneously a prince in the Holy Roman Empire and a *vassal*—a free man who entered into a formal personal relationship with a higher ranking free man, promising loyalty and deference (*fealty*) in exchange for either protection or a grant of land or revenue —to the king of France. Garrett Mattingly, a well-known diplomatic historian, describes the period this way:

Kings made treaties with their own vassals and with vassals of their neighbors. They received embassies (*i.e.*, ambassadors) from their own subjects and from the subjects of other princes, and sometimes sent agents who were in fact ambassadors in return. Subject cities negotiated with one another without reference to their respective sovereigns.

The overlapping and personal nature of feudal relationships is also emphasised by Hendrik Spruyt, a political scientist who has written an insightful analysis of the origins of the sovereign state. "One could simultaneously be the vassal of the German emperor, the French king, and various counts and bishops, none of whom necessarily had precedence over the other. . . . Consequently a vassal might be caught in crosscutting obligations that are very difficult to comprehend within our understanding of 'international' relations."

A real example of the complex personal relationships that characterised feudal linkage politics can be found in the crosscutting obligations of John Toul, who lived in the 12th century. Toul's feudal ties left him indebted to four nobles: Lord John of Arcis, Lord Enguerran of Coucy, the Count of Champagne, and the Count of Grandpre. Having four distinct sets of obligations created problems not only because it meant that there were multiple debts that could be called in at the same time, but also because it wasn't at all impossible that Toul would find himself in a situation in which he had ties to nobles on both sides of a conflict. If that happened, how was he to choose?

Since Medieval Europe was a hierarchical society, the first criterion for choosing which obligations to honor was the personal precedence, or standing, of the nobles involved. Both the Count of Champagne and the Count of Grandpre ranked significantly above Lord John of Arcis and Lord Enguerran of Coucy, so in any war involving either of the first two against either of the second two, Toul's responsibilities were clear: to come to the aid of Champagne or Grandpre.

But what if the war were between the Count of Champagne and the Count of Grandpre? Here the hierarchical nature of medieval society provided a more complex answer. Because the two counts were of such high status, the norms of feudal society led Toul to believe he ought to send help to both if each called on him to honor his oath of fealty. However, while both lords would get Toul's help, his obligations to Grandpre took precedence over his obligations to Champagne. Consequently, both the number of knights he would have to send to each and which lord Toul would personally fight alongside depended on whether the grievances were personal. In John of Toul's declaration of fealty his specific obligations were laid out in advance:

If it should happen that the count of Grandpre should be at war with the countess and count of Cssshampagne for his own personal grievances, I will personally go to the assistance of the count of Grandpre and will send to the countess and count of Champagne, if they summon me, the knights I owe for the fief which I hold of them. But if the count of Grandpre shall make war on the countess and count of Champagne on behalf of his friends and not for his personal grievances, I shall serve in person with the count and countess of Champagne and I will send one knight to the count of Grandpre to give the service owed from the fief which I hold of him. But I will not myself invade the territory of the count of Grandpre.

If the issues were personal, Toul would fight with Grandpre against Champagne and Toul's own knights, who he was obligated to send to Champagne. Change the occasion for Grandpre's declaration of war from personal to non-personal grievances, and Toul would fight with Champagne and Grandpre would receive only one of Toul's knights.

When assessing the implications of feudal political arrangements, it is important to remember a point mentioned above: During the medieval period the nobility had the exclusive right to bear arms and to mobilize what were, in effect, private armies. Because the nobility were also responsible for secular governance and law enforcement, the crosscutting and overlapping feudal obligations outlined above created a type of cross-arena politics totally unlike the links between domestic and foreign politics that characterize the modern state system. The complexity of these linkages was increased by the connections between the nobility and the Church, the other great institution of politics and governance.

While factions within the secular nobility and the Church made and broke coalitions in pursuit of their sometimes compatible and sometimes conflicting preferences, the people who generated the majority of the wealth in medieval Europe—the peasantry, who were typically tied to the manors as serfs, and the craftsmen and merchants in the towns (called burghers from burgh, meaning borough or town)—were systematically excluded from governance. According to contemporary beliefs, this political exclusion and economic exploitation were the necessary result of a natural hierarchy in which serfs and burghers served as workers underneath the nobles (who were supposed in turn to be the defenders of the faith) and the clergy.

When one reflects on how these separate pieces of the medieval puzzle fit together by the beginning of the High Middle Ages (c.1000), it is clear that in many ways Europeans lived in a mutually reinforcing network of religious, political, and economic relationships. However, given the right catalysts, there were two potential sources of pressure for change that could destabilize these arrangements. First, while there were some opportunities for upward mobility by individual burghers and peasants (especially if they could perform notable military service), burghers and peasants were clearly the economic and political losers in the existing arrangements. Whether or not they would choose to challenge the system depended, then, on their preferences, their perceived power, and the range of potential coalition partners. On all three dimensions the burghers were closer to turning into challengers than were the peasants, whose ignorance and poverty made them more likely to accept the legitimacy of the established order, less likely to believe that positive change was possible, and less attractive as coalition partners. The second potential source of internally driven change in the medieval system was the struggle between the Church and the Holy Roman Empire. Each claimed a right to exercise universal leadership within Christendom. Even as they continued to form a series of temporary coalitions to achieve short-term objectives, those incompatible long-term preferences led the pope and emperor to distrust each other's motives and to fear any significant increases in the other's power.

The Old Arrangements Unravel

The central role of the conflict between the pope and the emperor in undermining feudal relationships and opening up an opportunity for the rise of the state is well known by historians and political scientists.

The emperor's principal political and economic base was in German-speaking parts of central Europe, but he also had large holdings in northern and, intermittently, southern Italy. During the High Middle Ages, the growth of trade made the cities in the emperor's Italian provinces so wealthy that they generated more revenue than he got from his German feudal relationships and perhaps, according to some historical research, even more revenue than the French and English kings could extract from their vassals. These financial incentives for expanding the empire into the papal states, the areas in Italy controlled directly by the pope, were reinforced by two additional considerations. First, the pope and the emperor made incompatible claims for universal leadership throughout Christendom.

Second, the pope regularly used church ties to powerful lords in central Europe to build coalitions that resisted the emperor's efforts to gain firm control of his German-speaking territories. As a result, the pope was the biggest obstacle to both the emperor's political position and his policy objectives. Everything in this strategic situation pointed toward protracted conflict: high stakes, reinforcing political and policy incentives, and access to resources that could be used to sustain a challenge over a long period of time. It lasted from 1046 to 1356, when the emperor agreed – in an announcement called the Golden Bull – both to drop his claim to additional land in Italy and to end his efforts to centralize the empire.

The centuries-long conflict between the pope and the emperor exhausted the only two claimants to universal authority in medieval Europe. Recent research suggests that the destabilising effects of this conflict were greatly magnified by a substantial increase in long-distance trade that began during the 11th century. Why would increased trade undermine feudalism? Increased trade led to the rebirth of towns throughout Europe, which both ended the economic stranglehold of the manorial system and increased the political importance of the growing numbers of merchants and urban craftsmen who together made up the burghers. Economic growth gave burghers the resources to be key actors in coalitions that tried to fill the opening created by the debilitating struggle between the emperor and the pope. They also had compelling reasons to prefer a change in existing arrangements. The overlapping and crosscutting nature of feudal arrangements meant that merchants were constantly harassed by the competing claims of a wide variety of secular and church elites for a share of the new wealth. Moreover, elites from the governing classes imposed different rules for trade, different systems of money, and different standards for measuring the weight and volume of goods.

This situation produced a natural "burgher coalition" between merchants and the craftsmen whose goods they sold. It also produced merchant-led efforts to find allies outside the towns that could help them simplify the system. The coalitions they formed in different parts of Europe created what were, in effect, the three principal contenders to replace feudalism: (1) the claim of French kings to a large territorial state with exclusive jurisdiction over domestic secular issues; (2) a system of city-leagues in the Holy Roman Empire; and (3) the city-state system in Italy.

The Three Contenders to Replace Feudalism

The Large Territorial State. French kings had a long-standing preference for expanding their access to resources and strengthening their claim to legal and political supremacy in secular matters over the higher nobility and the Church. However, until the growth of towns and the rise of burghers as political actors, they were unable to overcome the blocking coalitions put together by the nobility and the Church. The burghers wanted predictability and common standards to promote trade. However, unlike the burghers in Germany (whose trade generated enough revenue to build city leagues) and those in Italy (whose cities were so rich that, once the papacy and the Holy Roman Empire went into decline, they could afford to go it alone as city-states), French burghers needed a powerful coalition partner. They found that partner in a succession of French kings, who wanted access to new resources that would enable them to build a strong central bureaucracy and buy off any nobles who were too powerful to control. They particularly wanted resources that were generated outside of agriculture, which was controlled by the nobility under the manorial system.

Members of the nobility, meanwhile, inadvertently undermined their own long-term political position by accepting the short-term gains created by the king's offer to let them substitute payments in money for personal military service. This substitution undermined the perceived legitimacy of the nobility's historic claim to a privileged position based on their role as protectors of the faith. It also enabled the king to pay mercenaries to staff a state-controlled military. By the time the higher nobility realised that they had cooperated in their own marginalisation, it was too late.

By the end of the 13th century, the coalition between French kings and the towns (in which the king was very much the senior partner) against the nobility and the Church put French monarchs in a position to buy the acquiescence of the nobles by exempting them from royal taxes and, when necessary, bribe them with pensions and other payments. Having coalesced with the burghers and bought off the nobility, French kings were able to make their claim to territorial sovereignty stick. Significantly, the effectiveness of the first claims to sovereignty depended very much on the kings' willingness to purchase the cooperation of the great nobles. As we discuss later, in the sixteenth century some monarchs unilaterally tore up this deal and tried to crush the ability of nobles to challenge them. This attempt to change the distribution of power so that kings could command obedience—rather than relying on coalitions to build support through mutually acceptable exchanges—produced rebellion and war.

The City Leagues. The strategic situation in the Holy Roman Empire produced a quite different set of political coalitions to replace feudal arrangements. There the emperor, worried about potential coalitions between the nobility and the pope and pressured to gain access to the resources he needed to sustain recurring invasions of Italy, chose to ally with the nobility. In return for their financial and political support during his thirteenth-century invasions of Italy, the emperor offered the nobility increased control over their peasants and the towns.

The peasants did not have the resources to mount an effective resistance, but the towns did. With more lucrative trade patterns and a stronger set of cities outside the control of the monarch than existed in France, German cities formed a series of ten defensive alliances called leagues, the most important of which was the Hanseatic League (named after the Hanses, groups of merchants that met to plan joint policies to promote trade). The Hanseatic League's membership varied between seventy-seven and two hundred cities; another key league, the Swabian-Rhenisch League, had eighty-nine. The leagues levied their own taxes on members, made binding decisions on a one-city, one-vote basis, negotiated treaties, and raised armies that were frequently numerically superior to those of the princes attacking them.

The problem for the leagues was the difficulty they had in sustaining coordinating action. For instance, in the Hanseatic League the central decision-making body usually met only every couple of years, and never more often than once a year. In the intervals between meetings, authority was delegated to local representatives. Consequently, while the leagues could form blocking coalitions, league policy making was too decentralised for separate towns to act together as a unified faction within a winning coalition. As a result, the Holy Roman Empire survived, but it was fragmented and frequently ineffective.

The City States. In Italy, feudal arrangements were replaced by a city-state system during the Renaissance. Trade made the Italian cities the biggest and wealthiest in Europe. Each of the most important—Venice, Florence, Milan, and Genoa—individually had military and financial resources greater than the most powerful German city leagues, which had to pool the resources of over seventy towns. Genoa, for instance, was able to mobilize 200 warships and 40,000 men in 1295.

The development of a city-state system in Italy was due to more than the value of their trade routes. Burghers in Italian cities were able to form coalitions with many key members of the Italian nobility who, unlike their French and German counterparts, often moved into town and became part of the urban elite, investing in trade and finance even as they maintained their agricultural holdings. Burghers and the urban nobility were also drawn together by their shared fear of the Church and the Holy Roman Empire, both of which coveted the independent cities' riches. With the burghers usually the lead faction, the urban coalitions began to create communes (self-governing communities) as early as 1081. By 1200 there were from 200 to 300 independent communes in northern Italy alone.

Perversely, the very richness of the Italian trade created incentives for the more powerful cities to expand, gobbling up weaker communes and fighting with each other even as they intrigued against their common enemies, the emperor and the pope. The pope and the emperor, meanwhile, sought allies among the cities in their continuing struggle to dominate Christendom. After several centuries of conflict and consolidation, the exhaustion of the Holy Roman Empire (after its failed invasions of Italy in the thirteenth century) and the collapse of papal authority between 1309 and 1417 (as a result of the Avignon captivity and the Great Schism) profoundly changed the political stage in Italy. The major city-states were the only key actors left standing on the Italian peninsula.

The Triumph of the Large Territorial State as the Successor to Feudalism

The feudal political system collapsed under the combined weight of the development of the city-state system in Italy, the city-leagues in the Holy Roman Empire, and the territorial state in France. Of these three possible replacements for feudalism, the territorial state proved to be the most adaptable and effective model. Part of its competitive advantage was a simple question of scale: the sheer magnitude of the military resources it could mobilize. But the large territorial had other advantages over its competitors. The city leagues, which had very decentralised institutions, had great difficulty sustaining coordinated action. As for the great Italian city states, while some were major military powers and they could decide and act quickly, the systems of trade they depended on did not exist in many other parts of Europe.

The Italian city-state system could not, therefore, serve as a general model. Finally, the large territorial state was simply better at a wide range of important political tasks. It was better at creating widely acceptable units of money and standardising systems of weights and measures for trade. It was better at raising money, establishing judicial systems, and organising state-controlled militaries that could gradually replace private armies. It was better at implementing treaties and building a system of mutual diplomatic recognition. For all these reasons, it was the state that came to dominate European politics.

Rulers were sovereign and people were subjects under the legitimising norms of the Westphalian settlement. To these norms, classical-balance-of-power diplomacy added the goal of preventing preponderance to preserve the survival of the key actors (the major military powers) in 17th and 18th century Europe. Reciprocal compensation or reshuffling populations from one state to another after a war was one of the major tools dynastic rulers used to keep the system in "balance." After the defeat of Napoleon, the victors sought to re-balance the distribution of military power through one of the most systematic efforts at reciprocal compensation in the history of the state system. If you lived in Europe in this period, which dynasty governed the territory you lived in had nothing to do with your preferences and everything to do with reciprocal compensation.

People living in the western part of northern Italy (the Piedmont) became part of a larger Kingdom of Piedmont-Sardinia to shrink France. The rest of northern Italy was transferred to the Austrian Empire to increase the resources available to Austria in counterbalancing both France and Russia. People living in Belgium (formerly the Austrian Netherlands) were attached to the Netherlands to strengthen the barrier to the north of France.

The most complex negotiations centered on the organisations of the states in the German Confederation and the boundaries between Russia, Prussia, and Austria. Indeed, this area was so complex that the negotiators set up a Demography Committee to analyze who went where. Table reproduces Prussia's proposal for finding the appropriate number of subjects for the Prussian king. Lines 1-25 in the first part of the table show Prussia's estimate of the number of subjects the Prussia king had lost and regained between Napoleon's defeat of Prussia in 1805 and the peace conference in 1815. As you can see, Prussia estimated that the end of the war left the king short 3,180,215 subjects. To these the next section in the document adds an additional 231,500 subjects that ongoing negotiations had temporarily allocated to other states, producing a grand total of 3,411,715 subjects that the Prussian king demanded be added to his domains.

The next section (with lines numbered 1-8) shows where the Prussians proposed to get the number of additional subjects they believed their king deserved. Some were in the Westphalian area and the west bank of the Rhine River, including the city of Cologne. This territory was highly desirable because, although it was separated from Prussia by a number of independent German principalities, it put

Prussia next to France. It also gave Prussia a significant increase in resources in an area that did not threaten Austria. The eastern boundaries were more complicated because the relative military positions of Prussia, Russia, and Austria were directly affected. At an earlier stage of the negotiations, Prussia had been willing to cede central Poland to Russia in exchange for the opportunity to get most of the land in Saxony, which was between Prussia and Austria. That option was, however, staunchly opposed by the Austrians because it would leave them worse off relative to both Russia and Prussia. A coalition among Austria, France, and Britain forced a compromise that gave Russia a bit less of Poland and Prussia a bit less of Saxony.

4

Evolution of the Contemporary Political Pattern

After taking this course you should have a basic understanding of what produced 200-odd "sovereign" states. This unit should briefly describe the development of the state idea in Europe and its diffusion to the rest of the world.

Territorial Principles of the Modern State System

A useful starting point is the sixteenth-to-seventeenth century's political pattern in western/central European. The continent was dominated two distinct types of countries. One the incipient national states such as England, France, Spain, and Portugal and the other the empires in central and Eastern Europe. The Peace of Westphalia (1648), held that the Prince of any realm could determine the religion of that realm, as part of an arrangement that governed how territorial units in the Holy Roman Empire would relate to one another. This gave birth to a notion of sovereignty based in law. This legal principle became the foundation on which all units were to relate to one another, and the strong de facto sovereign arrangements of the west ensured that sovereignty was understood to be all encompassing.

The sovereignty principle is significant because it provided a theoretical foundation for carving territory into largely autonomous governmental units. This meant that the exercise of power was no longer seen in human hierarchical terms, but instead was to be exercised at a single scale-that of the state. However, as long as authority was vested in absolutist rulers and institutions the system was subject to warfare and collapse.

The other key ingredient to the future of the European state system was the doctrine of nationalism which the idea that each ethno-cultural community (nation) had the right to control its own affairs, and that the exercise of power ultimately rested with the members of that community. These nations were said to possess an immortal sprit that was more important that individuals. Furthermore nationalists believe that all progress and creative energy comes from the national spirit and the nation can demand supreme loyalty of its members. Further more the ideal form of government is where nations govern the territory they occupy the nation state.

The actual pattern of people in Europe forced intellectuals to argue that nations could develop in a variety of ways. Some were diverse people knit together in centralised states (the English, the French, and the Spanish), some were the product of nineteenth-century movements to unify diverse peoples based on some sense of cultural continuity (*e.g.*, the Germans and the Italians), some were the product of early-twentieth-century movements to free a group from dominance by another self-defined nation (the Irish and the Norwegians), and some were the product of movements to achieve self-determination from empires (the Serbs, Bulgarians and Croatians). In the United States the concept of nationalism calls for the blending together of very diverse people into a new nation.

The nation-state ideal has become a pervasive notion undergirding the modern state system but students should understand the gap between the nation-state ideal and the multi-cultural reality that lies behind it. The vast majority of the countries of the world are not nation-states in the original meaning of that term. Today we learn about Russians fighting Chechens, Palestinians seeking their own state, Basque separatists demanding greater autonomy from Madrid, Tamils and Singhalese fighting one another in Sri Lanka, and many more.

Colonialism and Imperialism World Systems

Theory holds that periods of colonial activity are determined by conditions in the core region of the world (Europe, Japan and the United States). There were two phases of large-scale colonialisation. The first lasted from 1415-1800 and was dominated by trading companies except in Latin America. In that region the Spanish imposed the rule of the monarch directly using techniques from the reconquista policy, which they developed to retake the Iberian Peninsula from the Moors. During this period colonialists focused on the Americas and South Asia. The Russians directed their energy eastward into Siberia. The second phase was the late 19th century to post WWII. During it the colonialists focused on occupation and government lands in Africa, Asia and the Pacific. The first wave was characterised by conquest, plunder, slavery, and annihilation of indigenous people. For example the Aztecs declined from 13 to 2 million by 1600. The second phase was less destructive of societies and economic exploitation is preferred to military conquest and rule.

Why periods of expansion? Colonialism resulted because of events in the core. When the core is insatiable there is an expansion of colonial governments. When the core is stable there is a contraction of colonial activity. When stablility in core exists an individual hegemonic power can control the world without colonialism. This is viewed as a better alternative to colonialism because formal colonies are expensive. Hegemony exists when one core power controls production, commerce financial and political leadership. It owns the large share of world production. Its currency is universal and its primate city is the financial center of the world. Such periods are characterised by peace and universal ideologies such as free trade. Hegemonic power relies on economic mechanisms to extract surplus value from the periphery.

Hegemons fall because rival powers can focus on capital accumulation while the hegemon is forced to spend its wealth maintaining political and military organisation. Without a dominant power conflicts increase.

The historical geographer Donald Meinig described four types of colonial landscapes. In the Latin American case, extensive colonial influences date back farther than in the rest of the areas. Spanish and Portuguese colonialism in the Americas is associated with decimation of indigenous populations but, in the Spanish case in particular, there was also considerable intermarriage with indigenous peoples. The Spanish set up an administrative system in South America to facilitate the administration of a vast area and as well as the extract wealth from it. The administrative units bore some relationship to the physical character of the region, but none to the indigenous ethnic pattern. These units became the basis for the modern pattern of states in Latin America. The current states emerged in the early nineteenth century when Spain's declining power coincided with the emergence of a political class in Latin America that wanted to be free of Spanish control.

In South and Southeast Asia the European colonists did not have a demographic impact on local peoples, nor were they powerful enough to claim major land empires in the early centuries of the colonial era. Instead, they set up key coastal bases and they developed a highly elabourate trade network focused on those bases. In the late nineteenth century Europeans were finally able to control large areas in these regions.

These two systems provided the framework for the current political pattern, but in Southeast Asia, they were not completely disconnected from local ethno-political patterns. Instead, the European colonial bases were frequently ports at the mouths of major rivers, which drained basins where rather homogeneous groups lived (Burmese, Vietnamese, etc.). The states that emerged in the mid-twentieth century, while encompassing many minorities, often had a single large ethno-cultural majority group. The European colonials had a practice of bringing peoples from one colony to help administer another colony. This explains, for example, the large number of Indians in cities such as Rangoon.

Africa experienced a different form of colonialism. European trading posts and some colonial ports were established along various parts of the African as early as the 16th century but in last two decades of the nineteenth century that the Europeans participated in an unprecedented land grab on the part of several European powers. The geographer Donald Meinig called these new colonies the "nationalist empires" because they were established by European owners for nationalist goals. That is each power wanted as much land as it could get. The resulting pattern of political boundaries was unrelated to cultural patterns among the indigenous Africans. The African colonies were also the last to gain independence-many as late as the 1960s. The new states were based on colonial boundaries and had little administrative/governmental infrastructure.

The United States, Canada, and Australia present another pattern of colonialism. Because they were thought to have a climate suitable for European settlers they were all destinations for European migrants. The settlers ignored the rights of the indigenous population and treated these regions as effectively empty areas. These colonies were to provide a place where migrants from the colonial power could make a home and increase the power of the colonial power. By expansion of settlement and independence movements these colonies created countries that fulfilled the dreams of the settlers, but they largely destroyed indigenous patterns and institutions.

These four types of colonialism led to the creation of political patterns in different parts of the world. The leadership of newly independent colonies faced a dilemma. Their countries units entered a world political system based (at least theoretically) on the concepts of sovereignty and the nation-state. But the economic dependencies that had developed during the colonial period were difficult to shed and their sovereignty was often as much a fiction as a reality. At the same time, the legitimacy of state leaders was tied to their ability to exert power in the name of "nations" and in the process created another type of fiction. These issues link the political geography segment of the course focused on global economic patterns, for understanding the geographical dynamics of the global economy.

In many former colonies rulers can trace roots to colonial social structures, and many of the colonial powers remain actively involved with their former colonies through formal associations of ex-colonies (*e.g.*, the British Commonwealth) or through more informal mechanisms of influence and control. During the Cold War powerful states played off so-called Third World states against one another, and supported internal developments that fit a geopolitical game plan.

5

The Concept of Sovereign State

A Sovereign state is a state with a defined territory on which it exercises internal and external sovereignty, a permanent population, a government, independence from other states and powers, and the capacity to enter into relations with other sovereign states. It is also normally understood to be a state which is not dependent on, or subject to any other power or state. While in abstract terms a sovereign state can exist without being recognised by other sovereign states, unrecognised states will often find it hard to exercise full treaty-making powers and engage in diplomatic relations with other sovereign states.

Since the late 19th century, virtually the entirety of the world's inhabitable land has been parceled up into areas with more or less definite borders claimed by various states. Earlier, quite large land areas had been either unclaimed or uninhabited, or inhabited by nomadic peoples who were not organised as states. However, even within present-day states there are vast areas of wilderness, like the Amazon Rainforest, which are uninhabited or inhabited solely or mostly by indigenous people (and some of them remain uncontacted). Also, there are states which do not hold *de facto* control over all of their claimed territory or where this control is challenged (as in the 2006 civil war in Somalia).

Currently the international community comprises more than 200 sovereign states, the vast majority of which are represented in the United Nations. These states form what international relations theorists call a system, where each state takes into account the behavior of other states when making their own calculations. From this point of view, states embedded in an international system face internal and external security and legitimation dilemmas. Recently the notion of an international community has been developed to refer to a group of states who have established rules, procedures, and institutions for the conduct of their relations. In this way the foundation has been laid for international law, diplomacy, formal regimes, and organisations.

Sovereignty is a term that is frequently misused. Lassa Oppenheim said "There exists perhaps no conception the meaning of which is more controversial than that of sovereignty. It is an indisputable fact that this conception, from the moment when it was introduced into political science until the present day, has never had a meaning which was universally agreed upon." In the opinion of Justice Evatt of the High Court of Australia "sovereignty is neither a question of fact, nor a question of law, but a question that does not arise at all."

In casual usage, the terms "country", "nation", and "state" are often used as if they were synonymous; but in a more strict usage they can be distinguished:

- Nation denotes a people who are believed to or deemed to share common customs, origins, and history. However, the adjectives national and international are frequently used to refer to matters pertaining to what are strictly sovereign states, as in national capital, international law.
- State refers to the set of governing and supportive institutions that have sovereignty over a definite territory and population.

DIPLOMATIC RECOGNITION

Diplomatic recognition in international law is a unilateral political act with domestic and international legal consequences, whereby a state acknowledges an act or status of another state or government. Recognition can be accorded either *de facto* or *de jure*, usually by a statement of the recognising government.

Recognition of States and Governments

Diplomatic recognition must be distinguished from recognition of states and their governments. The fact that states do not maintain bilateral diplomatic relations does not mean that they do not recognize or treat one another as states. A state is not required to accord formal recognition to any other state, but it is required to treat any entity that meets certain requirements as a state. A state has a responsibility to not recognize as a state any entity that has attained the qualifications for statehood by violating the prohibition on the threat or use of force in the UN Charter. States can exercise their recognition powers either explicitly or implicitly. The recognition of a government implies recognition of the state it governs, but not vice versa.

De facto recognition of states, rather than de jure, is rare. De jure recognition is stronger, while de facto recognition is more tentative and only recognises that a government exercises control over a territory. An example of the difference is when the United Kingdom recognised the Soviet Union de facto in 1921, but de jure only in 1924. Another example is the state of Israel in 1948, whose government was immediately recognised de facto by the United States and three days later by Soviet de jure recognition. Renewing recognition of a government is not necessary when it changes in a normal, constitutional way (such as an election or referendum), but is necessary in the case of a coup d'etat or revolution. Recognition of a new government by other states can be important for its long term survival. For instance, the Taliban government of the Islamic State of Afghanistan, which lasted from 1996 to 2001, was recognised by only Pakistan, the United Arab Emirates, and Saudi Arabia, while far more had recognised the government of ousted President Burhanuddin Rabbani. The Disputed territories of Jammu and Kashmir and Arunachal Pradesh of the Republic of India are not recognised by either Pakistan or the People's Republic of China, but are recognised by Russia.

Recognition can be implied by other acts, like the visit of the head of state, or the signing of a bilateral treaty. If implicit recognition is possible, a state may feel the need to explicitly proclaim that its acts do not constitute diplomatic recognition, like when the United States commenced its dialogue with the Palestine Liberation Organisation in 1988. The doctrine of non-recognition of illegal or immoral situations, like territorial gains achieved by force, is called the Stimson Doctrine, and has become more important since the Second World War, especially in the United Nations where it is a method of ensuring compliance with international law for instance, in the case of Rhodesia in 1965. Withdrawal of recognition of a government is a more severe act of disapproval than the breaking of diplomatic relations.

Recognition of Governments

Besides recognising other states, states also can recognize the governments of states. This can be problematic particularly when a new government comes to power by illegal means, such as a coup d'etat, or when an existing government stays in power by fixing an election. States once formally recognised both the government of a state and the state itself, but many no longer follow that practice, even though, if diplomatic relations are to be maintained, it is necessary that there be a government to engage in diplomatic relations with. Countries such as the United States answer queries over the recognition of governments with the statement: "The question of recognition does not arise: we are conducting our relations with the new government."

Unrecognised State

Several of the world's geo-political entities lack general international recognition, but wish to be recognised as sovereign states. The degree of *de facto* control these entities exert over the territories they claim varies. Most are subnational regions with an ethnic or national identity of their own that have separated from the original parent state. Such states are commonly referred to as "break-away" states. Some of these entities are in effect internally self-governing protectorates that enjoy military protection and informal diplomatic representation abroad through another state to prevent forced reincorporation into their original states. Note that the word "control" in this list refers to *control* over the area *occupied*, not *occupation* of the area *claimed*. Unrecognised countries may have either full control over their occupied territory, or only partial control (such as Western Sahara). In the former, the *de jure* governments have little or no influence in the areas they claim to rule, whereas in the latter they have varying degrees of control, and may provide essential services to people living in the areas.

Other Types of Recognition

Other elements that may be recognised, include occupation or annexation of territory, or belligerent rights of a party in a conflict. Recognition of the latter does not imply recognition of a state. Examples of recognition of belligerent status include:

- The United Kingdom recognised the Confederate States of America as a belligerent in the first month of the American Civil War.
- Bolivia, Colombia, Ecuador, Peru and Venezuela recognised the Sandinista National Liberation Front as a belligerent in Nicaragua's civil war in June, 1979.
- France and Mexico recognised the FMLN as a belligerent in the civil war in El Salvador on August 28, 1981.

MONTEVIDEO CONVENTION

The Montevideo Convention on the Rights and Duties of States was a treaty signed at Montevideo, Uruguay on December 26, 1933, at the Seventh International Conference of American States. At this conference, United States President Franklin D. Roosevelt and Secretary of State Cordell Hull declared the so-called Good Neighbor Policy, which opposed U.S. armed intervention in inter-American affairs. This was a FDR's diplomatic attempt to reverse the perception of "Yankee imperialism," brought about by policies instituted (largely) by his predecessor, President Herbert Hoover. The convention was signed by 19 states, 3 with reservations.

TEXT OF THE CONVENTION

ARTICLE 1

The state as a person of international law should possess the following qualifications:

- A permanent population;
- A defined territory;
- Government; and
- Capacity to enter into relations with the other states.

ARTICLE 2

The federal state shall constitute a sole person in the eyes of international law.

Article 3

The political existence of the state is independent of recognition by the other states. Even before recognition the state has the right to defend its integrity and independence, to provide for its conservation and prosperity, and consequently to organize itself as it sees fit, to legislate upon its interests, administer its services, and to define the jurisdiction and competence of its courts.

The exercise of these rights has no other limitation than the exercise of the rights of other states according to international law.

Article 4

States are juridically equal, enjoy the same rights, and have equal capacity in their exercise. The rights of each one does not depend upon the power which it possesses to assure its exercise, but upon the simple fact of its existence as a person under international law.

Article 5

The fundamental rights of states are not susceptible of being affected in any manner whatsoever.

Article 6

The recognition of a state merely signifies that the state which recognises it accepts the personality of the other with all the rights and duties determined by international law. Recognition is unconditional and irrevocable.

Article 7

The recognition of a state may be express or tacit. The latter results from any act which implies the intention of recognising the new state.

Article 8

No state has the right to intervene in the internal or external affairs of another.

ARTICLE 9

The jurisdiction of states within the limits of national territory applies to all the inhabitants.

Nationals and foreigners are under the same protection of the law and the national authorities and the foreigners may not claim rights other or more extensive than those of the nationals.

ARTICLE 10

The primary interest of states is the conservation of peace. Differences of any nature which arise between them should be settled by recognised pacific methods.

ARTICLE 11

The contracting states definitely establish as the rule of their conduct the precise obligation not to recognize territorial acquisitions or special advantages which have been obtained by force whether this consists in the employment of arms, in threatening diplomatic representations, or in any other effective coercive measure. The territory of a state is inviolable and may not be the object of military occupation nor of other measures of force imposed by another state directly or indirectly or for any motive whatever even temporarily.

ARTICLE 12

The present Convention shall not affect obligations previously entered into by the High Contracting Parties by virtue of international agreements.

ARTICLE 13

The present Convention shall be ratified by the High Contracting Parties in conformity with their respective constitutional procedures. The Minister of Foreign Affairs of the Republic of Uruguay shall transmit authentic certified copies to the governments for the aforementioned purpose of ratification. The instrument of ratification shall be deposited in the archives of the Pan American Union in Washington, which shall notify the signatory governments of said deposit. Such notification shall be considered as an exchange of ratifications.

Article 14

The present Convention will enter into force between the High Contracting Parties in the order in which they deposit their respective ratifications.

Article 15

The present Convention shall remain in force indefinitely but may be denounced by means of one year's notice given to the Pan American Union, which shall transmit it to the other signatory governments. After the expiration of this period the Convention shall cease in its effects as regards the party which denounces but shall remain in effect for the remaining High Contracting Parties.

Article 16

The present Convention shall be open for the adherence and accession of the States which are not signatories. The corresponding instruments shall be deposited in the archives of the Pan American Union which shall communicate them to the other High Contracting Parties. In Witness Whereof, the following Plenipotentiaries have signed this Convention in Spanish, English, Portuguese and French and hereunto affix their respective seals in the city of Montevideo, Republic of Uruguay, this 26th day of December, 1933.

Reservations

The Delegation of the United States of America, in signing the Convention on the Rights and Duties of States, does so with the express reservation presented to the Plenary Session of the Conference on December 22, 1933, which reservation reads as follows:

The Delegation of the United States, in voting "yes" on the final vote on this committee recommendation and proposal, makes the same reservation to the eleven articles of the project or proposal that the United States Delegation made to the first ten articles during the final vote in the full Commission, which reservation is in words as follows:

"The policy and attitude of the United States Government toward every important phase of international relationships in this hemisphere could scarcely be made more clear and definite than they have been made by both word and action especially since March 4. I have no disposition therefore to indulge in any repetition or rehearsal of these acts and utterances and shall not do so. Every observing person must by this time thoroughly understand that under the Roosevelt Administration the United States Government is as much opposed as any other government to interference with the freedom, the sovereignty, or other internal affairs or processes of the governments of other nations.

"In addition to numerous acts and utterances in connection with the carrying out of these doctrines and policies, President Roosevelt, during recent weeks, gave out a public statement expressing his disposition to open negotiations with the Cuban Government for the purpose of dealing with the treaty which has existed since 1903. I feel safe in undertaking to say that under our support of the general principle of non-intervention as has been suggested, no government need fear any intervention on the part of the United States under the Roosevelt Administration.

I think it unfortunate that during the brief period of this Conference there is apparently not time within which to prepare interpretations and definitions of these fundamental terms that are embraced in the report. Such definitions and interpretations would enable every government to proceed in a uniform way without any difference of opinion or of interpretations. I hope that at the earliest possible date such very important work will be done. In the meantime in case of differences of interpretations and also until they (the proposed doctrines and principles) can be worked out and codified for the common use of every government, I desire to say that the United States Government in all of its international associations and relationships and conduct will follow scrupulously the doctrines and policies which it has pursued since March 4 which are embodied in the different addresses of President Roosevelt since that time and in the recent peace address of myself on the 15th day of December before this Conference and in the law of nations as generally recognised and accepted".

The delegates of Brazil and Peru recorded the following private vote with regard to article 11:

> "That we accept the doctrine in principle but that we do not consider it codifiable because there are some countries which have not yet signed the Anti-War Pact of Rio de Janeiro 4 of which this doctrine is a part and therefore it does not yet constitute positive international law suitable for codification".

6

Traditional Systems of Governance and the Modern State

African societies, throughout the centuries, have been organised on the basis of a social contract whereby people come together to form a state or nation because they believe that, through their combined efforts, they will be more able to realize their common aspirations for peace and security, which are essential for their physical and spiritual welfare and progress, both as individuals and as a community. It is to achieve these objectives that the people agree collectively to surrender to a king or ruler the power to control their lives and to organize and regulate activities within their society. In the process, they have always had clear understandings and agreements regarding the ideas and principles that underlie their political systems and on the basis of which power and authority are to be exercised by the various elements of government. By traditional systems, I refer to genuine traditional institutions, uncontaminated by colonial or post-independence modifications or distortions. Most observers of traditional African political systems recognize two main forms, namely the non-centralised or fragmented traditional state and the centralised state.

In these states, there was no sovereign in the Non-centralised traditional states: Austinian sense. Techniques of social control revolved around what Meyer Fol1es called the "dynamics of clanship". The normative scheme consisted of elabourate bodies of well-established .rules of conduct, usually enforced by heads of fragmented segments, and in serious or subversive cases, by spontaneous community action. Examples are the', 'Talle "nsi" of Northern Ghana, the Sukuma of Tanzania, the Nuer of Southern Sudan, the of Nigeria and the Kikuyu of Kenya. For the purposes of our discussion we should two major features of this system: existence of well defined nonns despite the absence of a hierarchical system by a sovereign; direct and pronounced participation of people -members of clans, segments and so on in decision making assuring a visible democratic process.

Centralised States: The centralised states such as Asante and Mole-Dabgani of Ghana, Yoruba land of Nigeria, Zulus of South Africa, Barotse of Zambia and Baganda of Uganda had a more structured and sophisticated political system. These states were organised under well-entrenched, highly structured and sophisticated political authorities.

They had all the elements of an Austinian state-a political sovereign baked by well-organised law enforcement agencies and habitually obeyed by the citizenry. Infraction of well-legal norms attracted swift sanctions imposed by state officials. But the king, chief or the political sovereign, ruled with his council of elders and advisors in accordance with the law, and although autocracy was not unknown, the rule of law was a cardinal feature of their system of governance. The king was ultimately accountable and liable to deposition upon the violation of norm is considered subversive of the entire political system or particularly heinous. In many cases the political structures were complemented by hierarchy of courts presided over by the king, the head chief or the village chief. The concept of law in these states was, in substance, hardly distinguishable from that of a modern state. In most of these states, there was provision for participation in decision-making by groups of the citizenry either indirectly through the heads of their clans' lineages or families; or more directly through various types of organisations like the Asafo Companies of the Fantes in Ghana.

Eligibility for installation as king or chief was limited to certain royal families but among many states of Ghana the institution of king-makers was not unlike the Electoral College in some other countries. The Queen mother played a critical role as the custodian of the and the person who pronounced on the eligibility of conditions for "royal register" chiefly office.

MULTIPLICITY OF SYSTEMS

It is evident from the theme of this Session and my remarks that there are various systems of traditional governance in Africa. Just as there have been and remain different forms and orientations of western democracy, so there were different forms and institutions of government among the various ethnic groups and societies in different parts of Africa.

But, in spite of the unavoidable variations, the different forms of African traditional governance had a number of important common elements and features. Invariably, they almost always involve the devolution of power by ascription. A person inherits governmental authority or position mainly by virtue of membership of a particular family or clan.

However, in many cases, the choice of the political leader is based not solely on the circumstance of birth, but involves other criteria, such as the character or other personal qualities. Where this is the case, there usually is an election between several eligible persons from the same family or clan.

The people who exercised governmental authority were referred to by various names in different parts of a Africa, such as kings, chiefs, elders, leopard skin chiefs, emirs and so on. In all cases, they ruled or governed their societies with t he assistance of lower-rank rulers, a s well as a large number and levels of advisers who for the most part, a is occupied their positions by virtue of their family or clan origins and status.

It is worth emphasising that this mechanism ensures that the king or chief does not rule arbitrarily. A though the king or chief has the final word, he is bound to consult very regularly, and decisions are reached by consensus without formal votes. In this connection, although a chief is elected and installed for life, his continued stay in office is subject to good conduct.

It is not my intention to glorify our traditional systems. But I am concerned to point out that democracy was not alien to all traditional African systems, and the rule of law, which provided checks and balances in the political system and imposed restraints on authoritarian rule, was a prominent feature of most traditional African systems. However, this presentation is not about our traditional systems in their pristine purity before the colonial and post-independence impact. It is very much about the role of these systems under modern political and constitutional dispensations in Africa.

THE FUNTIONS OF THE TRADITIONAL RULER

Before the advent of colonial rule, the traditional leader's role encompassed numerous functions which revolved around the cardinal theme of guiding, protecting, defending and providing for the needs of the society he served.. He was the intemlediary between the departed ancestors, the living and the yet unborn.

These holistic approaches involved religious, military, legislative, executive, judicial, social and cultural features. Leadership was however predicated on a set of well articulated norms and mechanisms. The multifarious functions were exercised with specific functionaries whose role was hallowed by ancient custom. Sometimes these were elders or councilors, or communal groups or judicial institutions or state or drummers. Each entity perfonned its assigned role in accordance with customary law.

The military role of the traditional leader was accentuated by the frequent incidence of inter-ethnic wars or the nonnal process of acquiring territory for statehood. But in this function, the welfare of the people was paramount. Any chief who ignored this forfeited the trust of his people and was liable to deposition.

TRADITIONAL AUTHORITY IN COLONIAL AND POST COLONIAL ERAS

The colonial and post-independence eras had a profound impact on traditional institutions, in particular chieftaincy. The colonial system ostensibly enhanced chieftaincy through the system of indirect rule particularly in Nigeria and Ghana. But the perception that chiefs and kings ultimately derived their power from the colonial power eventually undermined their power. In some African countries the colonial authorities appointed chiefs directly thereby underscoring the uncomfortable fact that they were colonial creations, which were ultimately abolished with the demise of colonial rule far as post-colonial African regimes were concerned, it is hardly contestable that they saw traditional authorities as a dangerous bastion of rival political power and largely succeeded in dismantling or attenuating their authority. Examples exist in Liberia and other African states. The reality is that in most African states our traditional ,systems have been divested of their formal executive, economic and judicial powers except in narrowly defined areas.

Even more critical, they have been denied the requisite resources for effective functioning, although the institution of chieftaincy has been guaranteed in some constitutions such as Ghana's. in spite of all these moves, it is paradoxical that in a number of African countries, chieftaincy is attracting academics, civil servants, business leaders and teachers. In Nigeria, Ghana, Uganda, Lesotho, and Swaziland and in South Africa, the traditional leadership position is becoming more competitive than probably ever before. It would be illuminating to find out why the situation is changing so fast.

TRADITIONAL AUTHORITY TODAY

Admittedly, the chief of today cannot act in the way his predecessors behaved. He is neither the military leader nor the legislator that he once was. Except in very limited areas, he has no judicial functions or executive powers of any significance. But this does not mean that the chief has no meaningful role in the modem era. On the contrary, he has a vital role to play not just in his own domain, but also at the national level. This fact is recognised in the governmental system of Ghana, where the institution of chieftaincy is given an entrenched status in the 1992 Constitution other duties, chiefs are expected to provide advice to the central government and to participate in the administration of regions and districts. As symbols of unity in Ghanaian society, chiefs are constitutionally barred from active party politics.

Apart from these constitutional functions, chiefs have the moral obligation to contribute to the lives of their individual citizens in particular, and to the nationals of their country. These days, a chief is expected to lead his people in organising self-help activities and projects, and take the initiative in establishing institutions and programmes to improve the welfare of his people in areas such as health, educational, trade and economic or social development. These institutions and programmes are not intended to replace those that must be provided by the central and regional government, but rather to supplement them, especially in these days when the demands-of the people are such that it is unrealistic to expect that they can all be met from central government resources. The chiefs can and do playa vital role in development which at once enhances democracy and sustains good governance.

At a recent international conference on chieftaincy in Africa, held in Niger, there were numerous reports from African countries such a s Nigerià and South Africa as well as Ghana about the developmental roles of chiefs, mobilising their people for the execution of development projects, sensitising them to health hazards, promoting education, preaching discipline, encouraging various economic enterprises, inspiring respect for the law and urging the people to participate in the electoral process. Most of these efforts are done without fomlal recognition or financial support from Government. Modern African states have not all succeeded in establishing viable insurance schemes, comprehensive health and educational systems facilities for counseling the youth or role models in all fields of endeavour.

The modern chief, stripped of political and executive power and formal financial support, has to address these basic needs for his people using his ingenuity, diplomacy, power of motivation and sometimes his own personal resources have been most active in dispute resolution both in Africa generally and in Ghana particularly, where parties, disenchanted with the dilatory procedures of the formal courts, have clamoured for traditional techniques of resolution. Indeed dispute resolution would have been impossible without the active involvement of chiefs in all parts of Ghana. And it is my considered opinion that the absence of strong traditional systems in some African states, particularly in Liberia, Sierra Leone and Cote D'Ivoire, has contributed to the instability we see there today.

7

The Concept of Representation in Politics

In politics, representation describes how political power is alienated from most of the members of a group and vested, for a certain time period, in the hands of a small subset of the members. Representation usually refers to representative democracies, where elected officials nominally speak for their constituents in the legislature. Generally, only citizens are granted representation in the government in the form of voting rights; however, some democracies have extended this right further.

The concept of political representation is misleadingly simple: everyone seems to know what it is, yet few can agree on any particular definition. In fact, there is an extensive literature that offers many different definitions of this elusive concept. (Classic treatments of the concept of political representations within this literature include Pennock and Chapman 1968; Pitkin, 1967 and Schwartz, 1988.) Hanna Pitkin (1967) provides, perhaps, one of the most straightforward definitions: to represent is simply to "make present again." On this definition, political representation is the activity of making citizens' voices, opinions, and perspectives "present" in the public policy making processes. Political representation occurs when political actors speak, advocate, symbolize, and act on the behalf of others in the political arena. In short, political representation is a kind of political assistance. This seemingly straightforward definition, however, is not adequate as it stands. For it leaves the concept of political representation underspecified. Indeed, as we will see, the concept of political representation has multiple and competing dimensions: our common understanding of political representation is one that contains different, and conflicting, conceptions of how political representatives should represent and so holds representatives to standards that are mutually incompatible. In leaving these dimensions underspecified, this definition fails to capture this paradoxical character of the concept.

We first provide a general overview of the meaning of political representation, identifying the key components of this concept. The second is to highlight several important advances that have been made by the contemporary literature on political representation. These advances point to new forms of political representation, ones that are not limited to the relationship between formal representatives and their constituents. The third goal is to reveal several persistent problems with theories of political representation and thereby to propose some future areas of research.

Key Components of Political Representation

Political representation, on any account, will exhibit the following four components:

1. some party that is representing (the representative, an organisation, movement, state agency, *etc.*);
2. some party that is being represented (the constituents, the clients, *etc.*);
3. something that is being represented (opinions, perspectives, interests *etc.*) and
4. a setting within which the activity of representation is taking place (the political context).

Theories of political representation often begin by specifying the terms for each of these four components. For instance, democratic theorists often limit the types of representatives being discussed to formal representatives—that is, to representatives who hold elected offices. One reason that the concept of representation remains elusive is that theories of representation often apply only to particular kinds of political actors within a particular context. How individuals represent an electoral district is treated as distinct from how social movements or informal organisations represent. Consequently, it is unclear how different forms of representation relate to each other. This general agreement about the necessary components exhibited by political representation is somewhat misleading. For what exactly representatives *do* has been a hotly contested issue. In particular, a controversy has raged over whether representatives should act as *delegates* or *trustees*.

Delegate vs. Trustee

Historically, the theoretical literature on political representation has focused on whether representatives should act as *delegates* or as *trustees*. Representatives who are delegates simply follow the expressed preferences of their constituents. James Madison (1987) is one of the leading historical figures who articulated a delegate conception of representation. Trustees are representatives who follow their own understanding of the best action to pursue.

Edmund Burke (1967) is famous for arguing that Parliament is not a congress of ambassadors from different and hostile interests, which interest each must maintain, as an agent and advocate, against other agents and advocates; but Parliament is a deliberative assembly of one nation, with one interest, that of the whole... You choose a member, indeed; but when you have chosen him he is not a member of Bristol, but he is a member of Parliament (115).

Both the delegate and the trustee conception of political representation place competing and contradictory demands on the behavior of representatives. Delegate conceptions of representation require representatives to follow their constituent's preferences, while trustee conceptions require representatives to follow their own judgment about the proper course of action. Any adequate theory of representation must grapple with these contradictory demands.

Famously, Hanna Pitkin argues that theorists should not try to reconcile the paradoxical nature of the concept of representation. Rather, they should aim to preserve this paradox by recommending that citizens safeguard the autonomy of both the representative and of those being represented. Representatives must act in ways that safeguard the capacity of the represented to authorize and to hold their representatives accountable *and* uphold the capacity of the representative to act independently of the wishes of the represented. Objective interests are the key for determining whether the autonomy of representative and the autonomy of the represented have been breached. However, Pitkin never adequately specifies how we are to identify constituent's objective interests.

At points, she implies that constituents should have some say in what are their objective interests, but ultimately she merely shifts her focus away from this paradox to the recommendation that representatives should be evaluated on the basis of the reasons they give for disobeying the preferences of their constituents. For Pitkin, assessments about representatives will depend on the issue at hand and the political environment in which a representative acts. To understand the multiple and conflicting standards within the concept of representation is to reveal the futility of holding all representatives to some fixed set of guidelines.

In this way, Pitkin concludes that standards for evaluating representatives defy generalisations. Moreover, individuals, especially democratic citizens, are likely to disagree deeply about what representatives should be doing.

Pitkin's Four Views of Representation

Pitkin offers one of the most comprehensive discussions of the concept of political representation, attending to its contradictory character in her *The Concept of Representation*. This classic discussion of the concept of representation is one of the most influential and oft-cited works in the literature on political representation. Adopting a Wittgensteinian approach to language, Pitkin maintains that in order to understand the concept of political representation, one must consider the different ways in which the term is used. Each of these different uses of the term provides a different view of the concept. Pitkin compares the concept of representation to " a rather complicated, convoluted, three–dimensional structure in the middle of a dark enclosure." Political theorists provide "flash-bulb photographs of the structure taken from different angles". More specifically, political theorists have provided four main views of the concept of representation.

Unfortunately, Pitkin never explains how these different views of political representation fit together. At times, she implies that the concept of representation is unified. At other times, she emphasises the conflicts between these different views, *e.g.* how descriptive representation is opposed to accountability. Drawing on her flash-bulb metaphor, Pitkin argues that one must know the context in which the concept of representation is placed in order to determine its meaning. Apparently, the views of representation can expand or unduly constrain our understanding of representation depending on how the ways in which the term is used in contemporary politics.

For Pitkin, disagreements about representation can be partially reconciled by clarifying which view of representation is being invoked. Pitkin identifies at least four different views of representation: formalistic representation, descriptive representation, symbolic representation, and substantive representation. Each view provides a different approach for examining representation. The different views of representation can also provide different standards for assessing representatives.

So disagreements about what representatives ought to be doing are aggravated by the fact that people adopt the wrong view of representation or misapply the standards of representation. Pitkin has in many ways set the terms of contemporary discussions about representation by providing this schematic overview of the concept of political representation.

One cannot overestimate the extent to which Pitkin has shaped contemporary understandings of political representation, especially among political scientists. For example, her claim that descriptive representation opposes accountability is often the starting point for contemporary discussions about whether marginalised groups need representatives from their groups. Similarly, Pitkin's conclusions about the paradoxical nature of political representation support the tendency among contemporary theorists and political scientists to focus on formal procedures of authorisation and accountability (formalistic representation). In particular, there has been a lot of theoretical attention paid to the proper design of representative institutions.

This focus is certainly understandable, since one way to resolve the disputes about what representatives should be doing is to "let the people decide." In other words, establishing fair procedures for reconciling conflicts provides democratic citizens one way to settle conflicts about the proper behavior of representatives.

Four Views	Brief Description	Main Research Question within each View	Implicit Standards for Evaluating Representatives
1. Formalistic Representation	The institutional arrangements that precede and initiate representation. Formal representation has two dimensions: authorization and accountability	What is the institutional position of a representative?	None
(Authorization)	The means by which a representative obtains his or her standing, status, position or office.	What is the process by which a representative gains power (e.g. elections) and what are the ways in which a representative can enforce his or her decisions?	No standards for assessing how well a representative behaves. One can merely assess whether a representative legitimately holds his or her position.
(Accountability)	The ability of constituents to *punish* their representative for failing to act in accordance with their wishes (e.g. voting an elected official out of office) or the *responsiveness* of the representative to the constituents.	What are the sanctioning mechanisms available to constituents? Is the representative responsive towards his or her constituents' preferences?	No standards for assessing how well a representative behaves. One can merely determine whether a representative can be sanctioned or has been responsive.
2. Symbolic Representation	The ways that a representative "stands for" the represented — that is, the meaning that a representative has for those being represented.	What kind of response is invoked by the representative in those being represented?	Representatives are assessed by the degree of acceptance that the representative has among the represented.
3. Descriptive Representation	The extent to which a representative resembles those	Does the representative look like, have common interests with,	Assess the representative by the accuracy of

	being represented.	or share certain experiences with the represented?	the resemblance between the representative and the represented.
4. Substantive Representation	The activity of representatives—that is, the actions taken on the behalf of, in the interest of, as an agent of, and as a substitute for the represented.	Does the representative advance the policy preferences that serve the interests of the represented?	Assess a representative by the extent to which policy Outcomes advanced by a representative serve "the best interests" of their constituents.

In this way, theoretical discussions of political representation tend to depict political representation as primarily a principal-agent relationship. The emphasis on elections also explains why discussions about the concept of political representation frequently collapse into discussions of democracy. Political representation is understood as a way of 1) establishing the legitimacy of democratic institutions and 2) creating institutional incentives for governments to be responsive to citizens.

David Plotke (1997) has noted that this emphasis on mechanisms of authorisation and accountability was especially useful in the context of the Cold War. For this understanding of political representation (specifically, its demarcation from participatory democracy) was useful for distinguishing Western democracies from Communist countries. Those political systems that held elections were considered to be democratic. Plotke questions whether such a distinction continues to be useful. Plotke recommends that we broaden the scope of our understanding of political representation to encompass interest representation and thereby return to debating what is the proper activity of representatives.

Plotke's insight into why traditional understandings of political representation resonated prior to the end of the Cold War suggests that modern understandings of political representation are to some extent contingent on political realities. For this reason, those who attempt to define political representation should recognize how changing political realities can affect contemporary understandings of political representation. Again, following Pitkin, it would appear that our ideas about political representation are contingent on existing political practices of representation. Our understandings of representation are inextricably shaped by the manner in which people are currently being represented.

Changing Political Realities and Changing Concepts of Political Representation

As mentioned earlier, theoretical discussions of political representation have focused mainly on the formal procedures of authorisation and accountability within nation states, that is, on what Pitkin called formalistic representation. However, such a focus is no longer satisfactory due to international and domestic political transformations. Increasingly international, transnational and non-governmental actors play an important role in advancing public policies on behalf of democratic citizens—that is, acting as representatives for those citizens. Such actors "speak for," "act for" and can even "stand for" individuals within a nation-state. It is no longer desirable to limit one's understanding of political representation to elected officials within the nation-state.

After all, such officials do not necessarily possess "the capacity to act," the capacity that is most often used to identify who is acting as a representative. In other words, as the powers of nation-state have been diffused by international and transnational actors, elected representatives are no longer responsible for deciding or implementing the public policies that directly impact the citizens who authorised them. Given the role that International Non-Governmental Organisations play in the international arena, the representatives of dispossessed groups are no longer located in the formal political arena of the nation-state. Given these changes, the traditional focus of political representation, that is, on elections within nation-states, is insufficient for understanding how public policies are being made and implemented. The complexity of modern issues and the multiple locations of political power suggest that contemporary notions of accountability are inadequate. Grant and Keohane (2005) have recently updated notions of accountability, suggesting that the scope of political representation needs to be expanded in order to reflect contemporary realities in the international arena.

Domestic transformations also reveal the need to update contemporary understandings of political representation. Associational life—social movements, interest groups, and civic associations—is increasingly recognised as important for the survival of representative democracies. The extent to which interest groups write public policies or play a central role in implementing and regulating policies is the extent to which the division between formal and informal representation has been blurred. The fluid relationship between the career paths of formal and informal representatives also suggests that contemporary realities do not justify focusing mainly on formal representatives.

Given these changes, it is necessary to revisit our conceptual understanding of political representation, specifically of democratic representation. For as Jane Mansbridge has recently noted, normative understandings of representation have not kept up with recent empirical research and contemporary democratic practices. In her important article "Rethinking Representation" Mansbridge identifies four forms of representation in modern democracies: promissory, anticipatory, gyroscopic and surrogacy. Promissory representation is a form of representation in which representatives are to be evaluated by the promises they make to constituents during campaigns. Promissory representation strongly resembles Pitkin's discussion of formalistic representation.

For both are primarily concerned with the ways that constituents give their consent to the authority of a representative. Drawing on recent empirical work, Mansbridge argues for the existence of three additional forms of representation. In anticipatory representation, representatives focus on what they think their constituents will reward in the next election and not on what they promised during the campaign of the previous election. Thus, anticipatory representation challenges those who understand accountability as primarily a retrospective activity. In gyroscopic representation, representatives "look within" to derive from their own experience conceptions of interest and principles to serve as a basis for their action. Finally, surrogate representation occurs when a legislator represents constituents outside of their districts. For Mansbridge, each of these different forms of representation generates a different normative criterion by which representatives should be assessed. All four forms of representation, then, are ways that democratic citizens can be legitimately represented within a democratic regime. Yet none of the latter three forms representation operates through the formal mechanisms of authorisation and accountability.

Mansbridge's work holds an important insight for contemporary discussions of democratic representation. By specifying the different forms of representation within a democratic polity, Mansbridge teaches us that we should refer to the *multiple* forms of democratic representation. Democratic representation should not be conceived as a monolithic concept. Moreover, what is abundantly clear is that democratic representation should no longer be treated as consisting simply in a relationship between elected officials and constituents within her voting district. Political representation should no longer be understood as a simple principal-agent relationship. Andrew Rehfeld has gone farther, maintaining that political representation should no longer be territorially based. In other words, Rehfeld (2005) argues that constituencies, *e.g.* electoral districts, should not be constructed based on where citizens live.

Contemporary Advances

There have been a number of important advances to the concept of political representation. In particular, these advances call to question the traditional way of thinking of political representation as a principal-agent relationship. Most notably, Melissa Williams' recent work has recommended reenvisioning the activity of representation in light of the experiences of historically disadvantaged groups. In particular, she recommends understanding representation as "mediation." In particular, Williams identifies three different dimensions of political life that representatives must "mediate:" the dynamics of legislative decision-making, the nature of legislator-constituent relations, and the basis for aggregating citizens into representable constituencies. She explains each aspect by using a corresponding theme (voice, trust, and memory) and by drawing on the experiences of marginalised groups in the United States. For example, drawing on the experiences of American women trying to gain equal citizenship, Williams argues that historically disadvantaged groups need a "voice" in legislative decision-making. The "heavily deliberative" quality of legislative institutions requires the presence of individuals who have direct access to historically excluded perspectives.

In addition, Williams explains how representatives need to mediate the representative-constituent relationship in order to build "trust." For Williams, trust is the cornerstone for democratic accountability. Relying on the experiences of African-Americans, Williams shows the consistent patterns of betrayal of African-Americans by privileged white citizens that give them good reason for distrusting white representatives and the institutions themselves. For Williams, relationships of distrust can be "at least partially mended if the disadvantaged group is represented by its own members"(1998, 14). Finally, representation involves mediating how groups are defined. The boundaries of groups according to Williams are partially established by past experiences — what Williams calls "memory." Having certain shared patterns of marginalisation justifies certain institutional mechanisms to guarantee presence.

Williams offers her understanding of representation as mediation as a supplement to what she regards as the traditional conception of liberal representation. Williams identifies two strands in liberal representation. The first strand she describes as the "ideal of fair representation as an outcome of free and open elections in which every citizen has an equally weighted vote" (1998, 57). The second strand is interest-group pluralism, which Williams describes as the "theory of the organisation of shared social interests with the purpose of securing the equitable representation ... of those groups in public policies" (*ibid.*). Together, the two strands provide a coherent approach for achieving fair representation, but the traditional conception of liberal representation as made up of simply these two strands is inadequate. In particular, Williams criticises the traditional conception of liberal representation for failing to take into account the injustices experienced by marginalised groups in the United States.

Thus, Williams expands accounts of political representation beyond the question of institutional design and thus, in effect, challenges those who understand representation as simply a matter of formal procedures of authorisation and accountability. Another recent way of reenvisioning representation was offered by Nadia Urbinati

(2000, 2002). Urbinati argues for understanding *representation as advocacy.* For Urbinati, the point of representation should not be the aggregation of interests, but the preservation of disagreements necessary for preserving liberty. Urbinati identifies two main features of advocacy: 1) the representative's passionate link to the electors cause and 2) the representative's relative autonomy of judgment.

Urbinati emphasises the importance of the former for motivating representatives to deliberate with each other and their constituents. For Urbinati the benefit of conceptualising representation as advocacy is that it improves our understanding of deliberative democracy. In particular, it avoids a common mistake made by many contemporary deliberative democrats: focusing on the formal procedures of deliberation at the expense of examining the sources of inequality within civil society, *e.g.* the family. The benefit of Urbinati's understanding of representation is that it emphasises the importance of the domain of opinion and consent formation. In particular, this contemporary addition to the theoretical literature poses an agonistic conception of representation, one that emphasises the importance of disagreements and rhetoric to the procedures, practices, and ethos of democracy. Her account expands the scope of theoretical discussions of representation away from formal procedures of authorisation to the deliberative and expressive dimensions of representative institutions. In this way, those who recommend adopting an understanding of representation as advocacy provide a theoretical tool to those who wish to explain how non-state actors "represent."

Other political theorists have asked us to rethink our understanding of democratic representation. In *Inclusion and Democracy* Iris Marion Young asks us to rethink the importance of descriptive representation. Young warns that attempts to include more voices in the political arena can suppress other voices. She illustrates this point using the example of a Latino representative who might inadvertently represent straight Latinos at the expense of gay and lesbian Latinos (1986, 350). For Young, the suppression of differences is a problem for *all* representation (1986, 351). Representatives of large districts or of small communities must negotiate the difficulty of one person representing many. Because such a difficulty is constitutive of representation, it is unreasonable to assume that representation should be characterised by a "relationship of identity." The legitimacy of a representative is not primarily a function of his or her similarities to the represented. For Young, the representative should not be treated as a substitute for the represented. Consequently, Young recommends reconceptualising representation as *a differentiated relationship* (2000, 125-127; 1986, 357).

There are two main benefits of Young's understanding of representation. First, her understanding of representation encourages us to recognize the diversity of those being represented. Second, her analysis of representation emphasises the importance of recognising how representative institutions include as well as they exclude. Democratic citizens need to remain vigilant about the ways in which providing representation for some groups comes at the expense of excluding others.

Moreover, based on this way of understanding political representation, Young provides an alterative account of democratic representation. Specifically, she envisions democratic representation as a dynamic process, one that moves between moments of authorisation and moments of accountability (2000, 129). It is the movement between these moments that makes the process "democratic." This fluidity allows citizens to authorize their representatives and for *traces* of that authorisation to be evident in what the representatives do and how representatives are held accountable. The appropriateness of any given representative is therefore partially dependent on future behavior as well as on his or her past relationships. For this reason, Young maintains that evaluation of this process must be continuously "deferred." We must assess representation dynamically, that is, assess the whole ongoing processes of authorisation and accountability of representatives. Young's discussion of the dynamic of representation emphasises the ways in which evaluations of representatives are incomplete, needing to incorporate extent to which democratic citizens need to suspend their evaluations of representatives and the extent to which representatives can face unanticipated issues.

Another insight about democratic representation that comes from the literature on descriptive representation is the importance of contingencies. Here the work of Jane Mansbridge on descriptive representation has been particularly influential. Mansbridge recommends that we evaluate descriptive representatives by contexts and certain functions. More specifically, Mansbridge (1999, 628) focuses on four functions and their related contexts in which disadvantaged groups would want to be represented by someone who belongs to their group.

Those four functions are "(1) adequate communication in contexts of mistrust, (2) innovative thinking in contexts of uncrystallised, not fully articulated, interests, ... (3) creating a social meaning of 'ability to rule' for members of a group in historical contexts where the ability has been seriously questioned and (4) increasing the polity's de facto legitimacy in contexts of past discrimination." For Mansbridge, descriptive representatives are needed when marginalised groups distrust members of relatively more privileged citizens and when marginalised groups possess political preferences that have not been fully formed. The need for descriptive representation is contingent on certain functions.

Mansbridge's insight about the contingency of descriptive representation suggests that at some point descriptive representatives might not be necessary. However, she doesn't specify how we are to know if interests have become crystallised or trust has formed to the point that the need for descriptive representation would be obsolete. Thus, Mansbridge's discussion of descriptive representation suggests that standards for evaluating representatives are fluid and flexible.

Mansbridge's discussion of descriptive representation points to another trend within the literature on political representation—namely, the trend to derive normative accounts of representation from their function. Russell Hardin (2004) captured this trend most clearly in his position that "if we wish to assess the morality of elected officials, we must understand their function as our representatives and then infer how they can fulfill this function." For Hardin, only an empirical explanation of the role of a representative is necessary for determining what a representative should be doing. In *Ruling Passions*, Andrew Sabl (2002) links the proper behavior of representatives to their particular office. In particular, Sabl focuses on three offices: senator, organiser and activist. He argues that the same standards should not be used to evaluate these different offices. Rather, each office is responsible for promoting democratic constancy, what Sabl understands as "the effective pursuit of interest." Sabl (2002) and Hardin (2004) exemplify the trend to tie the standards for evaluating political representatives to the activity and office of those representatives.

Future Areas of Study

There are three persistent problems associated with political representation. Each of these problems identifies a future area of investigation. The first problem is the proper institutional design for representative institutions within democratic polities. The theoretical literature on political representation has paid a lot of attention to the institutional design of democracies. More specifically, political theorists have recommended everything from proportional representation (*e.g.* Guinier, 1994 and Christiano, 1996) to citizen juries (Fishkin, 1995). However, with the growing number of democratic states, we are likely to witness more variation among the different forms of political representation. There is likely to be much debate about the advantages and disadvantages of these different ways of representing democratic citizens.

This leads to a second future line of inquiry --- ways in which democratic citizens can be marginalised by representative institutions. This problem is articulated most clearly by Young's discussion of the difficulties arising from one person representing many. Young suggests that representative institutions can include the opinions, perspectives and interests of some citizens at the expense of marginalising the opinions, perspectives and interests of others. Hence, a problem with institutional reforms aimed at increasing the representation of historically disadvantaged groups is that such reforms can and often do decrease the responsiveness of representatives. For instance, the creation of black districts has created safe zones for black elected officials so that they are less accountable to their constituents. Any decrease in accountability is especially worrisome given the ways citizens are vulnerable to their representatives. Thus, one future line of research is examining the ways that representative institutions marginalize the interests, opinions and perspectives of democratic citizens.

In particular, it is necessary for to acknowledge the biases of representative institutions. While Schumpeter (1976) has long noted the class bias of representative institutions, there is little discussion of how to improve the political representation of the disaffected — that is, the political representation of those citizens who do not have the will, the time, or political resources to participate in politics. The absence of such a discussion is particularly apparent in the literature on descriptive representation, the area that is most concerned with disadvantaged citizens.

Anne Phillips (1995) raises the problems with the representation of the poor, *e.g.* the inability to define class, however, she argues for issues of class to be integrated into a politics of presence. Few theorists have taken up Phillip's gauntlet and articulated how this integration of class and a politics of presence is to be done. Of course, some have recognised the ways in which interest groups, associations, and individual representatives can betray the least well off (*e.g.* Strolovitch, 2004). And some (Dovi, 2003) have argued that descriptive representatives need to be selected based on their relationship to citizens who have been unjustly excluded and marginalised by democratic politics.

However, it is unclear how to counteract the class bias that pervades domestic and international representative institutions. It is necessary to specify the conditions under which certain groups within a democratic polity require enhanced representation. Recent empirical literature has suggested that the benefits of having descriptive representatives is by no means straightforward (Gay, 2002).

A third and final area of research involves the relationship between representation and democracy. Historically, representation was considered to be *in opposition with* democracy. When compared to the direct forms of democracy found in the ancient city-states, notably Athens, representative institutions appear to be poor substitutes for the ways that citizens actively ruled themselves. Barber (1984) has famously argued that representative institutions were opposed to strong democracy. In contrast, almost everyone now agrees that democratic political institutions are representative ones. Bernard Manin (1997) reminds us that the Athenian Assembly, which often exemplifies direct forms of democracy, had only limited powers. According to

Manin, the practice of selecting magistrates by lottery is what separates representative democracies from so-called direct democracies. Consequently, Manin argues that the methods of selecting public officials are crucial to understanding what makes representative governments democratic. He identifies four principles distinctive of representative government:

- Those who govern are appointed by election at regular intervals;
- The decision-making of those who govern retains a degree of independence from the wishes of the electorate;
- Those who are governed may give expression to their opinions and political wishes without these being subject of the control of those who govern;
- Public decisions undergo the trial of debate;
- For Manin, historical democratic practices hold important lessons for determining whether representative institutions are democratic.

While it is clear that representative institutions are vital institutional components of democratic institutions, much more needs to be said about the meaning of democratic representation. In particular, it is important not to presume that all acts of representation are equally democratic. After all, not all acts of representation within a representative democracy are necessarily instances of democratic representation.

Henry Richardson (2002) has recently explored the undemocratic ways that members of the bureaucracy can represent citizens. Similarly, it is unclear whether a representative who actively seeks to dismantle democratic institutions is representing democratically. Does democratic representation require representatives to advance the preferences of democratic citizens or does it require a commitment to democratic institutions? At this point, answers to such questions are unclear. What is certain is that democratic citizens are likely to disagree about what constitutes democratic representation.

One popular approach to addressing the different and conflicting standards used to evaluate representatives within democratic polities, is to simply equate multiple standards with democratic ones. More specifically, it is argued that democratic standards are pluralistic, accommodating the different standards possessed and used by democratic citizens. Theorists who adopt this approach fail to specify the proper relationship among these standards. For instance, it is unclear how the standards that Mansbridge identifies in the four different forms of representation should relate to each other. Does it matter if promissory forms of representation are replaced by surrogate forms of representation? A similar omission can be found in Pitkin: although Pitkin specifies there is a unified relationship among the different views of representation, she never describes how the different views interact. This omission reflects the lacunae in the literature about how formalistic representation relates to descriptive and substantive representation. Without such a specification, it is not apparent how citizens can determine if they have adequate powers of authorisation and accountability.

Currently, it is not clear exactly what makes any given form of representation consistent, let alone consonant, with democratic representation. Is it the synergy among different forms or should we examine descriptive representation in isolation to determine the ways that it can undermine or enhance democratic representation? One tendency is to equate democratic representation simply with the existence of fluid and multiple standards. While it is true that the fact of pluralism provides justification for democratic institutions as Christiano (1996) has argued, it should no longer presumed that all forms of representation are democratic since the actions of representatives can be used to dissolve or weaken democratic institutions. The final research area is to articulate the relationship between different forms of representation and ways that these forms can undermine democratic representation.

Theories of Representation

The most groundbreaking work on this subject was done by Hanna Fenichel Pitkin who established four theories of representation:

1. Formalistic Representation, including:
    - Authorisation
    - Accountability
    - Symbolic Representation

- Descriptive Representation, and
- Substantive Representation

Representation by Population

In this method, elected representatives will be chosen by more or less numerically equivalent blocks of voters. This is not always practical for historical and current political reasons, and sometimes is impractical purely on the basis of logistics, as in regions where travel is difficult and distances are long. The shortened term "rep-by-pop" is used in Britain but is relatively uncommon in U.S.

Historically rep-by-pop is the alternative to rep-by-area. However, in the colonial countries, the geographic realities made a necessity of low-population electoral districts in order to give meaningful representation to remote communities, and only in urban and suburban areas has there been any success with applying rep-by-pop more or less evenly.

In the United States and other democracies, typically the lower house of a bicameral (two-chamber) system is based on population—more or less—while the upper House is based on area. Or, as it might be put in the United Kingdom, on title to land, as was originally the case with the old pre-Reforms House of Lords. In the Senate or the Lords, it does not matter how many people are living in your jurisdiction, it matters that you have the jurisdiction (by election, heredity or appointment—the US, the UK and Canada respectively).

Representation by Area

The principle of rep-by-pop, when brought in and promoted publicly, removed many archaic seats in the British House of Commons although some northern and rural counties necessarily still have variably lower populations than most urban ridings. Former British colonies like Canada and Australia also have rural and wilderness areas spanning tens of thousands of square miles, with fewer voters in them than a tiny urban-core riding. In the most extreme case, one riding of the Canadian parliament covers more than 2 million square kilometres, Nunavut, yet has less than one third the average number of voters for a riding, with a population of about 30,000. Making the riding larger would be difficult for the elected member, as well as for campaigning and also unfair to remotely rural constituents, whose concerns are radically different from those of the medium-sised towns that typically dominate the electorate in such ridings.

The American Constitution has built into it a series of compromises between rep-by-pop and rep-by-area: two Senators per state, at least one Representative per state, and representation in the electoral college. In Canada, provinces such as Prince Edward Island have unequal representation in Parliament (in the Commons as well as the Senate) relative to Ontario, British Columbia, and Alberta, partly for historical reasons, partly because those electoral allotments are constitutionally guaranteed, and partly because governments have simply chosen to under-represent certain voters and over-represent others.Until recent reforms, there were still many federal and provincial electoral districts in British Columbia and other provinces that had less than a few thousand votes cast, notably Atlin, covering the province's far northwest, with no more than 1,500. The area of the riding was about the size of New Brunswick and Nova Scotia combined, and larger than many American states. In practicality, the voters of the tiny communities scattered across the subarctic landscape, less than the population of a city block, had as much electoral clout as two Fraser Valley municipalities totaling up to 60,000 in population. The population imbalance between largely rural areas and overwhelmingly urban areas is one reason why the realities of representation by area still have sway against the ideal of representation by population.

Descriptive Representation

Descriptive representation, sometimes called passive representation or symbolic representation, is the idea that candidates in democratic elections should be elected to represent ethnic and gender constituencies, as well as other minority interest groups, rather than the population at large. According to this idea, an elected body should resemble a representative sample of the voters they are meant to represent concerning outward characteristics—a constituency of 50% women and 20% blacks, for example, should have 50% female and 20% black legislators. Generally, voting systems that obtain proportional representation also tend to achieve descriptive representation as well, however this can only be guaranteed to the extent that voting patterns reflect descriptive characteristics of the voters. If a particular trait is not a concern for voters or prospective candidates (for instance, eye colour), then an elected body will resemble a random sampling of the voters instead.

Some (Ulbig 2005) argue that cynicism and distrust towards government of disadvantaged minorities is partly due to not having representatives with similar characteristics. Supporters of this argument point out that as descriptive representation increases, distrust decreases. This can be the basis of laws imposing that half the candidates on a given list be women (for example in France since 2001) or of voluntary symbolic measures (Spain's current government has eight women and eight men). Opponents of such logic argue that practical policies may ultimately play a larger role, making such representative gestures irrelevant unless already done by a government considered favourable by the community. For example, only 2% of African-Americans supported the Bush administration despite the high-profile nominations of Colin Powell and Condoleezza Rice.

REPRESENTATIVE DEMOCRACY

Representative democracy is a form of government founded on the principle of elected individuals representing the people, as opposed to autocracy and direct democracy. The representatives form an independent ruling body (for an election period) charged with the responsibility of acting in the people's interest, but *not* as their proxy representatives not necessarily always according to their wishes, but with enough authority to exercise swift and resolute initiative in the face of changing circumstances. It is often contrasted with direct democracy, where representatives are absent or are limited in power as proxy representatives. A representative democracy that emphasises individual liberty is a liberal democracy. One that does not is an illiberal democracy.

Today, in liberal democracies, representatives are usually elected in multi-party elections that are free and fair. The power of representatives in a liberal democracy is usually curtailed by a constitution (as in a constitutional democracy or a constitutional monarchy) or other measures to balance representative power:

- An independent judiciary, which may have the power to declare legislative acts unconstitutional (*e.g.* constitutional court, supreme court)
- It may also provide for some deliberative democracy (*e.g.*, Royal Commissions) or direct popular measures (*e.g.*, initiative, referendum, recall elections). However, these are not always binding and usually require some legislative action—legal power usually remains firmly with representatives.
- In some cases, a bicameral legislature may have an "upper house" that is not directly elected, such as the Canadian Senate, which was in turn modeled on the British House of Lords.

The term republic may have many different meanings. It normally means a state with an elected or otherwise non-monarchical head of state, such as the Islamic Republic of Iran or Republic of Korea. Sometimes in the US it is used similar to liberal democracy. For example, "the United States relies on representative democracy, but its system of government is much more complex than that. It is not a simple representative democracy, but a constitutional republic in which majority rule is tempered."

In many representative democracies (Australia, Canada, the United Kingdom, etc.), representatives are most commonly chosen in elections by a plurality of those who are both eligible to cast votes and actually do so. A candidate has a plurality when he or she has won more votes than any other candidate in the race, but not necessarily most (more than 50%) of the votes cast. This is not the case in Australia, where the elected representatives of the house of representatives are elected by a system of preferential voting and require the support of 50% or more voters in a single round to be elected. While existing representative democracies hold such elections to choose representatives, in theory other methods, such as sortition (more closely aligned with direct democracy), could be used instead. Also, representatives sometimes hold the power to select other representatives, presidents, or other officers of government (indirect representation).

8

THE ORIGINS OF ELECTORAL SYSTEMS AND POLITICAL PARTIES

Political parties and electoral systems have been analysed both as a cause and as a consequence of each other. First, a long tradition of empirical studies has focused on the consequences of electoral systems on party systems. Maurice Duverger postulates that "old" political parties were created internally in elected (and also in non-elected) assemblies and parliamentary groups. In a social choice perspective, the origin of political parties is also found in an endogenous process in elected legislatures embodying incentives to form enduring voting coalitions. Empirical analyses of the numbers of political parties and their relations, typically focusing on democratic regimes during the second half of the 20th century, usually assume that political parties derive from elections and electoral systems that are given and can be taken as the independent variable in the explanatory framework.

An alternative approach has upside down this relationship by postulating that it is the parties that choose electoral systems and manipulate the rules of elections. According to this approach, the origin of the invention and adoption of different electoral rules and procedures, especially during the 19th and early 20th centuries, should be found in the incentives created by political party competition. In this approach it is assumed, thus, that it is the political parties that can be taken as given and work as the independent variable to explain the emergence of different electoral rules.

The present discussion tries to disentangle this discussion by specifying the type of assembly and electoral conditions that can be placed in the most remote origins of the creation of political parties. Specifically, I emphasize the role of traditional elections in multi member districts, with open ballot and plurality rule, in the initial creation of political parties. This understudied, 'originating' electoral system was used very widely in local and national assemblies in pre-democratic or early democratic periods before and during the 19th century; it is still probably the most common procedure in small community, condominium, school, university, and union assemblies and elections; and it has also been adopted in a few new democracies in recent times. This set of electoral rules appears indeed as almost 'natural' and 'spontaneous' to many communities when they have to choose a procedure of collective decision-making based on votes, especially because it permits a varied representation of the community.

The important point to be remarked here is that these traditional electoral rules, while being able to produce fair representation, they also create strong incentives for the formation of 'factional' candidacies or voting coalitions, in another word 'parties'. Under the 'originating' electoral system, factions or parties tend to induce 'voting in bloc' for a list of candidates, which may change election results radically. On some crucial cases, it was mostly as a consequence of this type of experience that different political leaders, candidates and parties began to seek for alternative, less intuitive or 'spontaneous' electoral rules able to produce less advantage for the faction or party best organised. This opened the way in more recent times for parties and politically motivated scholars to invent and choose new electoral systems.

The structure of the discussin is the following. First, the 'originating' electoral system based on multi-member districts, open ballot and plurality rule is defined and discussed. Second, a survey of the uses of this set of electoral rules and some of its variants in political elections in different parts of the world during remote and recent periods shows its wide spread. Third, a simple model of voting under this type of electoral system demonstrates the incentives to form factional or partisan candidacies. Fourth, a number of prominent, mostly negative reactions to the emergence of political parties during the 18th and 19th centuries are collected and reinterpreted in the light of this discussion. Fifth, a great variety of electoral rules and procedures invented since the second half of the 19th century is presented as directly derived from the 'originating' system in the intention to reduce its effects in favour of a single party. In the conclusion, the general relations between political parties and electoral systems are restated to account for the foundational stage here discussed.

The Originating Electoral System

The originating electoral system here analysed has been widely used, especially in relatively simple elections with rather homogeneous electorates, particularly at the beginning of modern suffrage regulations and for small-size local governments. Specifically, with some variants, it was used from the 13th century on in English town meetings and shire (county) courts (Bishop 1893), German and Swiss communes and cantons (Lloyd 1907), Italian communes, French municipalities, and from the 15th century on, also in provincial Estates and the Estates-General. During the 17th and 18th centuries it was also adopted in the British colonies in North America (Sydnor 1962, Pole 1971), as well as, by early 19th century, in Juntas and Cortes elections in Spain and in the Spanish and Portuguese colonies in the Americas.

This is basically the same type of electoral system that is typically used in many meetings and assemblies of modern housing condominiums, neighborhood associations, school and university boards and delegates, professional organisations, corporation boards, and students' and workers' unions. In these as well as in many of the traditional communities mentioned in the previous paragraph, individual representation was well suited to contexts of high economic and ethnic homogeneity in which it was relatively easy to identify common interests and priority public goods to be provided by the elect.

As will be detailed in the next section, the 'originating' system rules have also been widely used in larger-scale national and local political elections with limited suffrage rights or in new democratic experiments in more recent times. The essential elements of this electoral system are the following:

- Multi-member districts ($M > 1$).
- Open ballot ($V < M$).

- Plurality or majority rule.

Where:

M: District magnitude or number of seats to be filled;

V: Number of votes per voter.

The first element, multi-member districts, has been understudied in the recent political science literature on elections. Well established empirical 'tendencies' in the relation between electoral systems and party systems consider two basic types of electoral systems: one combining single member districts with majoritarian rules (which are associated to bipartism) and another combining multi member districts with proportional representation rules (corresponding to multipartism). In contrast, the combination of multi-member districts with majoritarian rules has attracted much less attention. Indeed this type of electoral system would be difficult to fit into the mentioned relationships since it permits an individual candidate-based, highly pluralistic representation which is characteristic of none of the other two types of electoral system mentioned (respectively associated to individual representation and to pluralistic representation, but not the two together). Variants of multi-member district elections include both direct voting (like in the old German communes and the English and North-American local assemblies) and indirect elections of delegates in several stages (more traditional in France, Italy, Spain and Latin America in remote periods).

The second element, open ballot, permits voters to choose individual candidates, not a partisan list. This is compatible with voting by both raising hands (like in traditional Swiss communes or English counties) and oral vote (like in colonial Virginia, for instance), even if this requires voting separately for a candidate for each seat.

Voting separately for individual candidates by raising hands or by oral vote, as well as the request of a second or further rounds for each seat, are procedures favouring this type of elections to be hold in an assembly of voters, where successive voting rounds can be held comfortably. An assembly of voters can also proceed with secret ballot (including early forms like typical English poll-books with the names of the candidates over and against which were set down the votes, or written ballots, already used in some North-American colonies since the 17th century). Distributing groups of voters among different booths within the same multi-member district, which may facilitate secret ballot, is also compatible with this type of system (as in most at-large local or state elections in the United States). Thus, all these alternative formulas –oral or written ballot, assembly or booth voting, second or further round rules— are compatible with the essentials of the electoral system here to be discussed.

An interesting variant refers to the number of candidates each voter can vote for. While in some cases the voter must vote for as many candidates as seats to be filled (V = M), an alternative common rule permits the voter to vote for up to as many candidates as seats (V < M), which is a limited form of approval voting (already used, for instance, in medieval England boroughs and in Italian communes). Voting for fewer candidates than seats has been called 'plumper', 'partial abstention' and other names, but 'limited approval' voting seems more in tune with well-established precise definitions and categories in modern electoral studies.

(Note: In contrast, standard approval voting permits to vote for up to all candidates but one, as presented in Brams and Fishburn 1978, 1983, Weber 1995, Colomer and McLean 1998. Interestingly, while an abundant literature exists on approval voting for single-winner elections, apparently nobody has studied approval voting for multiwinner elections, a variety much more widely used, as demonstrated here).

Other variants may imply a series of successive, 'staggered' single-seat elections or, as mentioned, may require voters in a multi-seat election to choose one candidate for each seat, typically among the corresponding subset of candidates previously allocated to each seat (a procedure sometimes called 'place' system in certain state and local elections in the United States). In spite of certain contrary interpretations, none of these procedures is equivalent to a series or a collection of single-member district elections.

While in single-member district elections the voter elect only one seat, in the variants of multi-member district elections now considered each voter still elects multiple seats. In staggered successive elections for a single seat each, voters can choose their preferred candidates, if they run again and again, in the same way as they can do it in a multi-member ballot. Remember that the system here identified implies no closed party lists of candidates, but individual-candidate votes. Even if parties present candidacies, the voters can choose candidates from different parties at successive single-seat elections in a similar way as they can do it in a multi-seat election with no party lists.

A prominent example in present times is the United States Senate, in which two-member districts with staggered single-seat elections permit the election of senators from two different parties in each district, as happens with high and increasing frequency. In 'place' systems forcing the voters to choose for each seat from a different subset of candidates, the margin of choice may be more limited. But if the voters' preferred candidates they would vote for in a multi-seat election are running for different seats, they can choose them as well. In any case, the voter can vote for candidates from different parties for different seats.

Regarding the third element, plurality rule is most common in this type of system, but absolute majority rule can also be used. Variants of the latter include a second or a third round by simple plurality or between the two or the three most voted candidates at the previous round (like in Ancient regime France). For several-round rules, the procedure may require the voter to vote separately for one candidate for each seat, but this may not alter substantially the expected consequences of the election on the variety of elected representatives, as discussed above.

Very Wide-spread Electoral Rules

Now we present a broad although surely incomplete survey of modern and current uses of the 'originating' electoral system in national and local political elections. The survey starts in Europe, including England, France, Spain and other countries, then it goes to the United States and Latin America, and it ends with a few notes on Russia and a few Asian and African countries.

England

Two member districts were largely used in English shires, towns and boroughs from the 13th century on. Still in 1867 three fourths of the English districts for the House of Commons elected two members, while the rest were either single or four-member districts. The proportion of multi-member districts was dramatically reduced to less than 10 per cent in 1885, but some survived still until 1949. In two-member districts the voter could use either two votes or only one. According to historians, during the period 1688-1866 borough elections were dominated by a desire to secure effective representation of the public or corporate interest, while there is contemporary evidence of a considerable degree of hostility towards parties and partisanship. The presence of political 'tendencies' was elusive and partial and included many labels –Radical, Whig, Liberal, Tory, Conservative, Peelite, Protectionist—rather than a few compact parties.

Multi-member districts and to some extent nonpartisan candidacies have survived in English local elections. According to the rules enforced from 2003 on, still about 60 per cent of local councils are elected in two-or three-member electoral districts, usually called wards or divisions. They include metropolitan councils in Manchester, Merseyside, South and West Yorkshire, Tyne and Wear, West Midlands, as well as the London boroughs, a number of unitary, borough, district and parish/town councils, as well as a recently increasing number of urban areas in county councils. A few districts use mixed systems of single and multi-member constituencies. Nowadays nation-wide political parties dominate local politics, but in 2000 still about 12 per cent of elected local councilors were independent. (Electoral Commission, 2004).

FRANCE

In France, the tradition of using multi-member districts in indirect elections for medieval Estates was maintained for post-revolutionary national assemblies during most of the 19th century. From 1789 to 1819, canton or arrondissement assemblies elected delegates to department assemblies, which in turn chose deputies. At least at the highest level, majority rule was established with three rounds of voting. Direct elections were introduced since 1848. Until 1873 and again in 1885, voters still met in departmental assemblies and used limited approval voting in a written ballot. Party lists were increasingly relevant, but individual-candidate voting was always feasible. The 'originating' system has survived in French small municipalities with less than 3,500 inhabitants, where the local councils are elected in a single multi-member municipal district with individual-candidate voting and majority runoff rule. For recently established regional councils, one fourth of councilors are also elected in a single regional district by majority runoff rule, but now using closed lists that produce a single-party overrepresentation.

Spain

Also in Spain multi-member districts were used for indirect elections to anti-French invasion Juntas in 1810 and for constitutional elections from 1812 to 1834. Parish-or judicial party-juntas chose electors, which in turn chose deputies (or, in the earliest regulations, groups of candidates further selected by lots). Voting was usually separate for each seat by majority runoff. Direct elections were held since 1837. In several elections until 1865, voters still met at district juntas to elect deputies by limited approval voting in a written ballot and majority rule. Mixed systems of single-and multi-member districts, the latter with limited approval voting, were used from 1878 to 1936. Since 1977, multi-member districts with individual-candidate ballot are used for the Spanish Senate, as well as in local elections for small municipalities with less than 250 inhabitants.

Rest of Europe

In the rest of Europe, experiences of nation-wide political elections in multi-member districts with majoritarian rules include the following. Indirect elections with this type of electoral system were held in Norway, with an average magnitude of three seats, from 1815 to 1903; in Portugal during most of the 19th century; in Sweden from 1866 to 1908, in all these cases with plurality rule; as well as in Switzerland from 1848 to 1917 with majority runoff rules.

Direct elections to the national lower chamber with this type of electoral system were held in Belgium, with very high district magnitudes up to 37 seats and majority runoff rule, from 1831 to 1898; in Greece, with either majority or plurality rules, from 1844 to 1923, as well as on two isolated occasions as late as 1933 and 1952; Netherlands used two-member districts and majority runoff rule during all the second half of the 19th century. While local elections in most

European countries are currently held by proportional representation rules, still a few use the 'originating' electoral system. In Belgium, municipal elections are held in multi-member districts, although voters can choose individual candidates only from within a party list. In Hungary, towns and villages with less than 10,000 inhabitants use a single municipal multi-member district, limited approval vote and plurality rule. Individual candidates not officially linked to a party are more successful in these districts than in mixed or proportional representation systems used in larger municipalities and counties (Benoit, 2001). In Norway, multimember local districts use individual-candidate ballots, although three-fourths of the chosen candidates must be from the same party list. In Switzerland, multi-member districts are used in seven cantons for the election of either the cantonal assembly or the cantonal government or both. (Council of Europe 1999).

United States

The English model of multi-member districts, individual vote and plurality rule was adopted in all the British colonies in North America for the lower houses of their legislatures. Since its inception in 1619, the House of Burgesses in Virginia used English-style two-member districts, later enlarged to up to eight seats. All the other colonies also used, for their assemblies, two, three, four or six-member districts, while South Carolina and New Jersey had districts with up to 10 and 20 members respectively. Government by town meeting was typical in New England, while parish and county districts were more usual in the South. From the 1720s on, the lower houses consolidated their position in the colonial governments and acquired greater autonomy. According to historians, a vast majority of legislators, who were elected on individual bases, exhibited habits of consensus not dissimilar to those of the independent members of the British parliament. (Dinkin 1993, Greene 1993).

With independence, state congresses were made larger than the colonial assemblies. Eight new state constitutions established congressional elections in multimember districts, while five adopted this formula for most of the districts but also introduced a few single-member districts. The U.S. Presidential College was elected mostly in state-wide districts since 1828. The House of Representatives was also initially elected mostly in either state-wide 'at-large' districts or in smaller multimember districts. From 1824 on state-level political parties began to emerge. They promoted voting 'in bloc' for a list of party candidates or the 'general ticket', which tended to create state single-party representation. In defensive reaction, the Whigs achieved to approve single-member districts as the general norm for electing the House across all the United States territory since 1842. But at least 16 states still used at-large districts during some periods between the 1840s and the 1960s.

At state and local levels, most representatives have been elected in multimember districts most of the time. At state level the peak was reached in 1962, when 41 of the 50 states elected more than half of total state legislators in the country in multi-member districts. In 2000, 15 state lower chambers and four state senates employ some multi-member districts, encompassing in total over 25 per cent of all state legislators (Jewell and Morehouse 2001).

At municipal level, the progressive-oriented National Municipal League recommended in 1899 the adoption of at-large districts to insulate local elections from the influence of state and national party politics, a recommendation largely followed, together with a non-partisan ballot, especially in the West and the South. In 1970, over 60 per cent of the cities and over 30 per cent of the counties elected their representatives in a single 'at-large' district (Cox 1984, Niemi, Hill and Grofman 1985). In the 1980s, at-large districts were used in 84 per cent of the largest central cities (Engstrom and McDonald 1986, Weaver 1984). It has been estimated that in about two-thirds of U.S. municipal elections, candidates run for office without party label (Cassel 1986).

The capability of at-large districts to produce a single-party "sweep" in the disadvantage of political, ethnic and gender minorities has been broadly discussed. Against traditional assumptions, it has been found that, at state level, multi-member district lower chambers provide representation more proportional to the ethnic minority population than either single-member districts lower chambers or single-member district upper chambers in their own states. Multi-member districts have also favoured female representation during some periods.

Latin America

The election of Juntas and new Spanish Cortes in 1810-1812, above mentioned, was extended to the Spanish colonies in North and South America with the same type of traditional electoral rules as in the metropolis. In particular, in New Spain (today's Mexico), for the election of representatives to both the Spanish Cortes and provincial councils, multi-member districts were defined as corresponding to traditional parishes and the preserved Indian republics. Similar experiences took place in Argentina in 1811 and, at the Portuguese Crown's call, in Brazil in 1821. After independence, multimember districts for the election of the lower chamber of the new congresses were widely, generally by plurality rule. Cases inc lude Argentina, with two-to 20-member districts in 1826 and again during the period 1853-1908; Brazil, with districts up to 20 and 37 seats from 1824 on, from 1860 on, and in 1890; Chile from 1833 on; Colombia from 1857 on; Costa Rica with a mixed system of two-member districts by plurality and others by proportional representation during the period 1913-1948; and Honduras with an average of tree-member districts during the period 1879-1954. (Colomer 2004c).

Russia

The first democratic election in Russia, in February 1917, was held according to the traditional system above referred to, in districts with magnitudes from one to 15 seats, approval vote, and majority rule with third-round plurality. During the Soviet era, the same type of elections in multi-member districts was held, but with the dictatorial rule of accepting only one candidate per office. In post-soviet Russia, starting in 1993, at least 24 regional democratic assemblies hold elections with multi-member districts, approval vote and plurality rule (in front to 114 regions with mostly single-member districts). In the majority of regions, electoral competition is dominated by independent individual candidates. But, according to the argument above mentioned which will be developed in the next section, it has been found that multi-member districts create incentives for the formation of coalition and political party candidacies more than single-member districts (Golosov 2003).

Asia and Africa

Both the colonial British legacy and the United States influence contributed to the adoption of multi-member district elections by plurality rule in a number of countries in Asia and the Pacific. New Zealand maintained a few tree-member districts during the period 1890-1905; the Philippines used also some multi-member districts in 1935 and 1949; in India about 90 districts (out of 400) elected two or three representatives each from 1950 to 1957; in Thailand a number of multi-member districts are also used since 1978. Probably under French influence, also Lebanon used multi-member districts, together with majority runoff rule, during the period 1943-1951, and again, with plurality rule, since 1953. Turkey used approval voting, in large districts with up to 27 seats, during the period 1946-1957. (Hicken and Kasuya 2003, Hicken 2004). A few countries in Africa have also adopted electoral rules including multimember districts and majoritarian rules. They include a few recent democracies: Mali and Senegal, both since 1992.

Endogenous Party Formation

The 'originating' electoral system above reviewed is able to produce a varied individual representation of the community. But at the same time it creates incentives for the coordination of candidacies and voting. Forming or joining a coordinated candidacy, usually called 'faction' or 'party', may increase the prospects of winning additional votes and seats. 'Party' is, thus, here defined in a minimalist way that is not substantially different from traditional meanings of 'faction' in early periods of voting and elections.

The distinction between faction and party can make more sense only in a further process of organisation and development of policy programs and ideology. Let us present a simple model in which an election is hold by a two-member district, individual-candidate voting, and simple plurality rule. Let us assume that there are four groups of voters, A, B, C and D, with different preferences over four candidates, W, X, Y and Z. The distribution of voters' preferences is relatively consensual because the 'intermediate' groups, B and C, encompass 70 out of 90 voters but the distribution is more polarised because it is the 'extreme' groups, A and D, that now encompass 70 voters (90 is taken in the example as the total number of voters to facilitate a majority of 50 without ties).

If all voters vote for two candidates according to their first and second preferences, the total number of votes received by each candidate makes the intermediate candidates X and Y the winners, observe that, although with different numbers of votes, this result is valid for the two distributions of voters, the consensual and the polarised ones. Every group of voters elects at least one of the candidates it has voted for; specifically, the voters of the 'intermediate' groups elect the two candidates they have voted for while the members of the 'extreme' groups elect their second most preferred candidate. Thus, none of the voters' groups is a total loser.

In the third column it is assumed, alternatively, that a 'party' is formed by candidates W and X. Let us assume that all voters vote now for all the candidates of the party including their first preference, that is, all voters preferring either W or X as the first preference vote now 'in bloc' for W and X, even if some of them would have preferred another candidate as second preference (Y in the example). The result is that now W and X become the winners –the party 'sweep'. Only three groups of voters elect now some candidate they have voted for; specifically, the members of the 'extreme' group A elect all the candidates they have voted for, the members of the 'intermediate' group B elect only their first preference, and the members of the other 'intermediate' group C elect only their second preference; in contrast, the members of group D do not elect now any of the candidates they have voted for.

It is important to remark that, in order to attain a party-sweep, it is not necessary that all voters –like in the model— or even most or many of them follow the advice of factional leaders to vote for all and only for the members of a list of candidates. It may be sufficient that a few people do it, since, even if they are few, they can make a difference, especially under simple plurality rule not requiring any specific threshold of votes to win.

The party sweep result might be more satisfactory than the previous individual candidate result for some voters in a polarised distribution (depending on how voters evaluate their relative satisfaction with their first and second preferences), but it is exclusionary for those members of the electorate who become total losers. Certainly, the party-sweep result is less collective satisfactory than the individual-candidate result in the consensual distribution, which, as noted above, is more typical of small local, early national, and professional communities having traditionally used this electoral system.

A logical reaction to the party sweep can be the formation of another 'party', say in this example with Y and Z, also able to make the voters voting in bloc for all the candidates of the party if they include their first preference. The fourth column shows the results of a two-party election. In this example, the winners are still W and X, but the losers are now closer to the winners in numbers of votes, which may make them persevere in their party candidacy in further elections in the expectation to turn over a few more votes and win in bloc. Similar results can be obtained if we assume somewhat different distributions of voters' preferences, voting by majority runoff rule, or other variations the reader may be interested to explore.

This stylised model may account for the endogenous formation of parties, initially conceived only as enduring candidacy and voting coalitions, in early elections and assemblies using the 'originating' electoral system. The model also suggests that the emergence of parties may produce sentiments of dissatisfaction and disappointment in comparison with previous experiences of voting for individual candidates, especially in largely consensual societies in which the formation of party candid aces may introduce political polarisation.

Note again that, in historical terms, voting 'in bloc' was not an institutionally induced behavior, but a party strategy-induced behavior. In the old fashion way, certain men more or less distinguished for their professional or other activities were announced as eligible by newspapers or offered themselves as candidates. Gradually, elected representatives turned to organize their supporters and present lists or tickets of candidates. The success of this new way may lie in the fact that 'party' candidacies and labels provide the voters very cheap information about their candidates, which may be more difficult to obtain about those candidates who are not labeled, especially in mass elections and relatively complex electorates. This may move voters to vote in bloc rather than for individuals weighed separately.

However, party inducements to voting in bloc were also crucially helped in some countries and periods by the form of ballot, which is of course an institutional feature of elections. In the earliest times above surveyed, oral voting or handwritten ballots facilitated to the voter the choice of individual candidates independently from their possible grouping or factional allegiance. At some moment, which can be roughly located around the 1830s and 1840s for Britain, the United States and a few countries in Western Europe, the parties began to print their own ballots, listing only their own candidates. The voter needed only to cast the paper in the ballot box without marking any candidate to vote for the entire list (the 'general ticket'). Typically the party ballots were of various sizes, colours, and shapes, and thus distinguishable to the election officials, the candidates, the party organisers and the rest of voters.

Still, splitting the vote between candidates from different parties was possible by crossing out and writing in names or by turning in multiple party ballots with votes marked on each. In fact, in 19th century England, about half of districts with two seats rendered 'split' representation of two different groupings (Cox 1984). But in the United States before 1890, a single party swept all the seats in almost 90 per cent of elections in multi-member districts (Calabrese 2000). Criticisms of party ballot were persistent.

In particular, the National Municipal League of the U. S., already mentioned above, defended non-partisan ballots in local government. In the words of one of its founders, with party candidacies "a small, but well-disciplined, energetic and unscrupulous minority can generally defeat the honorable and patriotic majority". If people are forced to vote in bloc, "while many voters find sentiments which they disapprove in each platform, they can see no alternative but to cast their ballots for one or the other, and thus seem to endorse and support ideas to which they are really opposed" (Richardson 1892, in Scarrow 2002).

The so-called 'Australian ballot' made again non-partisan voting for individual candidates relatively easier. The new ballot, which was now printed and distributed by the electoral authority, listed the candidates of all parties instead of only one. As its name tells, this new form of ballot was first introduced in the British colonies in Australia since 1856, as well as in New Zealand in 1870; it was adopted in Britain in 1872, Canada in 1874, Belgium in 1877, several states in the U.S. since 1888, and later in most other countries with democratic experience.

Under multi-member elections, the Australian ballot ensures secret vote if the procedure did include a booth where the voter could mark the ballot unobserved, but it also facilitates the choice of individual candidates independently from their party affiliation. In some cases, the ballot requires the voters to vote for each candidate they wanted to vote for; but in others it is also possible to vote for all candidates from a party with a single mark, which still favours bloc voting.

Against Factions

The emergence of factions and parties from within largely consensual elections and assemblies increased polarisation, made representation more biased, and in general decreased voters' satisfaction with political outcomes, as suggested by the formal model above discussed. In communities holding elections with the 'originating' system during the 18th and 19th centuries, reactions against factions and political parties were loudly and widely voiced, as will be reviewed below.

Initially, factions tended to be loose and fluctuating groupings of individuals who joined together to support a particular leader or policy, but from the beginning they were viewed with suspicion as destroyers of previously existing unity and consensus. Gradually, a tension was developing between the recurring suspicion of partisan divisions and the seeming inevitability of partisan organisation. Parties were eventually conceived as "unavoidable evils". But, as summarised by Susan Scarrow in her survey of critical perspectives on political parties, "even many avowed democrats were not favourably disposed toward the evolving realities of organised parties ... while political experience may have convinced many people of parties' inevitability and expediency, it was and is less effective in persuading everyone of their desirability" (Scarrow 2002: 4).

A number of early, prominent analyses and statements along this line can be reinterpreted in the light of the discussion presented in this article. In general, in classical political literature 'faction' is usually associated to bad intentions, in the disadvantage of general or at least broad collective interests. David Hume, in particular, early considered that "sects and factions (should) be detested and hated… (because they) subvert government, render law impotent, and beget the fiercest animosities" (Hume 1741).

Later on, however, he pondered that "to abolish all distinctions of party may not be practicable, perhaps not desirable, in a free government". Interestingly, when in the further period Hume had to face the undesirable but perhaps unavoidable existence of political parties, he turned to wish that government were in hands not of a single party but of multiple-party coalitions in order "to prevent all unreasonable insult and triumph of the one party over the other, to encourage moderate opinions, to find the proper medium in all disputes, to persuade each that its antagonist may possibly be sometimes in the right, and to keep a balance in the praise and blame, which we bestow on either side" (Hume 1758).

Perhaps it was Jean-Jacques Rousseau who better realised and anticipated the dramatic influence of factions in elections held in multi-member districts by plurality rule –as used in his natal Geneva. "When factions arise he observed in a rather well-known but diversely interpreted passage—, and partial associations are formed at the expense of the great association, the will of each of these associations becomes general in relation to its members, while it remains particular in relation to the community: it may then be said that there are no longer as many votes as there are men, but only as many as there are associations… Lastly, when one of these associations is so great as to prevail over all the rest, the result is no longer a sum of small differences, but a single difference; in this case there is no longer a general will, and the opinion which prevails is purely particular". Highly remarkably, also Rousseau pondered that if factions of parties were unavoidable, that is, "if there are partial societies, it is best to have as many as possible and to prevent them from being unequal" (Rousseau 1762).

A similar evolution can be detected in James Madison actually influenced by reading Hume who initially also condemned factions, but later on saw them as unavoidable and even a necessary evil.

Madison perceptively noted that, with parties organised, in small communities there would likely be a single dominant party embedded in local prejudices and schemes of injustice and "the smaller the number of individuals composing a majority, and the smaller the compass within which they are placed, the more easily will they concert and execute their plan of oppression". In contrast, greater political units would provide "the greater security afforded by a greater variety of parties, against the event of any one party being able to outnumber and oppress the rest... In an equal degree does the increased variety of parties comprised within the (large) Union increase this security" (Madison 1788, No. 10).

Madison surely had in mind previous experiences in the House of Delegates in Virginia, of which he had been a member, as other prominent leaders of the newly emerging United States, when they turned to organize new political parties at national level, took references in traditional factions and personalised cliques in local and state institutions holding elections with the 'originating' system. (Main 1973, Aldrich 1995).

The present analysis induces us to revise also an established interpretation of some statements by Honore Gabriel Riqueti, Count de Mirabeau, in his address to the provincial Estate of Provence in 1789, on the edge of the events that would trigger the Revolution in France. It must be remarked that the subject under discussion on that occasion was precisely the procedure to follow for the election of provincial representatives to the Estates-General. Mirabeau and his audience certainly had in mind the multi-member district, individual vote type of elections they were used to participate in at local and provincial levels.

He famously declared that "the Estates-General are to the nation what a chart is to its physical configuration; in all its parts and as a whole the copy should at all times have the same proportions as the original". In another passage of the same speech, Mirabeau stated, "the nation is not there (in the Estates' assemblies) if those who call themselves its representatives have not been chosen in free and individual elections, if the representatives of groups of equal importance are not equal numerically and in voting power... In order to know the will of the nation, the votes must be collected in such a way so as to prevent the mistake of taking the will of an estate for one other, or the particular will of certain individuals for the general will".

(Author's translation, with emphases added, from Mirabeau 1789, vol. 1: 7-8). These statements have been often interpreted as an early pronouncement in favour of the principles of proportional representation (for example, Hoag and Hallett 1926, McLean 1991, Colomer 2001). However, we should acknowledge that no explicit reference to new electoral rules of proportional representation was ever made by Mirabeau and that the discussion about these principles as potentially operative for allocating seats on the basis of votes did not start until several decades later. Putting Mirabeau's contribution in context, it may appear rather obvious that he was referring to elections held in multi-member districts by an open ballot favouring the choice of individual candidates and majority rule. He was alluding to the peril to impose only votes in bloc for each of the estates in a way that the aristocracy and the clergy would prevail over the whole nation. But note that Mirabeau stated that the at the time really existing elected assemblies "are" like a chart of the nation, and that they "should" keep being it. If they actually "were" like a chart is because they were elected in a way permitting such a representation (in the two senses of the word); that they "should" maintain that characteristic may be reasonably interpreted as a warning against the risk that they might cease being it and become partial, most likely as a consequence of voting in bloc for closed lists of candidates of each estate, grouping or faction.

The authors mentioned were among the most influential in constitution making and criticism in Britain, the emerging United States, revolutionary France, and indirectly in many other countries at the time. It is noteworthy to remark that they essentially coincided in the following observations.

- First, they valued positively traditional electoral systems based on multimember districts and individual-candidate voting—what I call here the 'originating' system–able to produce a faithful representation of the community, like "a mirror".
- Second, they realised that the formation of electoral factions or parties introduced more biased and partial representation than

previous practices based on individual votes for individual candidates.

- Third, they eventually acknowledged that in mass elections in large societies, in which the homogeneity of interests and values which prevailed in small, simple communities during the previous eras was decreasing, the formation of political factions was unavoidable and perhaps even necessary to make the political representation of a diversity of groups possible.
- Finally, they considered that once parties had began to intervene in the electoral process, the existence of multiple parties was better than the concentration of power in the hands of a single party, in the sense of re-establishing to some extent the previous capacity of elections to become "a mirror" of the society by giving representation to different groups. In other words, if parties were unavoidable, multipartism was better than single-party dominance or two-party alternation.

Derived Electoral Systems

To the extent that parties and fictionalisation were unavoidable, the re-establishment of broad electoral representation required the invention and introduction of new electoral rules different from the traditional, now obsolete system based on multi-member districts and majoritarian rules. During the first few decades of the 20th century, as surveyed above, the 'originating' electoral system had generally been replaced with alternative formulas. Multi-member elections with majoritarian rules basically survived at local level elections, although they also reappeared in a number of cases of new democracies without previous experience of competitive elections. Virtually all the new electoral rules and procedures that were created since the 19th century can be understood as innovative variations of the 'originating' system –which can be called 'originating' precise for this. They can be classified in three groups, depending on whether they changed the district magnitude, the ballot, or the rule. The first group of new electoral rules implied a change of the district magnitude from multi-member to single-member districts, of course keeping both individual candidate voting and majoritarian rules.

With smaller single-member districts a candidate that would have been defeated by a party sweep in a multi-member district may be elected. This system, thus, tends to produce more varied representation than multi-member districts with party closed lists, although less than multi-member districts with open ballot. In late 18th century, single-member districts were broadly introduced in Scotland and Wales and in lower proportions in England, although they did not become the general norm for all Britain until 1885. In the U.S., single-member districts were introduced in the state of Vermont in 1793 and gradually expanded to the rest of the country, especially for the election of the House of Representatives since 1842, as mentioned. Also France replaced multi-member districts with single-member districts for first time in 1820, but re-established both formulas back and forth during the rest of the 19th century.

The second group of new electoral rules implied new forms of ballot favouring individual-candidate voting despite the existence of party candidacies, while maintaining the other two essential elements of the traditional system: multi-member districts and majoritarian rules. Two variants of limited vote (with either several votes or a single vote per voter) were already proposed during the French Revolutionary Convention of 1793 by Jean-Antoine-Nicolas de Caritat, Marquis de Condorcet, and Antoine-Louis-Leon de Saint-Just, on behalf of the Girondin and the Jacobin factions, respectively, as alternatives to the traditional system of multi-member districts with equal number of votes as seats, but they were never applied. By limited vote, one party can sweep as many seats as votes the voter can vote for, but it is likely that the rest of seats will be won by candidates of different political affiliation.

The earliest experiences of limited vote in multi-member districts took place in Spain, first in the form of single-nontransferable vote, that is, with only one vote per voter, from 1865 on, and giving each voter two votes in three-seat districts from 1878 on. Limited vote was also early introduced in previously existing multi-member districts in Britain in 1868 and in Brazil in 1875. A different but related formula, the cumulative ballot, which permits the voter to give more than one vote to the same candidate, was also introduced in previously existing multi-member districts, first of all in the state of Illinois in 1869 and later in some Latin European and Latin American countries, as well as in a number of U.S. local elections.

Finally, the third group of new electoral rules implied the introduction of proportional representation (PR) formulas, which permit to maintain multi-member districts and in some variants also open or individual-candidate ballot. The first proposals for distributing seats among different parties in proportion to their votes were formulated, on the basis of a fixed amount or quota of votes worth a seat, by French mathematician Joseph-Diaz Gergonne in 1820, just when the old system based on multimember districts was substantially revised in France for first time, and by Philadelphia's activist Thomas Gilpin in 1844, together with strong criticism of the uses of party lists in traditional multi-member districts. (Gergonne 1829, Gilpin 1844).

As is better known, another early formula usually considered to belong to the group of proportional representation rules is the single-transferable vote (STV), which was successively proposed by English school-teacher Thomas W. Hill in 1821, Danish politician Carl-Christopher-Georg Andrae in 1855, and English lawyer Thomas Hare from 1857 on.

As the traditional 'originating' system, STV is used in multi-member districts with individual voting, although it requires each voter not only to select but to rank candidates. Another formula of proportional representation was presented by Belgian civil law professor Victor d'Hondt in 1878 and was initially adopted in Belgium in 1899. This and other PR formulas require, of course, multi-member districts and are also compatible with the another essential element of the 'originating' system: individual-candidate voting, as in open double vote, preferential voting and open ballot, the latter used in Switzerland since 1918.

Conclusion

In traditional analyses in political science, political parties have been presented as derived from previously existing assemblies, elections and electoral systems, rather than the other way round. The present article has documented this relationship, but it only appears to be valid in general terms for remote periods in which a very old electoral system based on multi-member districts, open ballot, and a majoritarian rule was used. This electoral system, while being able to produce a pluralistic representation, it did indeed create incentives for the formation of coordinated candidacies and voting coalitions, usually called 'factions', which were the most primitive form of political parties. However, once partisan candidacies, partisan voting in bloc and even partisan ballots emerged, political leaders, activists and politically motivated scholars began to search for alternative electoral systems able to reduce single-party sweeps and exclusionary victories.

This new period started developing well advanced the 19th century. It can be hold that, from that moment on, it was the previously existing political parties that chose, manipulated and promoted the invention of new electoral rules, including the Australian ballot, single-member districts, limited and cumulative ballots, and proportional representation rules, rather than the other way round. This trend in favour of more pluralistic electoral rules was in some sense a re-establishment of the varied, "like a mirror" representation of the community which had been characteristic of the multi-member district-based set of rules that I have suggested to call the 'originating' electoral system.

9

Electoral Systems and Voting Behaviour

A voting system or electoral system is a method by which voters make a choice between options, often in an election or on a policy referendum. A voting system contains rules for valid voting, and how votes are counted and aggregated to yield a final result. Common voting systems are majority rule, proportional representation or plurality voting with a number of variations and methods such as first-past-the-post or preferential voting. The study of formally defined voting systems is called voting theory, a subfield of political science, economics or mathematics.

With majority rule, those who are unfamiliar with voting theory are often surprised that another voting system exists, or that "majority rule" systems can produce results not supported by a majority. If every election had only two choices, the winner would be determined using majority rule alone. However, when there are three or more options, there may not be a single option that is preferred by a majority. Different voting systems may give very different results, particularly in cases where there is no clear majority preference.

Aspects of Voting Systems

A voting system specifies the form of the *ballot*, the set of allowable votes, and the *tallying method*, an algorithm for determining the outcome. This outcome may be a single winner, or may involve multiple winners such as in the election of a legislative body. The voting system may also specify how voting power is distributed among the voters, and how voters are divided into subgroups (constituencies) whose votes are counted independently. The real-world implementation of an election is generally *not* considered part of the voting system. For example, though a voting system specifies the ballot abstractly, it does not specify whether the actual physical ballot takes the form of a piece of paper, a punch card, or a computer display. A voting system also does not specify whether or how votes are kept secret, how to verify that votes are counted accurately, or who is allowed to vote. These are aspects of the broader topic of elections and election systems.

The Ballot

In a simple plurality ballot, the voter is expected to mark only one selection. Different voting systems have different forms for allowing the individual to express his or her vote. In ranked ballot or "preference" voting systems, such as Instant-runoff voting, the Borda count, or a Condorcet method, voters order the list of options from most to least preferred. In range voting, voters rate each option separately on a scale. In plurality voting (also known as "first-past-the-post"), voters select only one option, while in approval voting, they can select as many as they want. In voting systems that allow "plumping", like cumulative voting, voters may vote for the same candidate multiple times. Some voting systems include additional choices on the ballot, such as write-in candidates, a none of the above option, or a no confidence in that candidate option.

Candidates

Some methods call for a primary election first to determine which candidates will be on the ballot.

Weight of Votes

Many elections are held to the ideal of "one person, one vote," meaning that every voter's votes should be counted with equal weight. This is not true of all elections, however. Corporate elections, for instance, usually weight votes according to the amount of stock each voter holds in the company, changing the mechanism to "one share, one vote". Votes can also be weighted unequally for other reasons, such as increasing the voting weight of higher-ranked members of an organisation. Voting weight is not the same thing as *voting power*. In situations where certain groups of voters will all cast the same vote (for example, political parties in a parliament), voting power measures the ability of a group to change the outcome of a vote. Groups may form coalitions to maximize voting power.

In some German states, most notably Prussia and Sachsen, there was before 1918 a weighted vote system known as the Prussian three-class franchise, where the electorate would be divided into three categories based on the amount of income tax paid. Each *category* would have equal voting power in choosing the electors.

Status Quo

Some voting systems are weighted in themselves, for example if a supermajority is required to change the status quo. An extreme case of this is unanimous consent, where changing the status quo requires the support of every voting member. If the decision is whether to accept a new member into an organisation, failure of this procedure to admit the new member is called blackballing.

A different mechanism that favours the status quo is the requirement for a quorum, which ensures that the status quo remains if not enough voters participate in the vote. Quorum requirements often depend only on the total number of votes rather than the number of actual votes cast for the winning option; however, this can sometimes encourage dissenting voters to refrain from voting entirely to prevent a quorum.

Constituencies

Often the purpose of an election is to choose a legislative body made of multiple winners. This can be done by running a single election and choosing the winners from the same pool of votes, or by dividing up the voters into constituencies that have different options and elect different winners. Some countries, like Israel, fill their entire parliament using a single multiple-winner district (constituency), while others, like the Republic of Ireland or Belgium, break up their national elections into smaller multiple-winner districts, and yet others, like the United States or the United Kingdom, hold only single-winner elections. The Australian bicameral Parliament has single-member electorates for the legislative body (lower house) and multi-member electorates for its Senate (upper house). Some systems, like the Additional member system, embed smaller districts (constituencies) within larger ones.

The way constituencies are created and assigned seats can dramatically affect the results. Apportionment is the process by which states, regions, or larger districts are awarded seats, usually according to population changes as a result of a census. Redistricting is the process by which the borders of constituencies are redrawn once apportioned. Both procedures can become highly politically contentious due to the possibility of both malapportionment, where there are unequal representative to population ratios across districts, and gerrymandering, where electoral districts are manipulated for political gain. An example of this were the UK Rotten and pocket boroughs, parliamentary constituencies that had a very small electorate *e.g.* an abandoned town and could thus be used by a patron to gain undue and unrepresentative influence within parliament. This was a feature of the unreformed House of Commons before the Great Reform Act of 1832.

Multiple-winner Methods

Seats won by each party in the 2005 German federal election, an example of a proportional voting system. Most Western democracies use some form of multiple-winner voting system, with the United States and the United Kingdom being notable exceptions.

A vote with multiple winners, such as the election of a legislature, has different practical effects than a single-winner vote. Often, participants in a multiple winner election are more concerned with the overall composition of the legislature than exactly which candidates get elected. For this reason, many multiple-winner systems aim for proportional representation, which means that if a given party (or any other political grouping) gets X% of the vote, it should also get approximately X% of the seats in the legislature. Not all multiple-winner voting systems are proportional.

Proportional Methods

Truly proportional methods make some guarantee of proportionality by making each winning option represent approximately the same number of voters. This number is called a *quota*. For example, if the quota is 1000 voters, then each elected candidate reflects the opinions of 1000 voters, within a margin of error. This can be measured using the Gallagher Index.

Most proportional systems in use are based on party-list proportional representation, in which voters vote for parties instead of for individual candidates. For each quota of votes a party receives, one of their candidates wins a seat on the legislature. The methods differ in how the quota is determined or, equivalently, how the proportions of votes are rounded off to match the number of seats.

The methods of seat allocation can be grouped overall into highest averages methods and largest remainder methods. Largest remainder methods set a particular quota based on the number of voters, while highest averages methods, such as the Sainte-Lague method and the d'Hondt method, determine the quota indirectly by dividing the number cf votes the parties receive by a sequence of numbers. Independently of the method used to assign seats, party-list systems can be *open list* or *closed list*. In an open list system, voters decide which candidates within a party win the seats. In a closed list system, the seats are assigned to candidates in a fixed order that the party chooses. The Mixed Member Proportional system is a mixed method that only uses a party list for a subset of the winners, filling other seats with the winners of regional elections, thus having features of open list and closed list systems. In contrast to party-list systems, the Single Transferable Vote is a proportional representation system in which voters rank individual candidates in order of preference. Unlike party-list systems, STV does not depend on the candidates being grouped into political parties. Votes are transferred between candidates in a manner similar to instant runoff voting, but in addition to transferring votes from candidates who are eliminated, excess votes are also transferred from candidates who already have a quota.

Semi Proportional Methods

An alternative method called Cumulative voting (CV) is a semi proportional voting system in which each voter has n votes, where n is the number of seats to be elected (or, in some potential variants, a different number, *e.g.* 6 votes for each voter where there are 3 seats). Voters can distribute portions of their vote between a set of candidates, fully upon one candidate, or a mixture. It is considered a *proportional* system in allowing a united coalition representing a *m/(n+1)* fraction of the voters to be guaranteed to elect *m* seats of an *n*-seat election. For example in a 3-seat election, 3/4 of the voters (if united on 3 candidates) can guarantee control over all three seats. (In contrast, plurality at large, which allows a united coalition (majority) (50%+1) to control all the seats.)

This ballot design, used in cumulative voting, allows a voter to split his vote among multiple candidates. Cumulative voting is a common way of holding elections in which the voters have unequal voting power, such as in corporate governance under the "one share, one vote" rule. Cumulative voting is also used as a multiple-winner method, such as in elections for a corporate board. Cumulative voting is not fully proportional because it suffers from the same spoiler effect of the plurality voting system without a run-off process. A group of like-minded voters divided among "too many" candidates may fail to elect any winners, or elect fewer than they *deserve* by their size. The level of proportionality depends on how well-coordinated the voters are. Limited voting is a multi-winner system that gives voters fewer votes than the number of seats to be decided. The simplest and most common form of limited voting is Single Non-Transferable Vote (SNTV). It can be considered a special variation of cumulative voting where a full vote cannot be divided among more than one candidate. It depends on a statistical distributions of voters to smooth out preferences that CV can do by individual voters.

For example, in a 4-seat election a candidate needs 20% to guarantee election. A coalition of 40% can guarantee 2-seats in CV by perfectly splitting their votes as individuals between 2 candidates. In comparison, SNTV tends towards collectively dividing 20% between each candidate by assuming every coalition voter flipped a coin to decide which candidate to support with their single vote. This limitation simplifies voting and counting, at the cost of more uncertainty of results.

Nonproportional and Semi Proportional Methods

Many multiple-winner voting methods are simple extensions of single-winner methods, without an explicit goal of producing a proportional result. Bloc voting, or *plurality-at-large*, has each voter vote for *N* options and selects the top *N* as the winners. Because of its propensity for landslide victories won by a single winning slate of candidates, bloc voting is nonproportional. Two similar plurality-based methods with multiple winners are the Single Non-Transferable Vote or SNTV method, where the voter votes for only one option, and cumulative voting, described above. Unlike bloc voting, elections using the Single Nontransferable Vote or cumulative voting may achieve proportionality if voters use tactical voting or strategic nomination.

Because they encourage proportional results without guaranteeing them, the Single Nontransferable Vote and cumulative voting methods are classified as *semiproportional*. Other methods that can be seen as semiproportional are *mixed methods*, which combine the results of a plurality election and a party-list election. Parallel voting is an example of a mixed method because it is only proportional for a subset of the winners.

Single-winner Methods

Single-winner systems can be classified based on their ballot type. In one vote systems, a voter picks one choice at a time. In ranked voting systems, each voter ranks the candidates in order of preference. In rated voting systems, voters give a score to each candidate.

Single or Sequential Vote Methods

An example of runoff voting. Runoff voting involves two rounds of voting. Only two candidates survive to the second round. The most prevalent single-winner voting method, by far, is plurality (also called "first-past-the-post", "relative majority", or "winner-take-all"), where each voter votes for one choice, and the choice that receives the most votes wins, even if it receives less than a majority of votes.

Runoff methods hold multiple rounds of plurality voting to ensure that the winner is elected by a majority. Top-two runoff voting, the second most common method used in elections, holds a runoff election between the two highest polling options if there is no absolute majority (50% plus one). In elimination runoff elections, the weakest candidates are eliminated until there is a majority.

A primary election process is also used as a two round runoff voting system. The two candidates or choices with the most votes in the open primary ballot progress to the general election. The difference between a runoff and an open primary is that a winner is never chosen in the primary, while the first round of a runoff can result in a winner if one candidate has over 50% of the vote. In the Random ballot method, each voter votes for one option and a single ballot is selected at random to determine the winner. This is mostly used as a tiebreaker for other methods.

Ranked Voting Methods

In a typical ranked ballot, a voter is instructed to place the candidates in order of preference. Also known as *preferential voting methods*, these methods allow each voter to rank the candidates in order of preference. Often it is not necessary to rank all the candidates: unranked candidates are usually considered to be tied for last place. Some ranked ballot methods also allow voters to give multiple candidates the same ranking.

The most common ranked voting method is instant-runoff voting (IRV), also known as the "alternative vote" or simply preferential voting, which uses voters' preferences to simulate an elimination runoff election without multiple voting events. As the votes are tallied, the option with the fewest first-choice votes is eliminated. In successive rounds of counting, the next preferred choice still available from each eliminated ballot is transferred to candidates not yet eliminated. The least preferred option is eliminated in each round of counting until there is a majority winner, with all ballots being considered in every round of counting.

The Borda count is a simple ranked voting method in which the options receive points based on their position on each ballot. A class of similar methods is called positional voting systems. Other ranked methods include Coombs' method, Supplementary voting, Bucklin voting, and Condorcet method.

Condorcet methods, or *pairwise methods*, are a class of ranked voting methods that meet the Condorcet criterion. These methods compare every option pairwise with every other option, one at a time, and an option that *defeats* every other option is the winner. An option defeats another option if a majority of voters rank it higher on their ballot than the other option.

These methods are often referred to collectively as *Condorcet methods* because the Condorcet criterion ensures that they all give the same result in most elections, where there exists a *Condorcet winner*. The differences between Condorcet methods occur in situations where no option is undefeated, implying that there exists a cycle of options that defeat one another, called a Condorcet paradox or Smith set. Considering a generic Condorcet method to be an abstract method that does not resolve these cycles, specific versions of Condorcet that select winners even when no Condorcet winner exists are called *Condorcet completion methods*.

A simple version of Condorcet is Minimax: if no option is undefeated, the option that is defeated by the fewest votes in its worst defeat wins. Another simple method is Copeland's method, in which the winner is the option that wins the most pairwise contests, as in many round-robin tournaments. The Schulze method (also known as "Schwartz sequential dropping", "cloneproof Schwartz sequential dropping" or the "beatpath method") and Ranked Pairs are two recently designed Condorcet methods that satisfy a large number of voting system criteria. The Kemeny-Young method is a Condorcet method that fully ranks all the candidates from most popular to least popular.

Rated Voting Methods

On a rated ballot, the voter may rate each choice independently. Rated ballots allow even more flexibility than ranked ballots, but few methods are designed to use them. Each voter gives a score to each option; the allowable scores could be numeric (for example, from 0 to 100) or could be "grades" like A/B/C/D/F.

Rated ballots can be used for ranked voting methods, as long as the ranked method allows tied rankings. Some ranked methods assume that all the rankings on a ballot are distinct, but many voters would be likely to give multiple candidates the same rating on a rated ballot.

Range Voting

In range voting, voters give numeric ratings to each option, and the option with the highest total score wins.

Approval Voting

Approval voting, where voters may vote for as many candidates as they like, can be seen as an instance of range voting where the allowable ratings are 0 and 1.

Criteria in Evaluating Single Winner Voting Systems

In the real world, attitudes towards voting systems are highly influenced by the systems' impact on groups that one supports or opposes. This can make the objective comparison of voting systems difficult. To compare systems fairly and independently of political ideologies, voting theorists use *voting system criteria*, which define potentially desirable properties of voting systems mathematically.

It is impossible for one voting system to pass all criteria in common use. Economist Kenneth Arrow proved Arrow's impossibility theorem, which demonstrates that several desirable features of voting systems are mutually contradictory. For this reason, someone implementing a voting system has to decide which criteria are important for the election.

Using criteria to compare systems does not make the comparison completely objective. For example, it is relatively easy to devise a criterion that is met by one's preferred voting method, and by very few other methods. Doing this, one can then construct a biased argument for the criterion, instead of arguing directly for the method. There is no ultimate authority on which criteria should be considered, but the following are some criteria that are accepted and considered to be desirable by many voting theorists:

- Majority criterion— If there exists a majority that ranks (or rates) a single candidate higher than all other candidates, does that candidate always win?
- Monotonicity criterion— Is it impossible to cause a winning candidate to lose by ranking him higher, or to cause a losing candidate to win by ranking him lower?
- Consistency criterion— If the electorate is divided in two and a choice wins in both parts, does it always win overall?
- Participation criterion— Is voting honestly always better than

not voting at all? (This is grouped with the distinct but similar Consistency Criterion.)

- Condorcet critérion— If a candidate beats every other candidate in pairwise comparison, does that candidate always win? (This implies the majority criterion, above)
- Condorcet loser criterion— If a candidate loses to every other candidate in pairwise comparison, does that candidate always lose?
- Independence of irrelevant alternatives— If a candidate is added or removed, do the relative rankings of the remaining candidates stay the same?
- Independence of clone candidates— Is the outcome the same if candidates identical to existing candidates are added?
- Later-no-harm criterion— If, in any election, a voter gives an additional ranking, vote or positive rating to a less preferred candidate, can that additional ranking, vote or rating cause a more preferred candidate to lose?
- Reversal symmetry— If individual preferences of each voter are inverted, does the original winner never win?
- Polynomial time— Can the winner be calculated in a runtime that is polynomial in the number of candidates and the number of voters?
- Summability— How much information must be transmitted from each polling station to a central location in order to determine the winner? This is expressed as an order function of the number of candidates N. Slower-growing functions such as O(N) or O(N) make for easier counting, while faster-growing functions such as O(N!) might make it harder to catch fraud by election administrators.
- Allows equal rankings— Allows a voter to choose whether to rank any two candidates equally at any position on the ballot. This can reduce the prevalence of spoiled ballots due to overvotes, and can give a less-dishonest alternative to some tactical voting strategies.

In addition to the above criteria, voting systems are judged using criteria that are not mathematically precise but are still important, such as simplicity, speed of vote-counting, the potential for fraud or disputed results, the opportunity for tactical voting or strategic nomination, and, for multiple-winner methods, the degree of proportionality produced.

It is also possible to simulate large numbers of virtual elections on a computer and see how various voting systems compare in terms of maximum voter satisfaction, called in this context minimum Bayesian regret. Such simulations are sensitive to their assumptions, particularly with regards to voter strategy, but by varying the assumptions they can give repeatable measures that bracket the best and worst cases for a voting system. To date, the only such simulation to compare a wide variety of voting systems was run by a range-voting advocate and has not been peer-reviewed. Simulated elections in a two-dimensional issue space can also be graphed to visually compare election methods; this makes apparent issues like nonmonotonicity and clone-independence.

The New Zealand Royal Commission on the Electoral System listed ten criteria for their evaluation of possible new electoral systems for New Zealand. These included fairness between political parties, effective representation of minority or special interest groups, political integration, effective voter participation and legitimacy.

History

Early Democracy

Voting has been used as a feature of democracy since the 6th century BC, when democracy was introduced by the Athenian democracy. However, in Athenian democracy, voting was seen as the least democratic among methods used for selecting public officials, and was little used, because elections were believed to inherently favour the wealthy and well-known over average citizens. Viewed as more democratic were assemblies open to all citizens, and selection by lot (known as sortition), as well as rotation of office. One of the earliest recorded elections in Athens was a plurality vote that it was undesirable to "win": in the process called ostracism, voters chose the citizen they most wanted to exile for ten years. Most elections in the early history of democracy were held using plurality voting or some variant, but as an exception, the state of Venice in the 13th century adopted the system we now know as approval voting to elect their Great Council.

The Venetians' system for electing the Doge was a particularly convoluted process, consisting of five rounds of drawing lots (sortition) and five rounds of approval voting. By drawing lots, a body of 30 electors was chosen, which was further reduced to nine electors by drawing lots again. An electoral college of nine members elected 40 people by approval voting; those 40 were reduced to form a second electoral college of 12 members by drawing lots again. The second electoral college elected 25 people by approval voting, which were reduced to form a third electoral college of nine members by drawing lots. The third electoral college elected 45 people, which were reduced to form a fourth electoral college of 11 by drawing lots. They in turn elected a final electoral body of 41 members, who ultimately elected the Doge. Despite its complexity, the system had certain desirable properties such as being hard to game and ensuring that the winner reflected the opinions of both majority and minority factions. This process was used with little modification from 1268 until the end of the Republic of Venice in 1797, and was one of the factors contributing to the durability of the republic.

Foundations of Voting Theory

Voting theory became an object of academic study around the time of the French Revolution. Jean-Charles de Borda proposed the Borda count in 1770 as a method for electing members to the French Academy of Sciences. His system was opposed by the Marquis de Condorcet, who proposed instead the method of pairwise comparison that he had devised. Implementations of this method are known as Condorcet methods. He also wrote about the Condorcet paradox, which he called the *intransitivity of majority preferences*.

While Condorcet and Borda are usually credited as the founders of voting theory, recent research has shown that the philosopher Ramon Llull discovered both the Borda count and a pairwise method that satisfied the Condorcet criterion in the 13th century. The manuscripts in which he described these methods had been lost to history until they were rediscovered in 2001.

Later in the 18th century, the related topic of apportionment began to be studied. The impetus for research into fair apportionment methods came, in fact, from the United States Constitution, which mandated that seats in the United States House of Representatives had to be allocated among the states proportionally to their population, but did not specify how to do so. A variety of methods were proposed by statesmen such as Alexander Hamilton, Thomas Jefferson, and Daniel Webster. Some of the apportionment methods discovered in the United States were in a sense rediscovered in Europe in the 19th century, as seat allocation methods for the newly proposed system of party-list proportional representation. The result is that many apportionment methods have two names: for instance, *Jefferson's method* is equivalent to the d'Hondt method, as is *Webster's method* to the Sainte-Lague method, while *Hamilton's method* is identical to the Hare largest remainder method.

The Single Transferable Vote system was devised by Carl Andrae in Denmark in 1855, and also in England by Thomas Hare in 1857. Their discoveries may or may not have been independent. STV elections were first held in Denmark in 1856, and in Tasmania in 1896 after its use was promoted by Andrew Inglis Clark. Party-list proportional representation was first implemented to elect European legislatures in the early 20th century, with Belgium implementing it first in 1899. Since then, proportional and semi-proportional methods have come to be used in almost all democratic countries, with most exceptions being former British colonies.

The Single-winner Revival

Perhaps influenced by the rapid development of multiple-winner voting methods, theorists began to publish new findings about single-winner methods in the late 19th century. This began around 1870, when William Robert Ware proposed applying STV to single-winner elections, yielding instant runoff voting. Soon, mathematicians began to revisit Condorcet's ideas and invent new methods for Condorcet completion. Edward J. Nanson combined the newly described instant runoff voting with the Borda count to yield a new Condorcet method called Nanson's method. Charles Dodgson, better known as Lewis Carroll, published pamphlets on voting theory, focusing in particular on Condorcet voting.

He introduced the use of matrices to analyze Condorcet elections, though this, too, had already been done in some form in the then-lost manuscripts of Ramon Llull. He also proposed the straightforward Condorcet method known as Dodgson's method.

Ranked voting systems eventually gathered enough support to be adopted for use in government elections. In Australia, IRV was first adopted in 1893, and continues to be used along with STV today. In the United States in the early 20th century, various municipalities began to use Bucklin voting. Bucklin is no longer used in any government elections, and has even been declared unconstitutional in Minnesota.

Influence of Game Theory

After John von Neumann and others developed the mathematical field of game theory in the 1940s, new mathematical tools were available to analyze voting systems and strategic voting. This led to significant new results that changed the field of voting theory. The use of mathematical criteria to evaluate voting systems was introduced when Kenneth Arrow showed in Arrow's impossibility theorem that certain intuitively desirable criteria were actually mutually contradictory, demonstrating the inherent limitations of voting theorems. These circumscribe nonetheless to ordinal voting systems, and do not apply to cardinal ones like range voting, as John Harsanyi pointed out. Arrow's theorem is easily the single most cited result in voting theory, and it inspired further significant results such as the Gibbard-Satterthwaite theorem, which showed that strategic voting is unavoidable in certain common circumstances.

The use of game theory to analyze voting systems also led to discoveries about the emergent strategic effects of certain systems. Duverger's law is a prominent example of such a result, showing that plurality voting often leads to a two-party system. Further research into the game theory aspects of voting led Steven Brams and Peter Fishburn to formally define and promote the use of approval voting in 1977. While approval voting had been used before that, it had not been named or considered as an object of academic study, particularly because it violated the assumption made by most research that single-winner methods were based on preference rankings.

Post-1980 Developments

Voting theory has come to focus on voting system criteria almost as much as it does on particular voting systems. Now, any description of a benefit or weakness in a voting system is expected to be backed up by a mathematically defined criterion. Recent research in voting theory has largely involved devising new criteria and new methods devised to meet certain criteria.

Political scientists of the 20th century published many studies on the effects that the voting systems have on voters' choices and political parties, and on political stability. A few scholars also studied what effects caused a nation to change for a particular voting system. One prominent current voting theorist is Nicolaus Tideman, who formalised concepts such as strategic nomination and the spoiler effect in the independence of clones criterion. Tideman also devised the ranked pairs method, a Condorcet method that is not susceptible to clones. Also, Donald G. Saari has brought renewed interest to the Borda count with the books he has published since 2001. Saari uses geometric models of positional voting systems to promote the Borda count.

The increased availability of computer processing has increased the practicality of using the Kemeny-Young, ranked pairs, and Schulze methods that fully rank all the choices from most popular to least popular.

The advent of the Internet has increased the interest in voting systems. Unlike many other mathematical fields, voting theory is generally accessible enough to non-experts that new results can be discovered by amateurs, and frequently are.

The study of voting systems has influenced a new push for electoral reform that is going on today, with proposals being made to replace plurality voting in governmental elections with other methods. Various municipalities in the United States have begun to adopt instant-runoff voting in the 2000s. New Zealand adopted Mixed Member Proportional for Parliamentary elections in 1993 and Single Transferable Vote for some local elections in 2004. The Canadian province of British Columbia held two unsuccessful referenda (in 2005 and 2009) to adopt an STV system. The Province of Ontario held a

Referendum on October 10, 2007, on whether to adopt a Mixed Member Proportional system, which was defeated. An even wider range of voting systems is now seen in non-governmental organisations.

It has been argued and shown that more in-depth and fine-tuned voting systems lie at the core of the development of e-democracy, which consists of the digitisation of democratic processes, including voting. Electoral systems and voting behaviour is the first of three modules required for an AQA accredited AS level in Government and Politics. It introduces the reader to politics, and more specifically voting, by examining different electoral systems, affects of voting, determinants of electoral turnout and the composition of the electorate.

ELECTORAL SYSTEMS

INTRODUCTION

The predominant form of political participation in the United Kingdom is voting. It is from elections that governments derive their legitimacy and competitive elections are a defining feature of democracy. This necessitates a great interest in the multitude of methods by which governments are elected. Academics the world over have evaluated and discussed the vices and virtues of different systems, but a universal standard has yet to be achieved. Below the evidence advocating and opposing the various systems will be evaluated in addition to the debate surrounding electoral reform, an increasingly salient issue, following the election in 1997 of a Labour government committed to a referendum on reform of the electoral system.

FIRST-PAST-THE-POST

First-past-the-post (or simple plurality) is the electoral system utilised for General Elections in the United Kingdom. First-past-the-post is used to elect one candidate in a single member constituency, with the winning candidate requiring only one more vote than their nearest opponent. A widely celebrated characteristic of first-past-the-post is its history of creating large single party governments, and as the strength of a government is derived from the size of its majority, capable of strong governing. Furthermore, the strong and easily understood link between the electorate and their representative under first-past-the-post creates a climate in which the electorate can easily hold their representative accountable. The simplicity of first-past-the-post, requiring the voter to mark only an 'X' to indicate their favoured candidate, is a feature which allows first-past-the-post to ensure that votes are seldom wrongly cast reducing the extent to which electoral difficulties distort the representativeness of the election.

The results of use of first-past-the-post has generated considerable debate regarding electoral reform due to associated disadvantages. The ability to win an election without majority support has been the cause of much criticism of first-past-the-post by limiting the extent to which the candidate can be said to be representative of the electorate's wishes. In the 2005 General Election approximately 70% of votes cast were 'wasted', with 52% being cast in favour of losing candidates and 18% of votes were excess votes for winning candidates.

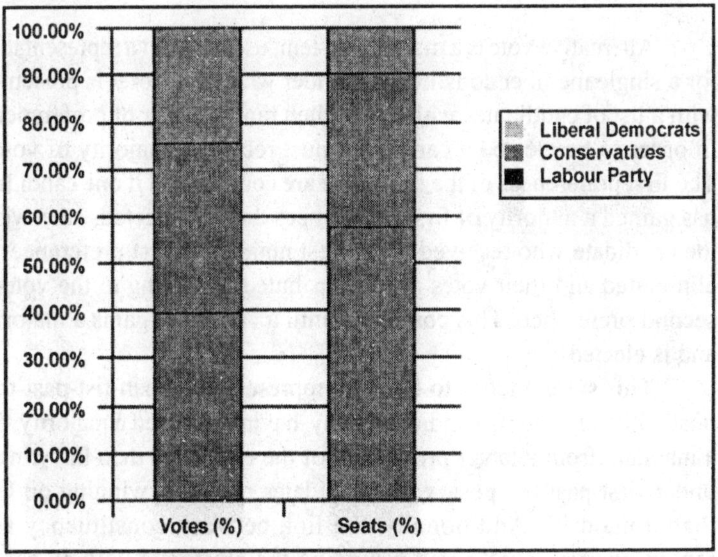

FIG. COMPARES THE PROPORTION OF SEATS AND THE PROPORTION OF VOTES FROM THE 2005 GENERAL ELECTION.

This leaves 52% of those who voted with a representative they did not vote for, generating significant criticism of the system. As with most systems the employment of first-past-the-post in elections can produce an appreciable bias, in this instance towards larger parties with geographically concentrated support.

The all-or-nothing nature of first-past-the-post with only one candidate being elected in each constituency creates a bias towards larger parties. Only candidates who can attain a simple majority in any constituency are elected, meaning that although a party may hold considerable support nation wide, the geographical disparity of their support can rule them out from acquiring a number of seats commensurate with their level of support. An excellent example of this is the Liberal Democrats who, despite obtaining over a fifth of the popular vote, received only a tenth of the seats in the House of Commons.

Alternative Vote

Alternative vote is a majority system, used to elect a representative for a single member constituency, under which the voter is presented with a list of candidates which they then rank in order of preferences. In order to be elected a candidate must receive a majority of votes. The first preferences of the electorate are counted and if one candidate has gained a majority of first preferences they are elected, otherwise, the candidate who received the fewest number of first preferences is eliminated and their votes are redistributed according to the voter's second preference. This continues until a candidate gains a majority and is elected.

This system tends to be more representative than fist-past-the-post with the winning candidate likely, having received a majority, got a mandate from a larger proportion of the electorate than the winner under first-past-the-post, with candidates routinely winning on less than a majority. Additionally, the link between constituency and representative is preserved providing the electorate with an easily identifiable contact by which they can address their grievances, something reduced under systems with multi-member constituencies.

Utilisation of alternative vote can present a significant bias in favour of centre parties who, on the basis of their policies being the least acrimonious, are able to win on 2nd and 3rd preferences.

SINGLE TRANSFERABLE VOTE

Single transferable vote is used to elect several representatives in a multi-member constituency under which candidates have to achieve a quote of votes to be elected. Voters are presented with a list of candidates who they rank in order of preference. The first preferences are then counted and if a candidate achieves the quota they are elected and the surplus votes redistributed, if, however, no candidate achieves the quota then the last placed candidate is eliminated and their votes redistributed, this continues until the prerequisite number of candidates have been elected.

$$\frac{\text{Quota = Number of Votes Cast}}{\text{Number of seats in the constituency } +1 \ +1}$$

This system, although not as representative as the list system, is significantly more representative than first-past-the-post or the majority systems.

10

International Relations: From the Cold War to the Globalised World

Arguably, the attacks against the united states on 11 September 2001 brought an unexpected close to the transitional phase that followed the end of the Cold War. But if the destruction of the Twin Towers in lower Manhattan and the near simultaneous attack on the Pentagon acted as a defining moment in our understanding of recent history, then what period came to a close on that particular day? Were the events of September 11 indeed the ultimate expression of fundamental change in the international system? In light of the cultural origins and religion-political motives of the suspected culprits, did the tragedies consequently act as a harbinger of a return to the "clash of civilisations," enunciated by the political scientist Samuel P. Huntington in 1993, with its concomitant religious and ethnic determinants? Or were the attacks not so much connected to the resurgence of old civilisational fault lines and their underlying antagonisms in the absence of bipolar ideological conflict but rather the consequence of a palpable U.S. unilateralism and, by extension, Western military and political preponderance in the decade after the Cold War?

Aside from the simple truth that watersheds in history constitute conceptual devices informed by individual preferences, the above questions cannot be conclusively answered at this stage, if only because historical analysis is predicated on an ex post facto assessment of events. Moreover, there is invariably no silver bullet, no single explanatory model that might provide a definitive answer to the occurrence of violent conflict of any kind at any stage in history. What is clear, however, is that after September 11 the time-honored myth of an invulnerable U.S. hegemon, secure between two oceans, has been debunked. Furthermore, the hopes of the early 1990s that growing international economic interdependence would provide the basis for a peaceful world order have not come to fruition. Instead, international politics has become highly complex and is marked by continuous change and a pervading sense of insecurity.

As the dissolution of the Soviet Union sent shockwave after shockwave through the regional as well as international environments, the forces of contending ideologies that had taken center stage for half a century gave way to a new, nascent international system. The United States had seemingly arrived at the apex of its global power: U.S. values, such as liberalism and democracy, spread around the globe; U.S. corporations were in the vanguard of building a new global economy; and U.S. military forces were in the forefront of international efforts to provide global stability. The irony was the fact that power had become more diffuse, and thus the U.S. ability to shape the global agenda had actually decreased. In the absence of a compelling nuclear logic of mutually assured destruction (MAD) inherent in the dualistic world of the Cold War, U.S. and, by implication, Western hegemony in international politics and economics would come under increasing pressure. Various events taking place during the decade after the end of the Cold War are suggestive of widespread skepticism, even hostility, toward the only superpower in the world.

In 1991, the U.S. led Coalition of Western powers was gearing up for military operations in the Persian Gulf region. Aside from the moral rationale for the Gulf War—wanting to protect tiny Kuwait from Iraqi military aggression—a vital interest of the West was at stake: A significant amount of the crude oil that lubricated the world's economic engine was produced in the fields of Kuwait. Western intervention and the stationing of multinational and, in particular, U.S. troops under the auspices of the Western powers in Saudi Arabia elicited widespread indignation among devout Muslims around the world. Simultaneously, and against the backdrop of an unprecedented economic boom, Asian states proved increasingly assertive and resilient vis-a-vis Western influence. Beyond their rising self-confidence, Asian states' policies in relation to China appear highly suggestive of a realignment of power in the region. As China is readying resources to substantiate its aspirations toward regional hegemony, most states of Southeast Asia are directing their attention toward Beijing. Will China—hailed as the greatest potential single market by economists—also supplant the Western powers in the global pecking order in the near future?

Also during the 1990s, Europe achieved unprecedented successes in its economic and political integration, going along with intensified Euroatlantic cooperation. The European Union (EU) introduced the single market and a single currency and became the largest trading bloc in the world. Yet at the same time, Europe witnessed ethnic conflicts at its doorstep, resulting from the fragmentation of the Balkans and the circumstance that Africa had long existed on the sidelines of global political concerns. The fact that a series of wars was, for all intents and purposes, fought in Europe's backyard is remarkable in and of itself—or so it appeared to many Europeans, who had not witnessed armed conflict in generations. The Balkans—the historic powder keg of Europe—once again erupted into political violence. In the wider context of the decline of the Yugoslav Federation, war was visited upon Bosnia (1992–1995), Croatia (1991–1995), and later Kosovo (1999). In Africa, tribal rivalries witnessed a bloody comeback, for example, in the genocidal war fought between the Hutu and Tutsi factions in Rwanda and Burundi in the early and mid-1990s.

Two attributes stand out in these wars: First, they were fought along ethnic lines within a state; second, multinational peacekeeping forces were deployed. In retrospect, two trends typical of the 1990s—the sharp increase of intrastate conflicts (as opposed to interstate conflicts) and the challenge to the sanctity of national sovereignty by the international community—constitute developments that have had, and continue to exert, significant influence on the conduct, nature, and understanding of international relations in the post–Cold War world.

Paradoxically, while patterns of conflict were reverting from ideological competition to ethnic and religious fault lines, the process of globalisation gave a new impetus to the neoliberal economic order that placed considerable power in the hands of multinational corporations and consequently further undermined the nation-state as unchallenged incumbent key actor in international relations. The world also became smaller due to increased connectivity and a concomitant interdependency, which in turn was caused by a revolution in information technology (IT).

Put simply, however, the problem with globalisation today is its uneven distribution: Whereas the full impact of the IT revolution was by and large a pervasive phenomenon in the West, many states of the former Soviet bloc in Eastern Europe were struggling to digest the shock of transitioning from a command economy to a free-market economy; for countries in the third world of Africa, Asia, and Latin America, the ostensible boon of globalisation was anything but. Instead, globalisation more often than not proved to be exacerbating the division between the haves and the have-nots of this world. Overall, the period between 1991 and today has brought much change to the international political and economic orders and can therefore appropriately be referred to as a "formative decade" during which we have witnessed the transition from the Cold War world into the globalised world of the early twenty-first century. But what did the international system of the Cold War look like in the time before 1991?

Between 1947 and 1991, the world witnessed a struggle between two fundamentally opposed value and social systems: socialist communism and liberal democracy. The two protagonists of this struggle, which in time would engulf the entire globe, were the Soviet Union and the United States.

By the end of World War II, each power had eclipsed the former Great Powers of Europe. The latter had dominated international politics for the greater part of the early modern period (roughly after 1500) but had been superseded by the two flanking powers of the pre–World War II era—the Soviet Union and the United States—among other reasons because their material bases were ravaged and their military power was depleted by 1945. By then, the former flanking powers were in the process of becoming superpowers, that is, political entities endowed with the capability of projecting their power globally. The end of World War II thus acted as the critical watershed between the prevailing modus operandi ante bellum in the international system and the new order of an incipient Cold War.

The old balance of power between the Great Powers of Europe had crumbled in the face of rampant nationalism and expansionism; the logic of the Cold War gave birth to the bipolar world, an international system in which the new superpowers maintained a precarious nuclear balance. In the immediate aftermath of World War II, the Cold War was at first centered in Europe. In only one decade, however, the Cold War became the defining feature of the international system. The conflict's second decade (roughly 1955–1965) brought the world to the brink of total destruction, but a significant step toward the relaxation of relations between the superpowers was achieved thereafter. After 1975 the world witnessed the coming of the Second Cold War, as well as a fundamental change in the international system, transforming it into a multipolar system as economic forces increasingly interlocked with political factors in shaping history. Finally, economic forces, as much as politics, determined the outcome of the Cold War: the Soviet Union ultimately paid a high price for communism and the concomitant command economy it had installed, whereas democracy and capitalism proved more durable in the West.

Aside from the two principal parties to the Cold War, there were those who gained and even more who lost. More often than not, for those caught between the rivals there was no recourse. They became the victims of the Cold War. It was no coincidence that the hot spots of the Cold War were located in the third world, where millions yearned for national independence only to struggle with massive impoverishment and political instability once they achieved it. To the superpowers, Europe as the terminus a quo (point of origin) of the Cold War did not present itself as a practicable battlefield for an important reason: the risk of escalation—conventional and nuclear—was too high. Whereas most battles of the Cold War were fought in Asia, the Middle East, and Africa, in Europe the Cold War evolved into a long peace. As of the late 1950s, the superpowers wooed developing countries with every intention of turning them into auxiliaries, thereby spreading and perpetuating the dynamic of the Cold War beyond its erstwhile limits.

The principal difference between previous wars, even global wars, and the Cold War was that the earlier wars (with the exception of the U.S. bombings of Hiroshima and Nagasaki in August 1945) had all been fought with conventional weapons, whereas the antagonists of the Cold War had nuclear arsenals at their fingertips. The destructiveness of nuclear weapons, to state the obvious, far exceeded that of any conventional weapon. If the equilibrium of the Cold War had ever been seriously disturbed—say, in the late 1970s—this subsequent attempt at composing a history of international relations would, in all probability, never have been written. More generally, the stakes and risks of the Cold War while it lasted were higher still than those for which World War II had been fought. Figuratively speaking, if the Cold War had ever turned hot, it literally would have been the war to end all wars, plunging the world into a nuclear holocaust of unprecedented levels. It is to the beginning of this story and its history that we now turn.

GLOBALISATION AND A WORLD PARLIAMENT

The Political Dimension of Globalisation and the Decline of the Sovereign State

Globalisation is the word which is on everyone's lips and is arousing the disquiet that comes from the prospect of deep and inevitable change. It is the word most commonly used to designate the new era that humankind has entered as a consequence of the revolution in production, communication, information and transportation technologies. Globalisation has been studied primarily as an economic process, while its political dimension has been largely neglected. The fact that the market has become global while governments have remained national is a contradiction that highlights the most significant change brought about by globalisation. In other words, globalisation has produced a shift of the borders between civil society and state. This means that it has opened a new space to civil society, that is that prepolitical area of social life which is the ground where individual interests assert themselves and clash, but which does not produce those mediating mechanisms between interests from which the need originates to promote the common weal. Therefore, private centers of power such as multinational corporations, non governmental organisations or criminal organisations have taken a global size and acquired an increasing freedom of action with regard to the regulating power of states. Here lies the root of the decline of the sovereign state, that will be overcome only through the establishment of new forms of statehood at world level. This is the condition that will allow to restore the pre-eminence of politics toward global civil society.

The Response of Governments: International Organisation

The response of governments to globalisation has been to pursue international co-operation, not because it is their inclination, but because they have no other choice. The expansion of the phenomenon of international organisation shows the way governments are going along to seek a solution to problems they cannot solve alone. The weakness of international organisations lies in their decision-making procedures, that are based on the principles of unanimity and veto, and in the lack of executive powers. The most widespread definition of this way of managing globalisation is the expression *global governance*. This is a formula that justifies the established world order, which is based on the principle of national sovereignty and on the dominance of multinational corporations in the world market and of the United States in world politics.

It is a formula that hides the illusion that a solution to the main international issues can be based on a mutual consent among sovereign states. Federalism is the antithesis of the internationalist approach. Its strength lies in the alternative goals of world government and international democracy. However distant and though they can be pursued gradually, these goals are the answer to the need to control globalisation and to start the process of establishing peace among nations through law.

The Decline of Democracy

When sovereign states decline, there is a parallel decline in democracy. The sharpest contradiction of our age lies in the fact that the problems on which the destiny of peoples depends, such as those of security, control of global economy, international justice or protection of the environment, have assumed international dimensions, where democratic institutions do not exist, while democracy still stops at state borders. In consequence, democratic institutions, having lost control of strategic decisions, confine themselves to govern secondary aspects of political life. The peoples are excluded from control of the questions which determine their future. In substance, we must face problems of global dimension, on which our destiny depends, while the world is still divided into independent sovereign states. The feeling widely shared by many citizens is that the most important decisions have migrated from the institutions they can control toward international centers of power, which are not submitted to any form of democratic control.

In conclusion, the decline of democracy has two aspects. On the one hand, national governments are unable to submit globalisation to democratic control. On the other hand, the democratic deficit prevents international organisations from being something more than the place where sovereign states co-operate to solve global issues. It is a contradiction that can only be overcome through iternational democracy, *i.e.* through the extension of democracy to state relations.

The Process of Democratisation in the World

The most revolutionary objective of our age is the democratisation of the United Nations, which would allow the government of the world to be removed from the control of the big powers and the other private centers of power, like multinational corporations, and put in the hands of all the peoples of the world. Of course, it is a long term objective that can only be achieved gradually.

The democratisation of the UN no longer appears a distant ultimate goal after the recent extraordinary advance of democracy in Eastern Europe, ex-Soviet Union, Asia and Latin America. Today, for the first time in history, over half of the countries of the world (120 according to the last Report of the Freedom House) have adopted a democratic form of government. Since the fall of fascist and communist regimes it seems that democracy has defeated all its alternatives. But the vacuum of power left by the fall of the blocs has opened the way to the revival of nationalism, that has triggered off a series of processes of disintegration of international organisations and multinational states and is threatening the new born democracies.

The Need for International Democracy

Democracy, precisely because it is fragmented among many national states, too small to assure the economic development and torn apart by international conflicts, is not the strong enough to prevent the authoritarian degeneration of its institutions. Only international democracy can submit international relations, which are still the ground of diplomatic and military clash among nations, to popular control. As a matter of fact, democracy and independence can be reconciled only within the framework of federal institutions that must be created both at regional and world level.

The European Parliament is the labouratory of international democracy. After its direct election it has increased its legislative powers and control powers over the Commission, understood as the potential European government. This means that the democratisation of the European Union has been a mighty tool for strengthening European institutions. It is worth recalling that the dilemma that arose during the process of European integration of strengthening first or democratising first the European Community has been solved in favour of the second horn. The same hypothesis can be formulated as regards the problem of the democratisation of the UN.

The Decline of the Political Parties

The great revolutionary transformations marking the milestones of mankind's progress in history, have never been promoted by the established powers. These powers try to rule the new course of events with old ideological schemes and with old institutions. Revolutionary change, which creates new institutions and higher forms of political coexistence, has always been the result of the storming into the political scene of new social forces. These forces provide a vehicle for new cultures, new values and new political institutions. While the political parties have lost their attraction force and their former capability for mobilisation, no longer succeeding in motivating commitment from young people, all over the world a non-governmental movement has grown. This expresses itself outside traditional channels of political representation and is a manifestation of a new dimension of political participation. It operates at all levels of political life (but more efficiently in local communities and at international level, where the limits of the established powers are more serious) in the sectors of peace, human rights, international justice, aid to development, environment, cultural goods, education, health and so on.

The decline of political parties is a consequence of the crisis of the sovereign state. Faced with the globalisation of social, economic and political life, national power offers an observation-post that obscures reality as it is and prevents the mastering of it. Political parties are prisoners of the national states: like boats in a stormy sea, they find themselves in the trough of the wave, where they cannot see the horizon.

Directed by powerless leaders, they depart from the real problems of humankind. Choked inside the tight limits of national states, the political decision-making loses any meaningful relation with real processes. Here lies the main root of the decadence of the moral and intellectual quality of the ruling class. When, in the debate among political parties, the great goals, those which make it possible to think of the future, are gone, politics deteriorates progressively in a mere power game which keeps at a distance the most dynamic and vital energies in society. The political parties represent for this reason politics without a future.

The Rise of the Global Civil Society Movements

On the other hand, the global civil society movements have tried to strengthen their influence over international politics. Wherever an international summit meeting gathers, a demonstration of the anti-globalisation movement is expected. These are citizens who protest against being excluded from representation within international organisations and pretend to have a say in international affairs. They are the most genuine manifestation of the world unification movement and of the necessity, largely felt by young people, to deal with the great dramas of mankind.

They are at present a varied mass of small and large groups, linked by a common situation (globalisation). It is a movement dragged by the current leading toward world unification, but lacking the instruments to rule this process. It is not yet aware of its institutional objectives, nor has it worked out a political strategy. It represents the future without politics. Two different positions can be distinguished. Some NGOs have taken on the role of opposing international organisations and globalisation itself, often resorting to violence, and consider the international organisations as irreformable. Other NGOs are integrated in the state system, are recognised by international organisations and behave according to a reformist attitude of mind. They participate in international conferences in an advisory capacity and exert real influence on negotiations.

The limit of these movements lies in that they have a sectorial perspective: each movement deals with one single problem. But to the extent that they interpret new needs and are the protagonists of a process tending to redefine actors and roles of political life, we can formulate the hypothesis that they can become the vanguard of international democracy.

Domestic and International Democracy

Is it true that the process of democratisation of the domestic order of states must be accomplished before we are able to start an action for the creation of a World Parliament? As was pointed out by Kant in his treatise on *Perpetual Peace*, the first condition for the formation of a World Federation is that the member states have a republican regime. In other words, without domestic democracy, an essential prerequisite of international democracy is lacking.

But the fact that the process of democratisation of state regimes all over the world has not been completed does not represent an obstacle to start the process of democartisation of the UN. If, in the logic of causal sequence, the democratisation of the different states has to precede the democratisation of the UN, in history these processes overlap. The six Western European countries that have founded the European Community did not wait for the democratisation of the institutions of all the states of Europe before starting the democratisation of the European Community. The completion of the European unification and the democratic transformation of its institutions has become possible today, because a small group of states started the process of construction of the European unity fifty years ago.

The European Federation: The Leading Country of International Democracy

There is no concealing the fact that the plan to bring globalisation under democratic control is meeting with formidable opposition not only on the part of the authoritarian regimes, but primarily on the part of the government of the United States, which will not let its power be lessened by the international organisations that it belong to, nor by movement arising in the global civil society. This shows that, to be a promoter of international democracy, it is not enough to have a democratic regime. The United States has so heavy world strategic commitments that it is unable to promote that design. To defeat the opposition of the United States, a center of power must emerge with the capability of supporting the plan for a world democratic order. It is reasonable to believe that Europe will play such a role.

The significance of the European unification lies in the overcoming of the nation-state, a form of political organisation that develops strength relations with the other states. Therefore it is fairly safe to assume that the European Union does not have, and in the future the European Federation will not have, hegemonic ambitions. On the other hand, Europe will hold sufficient power to releive the United States of some of its overwhelming world responsibilities and thus have the authority to persuade it to support the democatic reform of the UN. However, if it is to speak with a single voice, Europe must complete the process of federal unification. With a Parliament elected by universal suffrage, the European Federation can become the leading country of international democracy. Thus, it will be more inclined than any other political organisation to promote this experiment in the other great regions of the world and at world level (democratisation of the UN).

Many Competing Projects

The process of globalisation and the rise of the global civil society movements have been accompanied by a flowering of proposals addressing the question of the democratisation of the UN through the creation of an assembly which would represent the world citizens.

The problem to be solved is whether the traditional tool of a Parliament is appropriate to meet the exigency of popular representation at world level. I will take into consideration the most significant projects.

A Virtual World Parliament

A virtual World Parliament has been proposed as an alternative to a concrete World Parliament. Of course, the Internet can help in the exchange of ideas, the dissemination of information, the preparation of meetings and so on. Moreover, it can be used as a mobilisation network. It enabled a scattered mob to become the people of Seattle. But, in order to make his voice heard and to exercise a real influence on the political process, that people was obliged to materialize in the streets and squares of a city. In addition, the circulation of the images of the demonstrations organised at Seattle increased the political weight of the movement born in that city.

Likewise, the Internet cannot compensate or replace in any way the face to face relations which take place in a political assembly which physically gathers in a hall. The public space where the representatives of the people meet, participate in public dabates and take decisions is an irreplaceable aspect of democracy.

The Global Civil Society Forum

The Commission on Global Governance, in the report published in 1995 on the occasion of the 50th anniversary of the UN, proposed the creation of a permanent Global Civil Society Forum. It was conceived as the vehicle to voice the expectations emerging from the international civil society and to transmit them to the UN. More precisely it was proposed that the Forum should gather before the beginning of the annual session of the General Assembly and convey to it its claims.

This proposal reflects the impetuous growth of the global civil society movements and the exigency to build a body representing them at world level. The Millennium Forum, held from 22-26 May 2000 at the UN Building in New York, has represented the dress rehearsal of the Forum. It showed at the same time the potentialities and the limits of such initiative. It is not an exaggeration to state that it represented the first babble of global democracy. Awaiting the formation of a parliamentary body and political parties at world level (are the NGOs not movements anticipating political parties?), the Forum was an assembly representing as close as possible the peoples of the world or at least the most active part of them.

However, the limits of such an assembly must be pointed out. In the absence of international elections it is impossible to measure the degree of consent supporting the NGOs. The Forum would be lacking real democratic representativeness, being the expression of civil society movements and not of the will of the people, which can only come from an election based on a free competition among political parties. It can be compared to the medieval parliaments in which the orders were represented, not yet the people. And as these had the function of limiting the power of absolute sovereigns, likewise the Forum of Civil Society will limit the absolute power of the sovereign states ruling the UN. That is, as the medieval parliaments are distant forerunners of the contemporary ones, likewise the Forum of Civil Society may be an institution anticipating a World Parliament.

The WTO Parliamentary Assembly

The proposal to create a WTO Parliamentary Assembly has been drawn up by the Canadian WFM member organisation and received support within the Canadian and European parliaments. According to this proposal, the Assembly should be composed of members of national parliaments and should have consultative powers. The relevance of the proposal lies in the fact that it addresses the issue of the WTO's democratic deficit. Its limit lies in its sectorial approach: it is a partial response to the challenge of international democracy. The process of globalisation does not involve only trade flows, but concerns many other aspects of political, economic and social life, like security, international monetary and financial issues, poverty, human rights, environment, health, education and so on.

In fact, the WTO is facing new issues such as unemployment, international migration, social rights, child labour, health, environment, etc. These problems are different aspects of the activity of international economic organisations, but find no appropriate answer, in the absence of the necessary powers and because of the plurality of bodies dealing with these problems. It will therefore be necessary to increase the powers of the new international economic institutions, and also to create a centre to co-ordinate functions that are presently scattered in many institutions operating independently from each other (G8, IMF, WB, WTO, ILO, UNEP, etc.).

All this shows, in my opinion, that the problems concerning the strengthening and the democratisation of the UN must be addressed together. The UN, as a whole, should be entrusted with new tasks, particularly those related with the international commercial, monetary and financial relations, and a Parliament should be constituted in the fabric of the UN system. Therefore, if the goal to be pursued is the democratisation of the process of globalisation, the democratisation of the WTO is not enough.

The same conclusion can be reached if we consider the global civil society organisations. If it is true that the people of Seattle has begun to act during a meeting of the WTO in December 1999, it should be taken into account as well that in the movement born in Seattle converge a great variety of claims (peace, human rights, environment and so on), being each of them a response to the various aspects of globalisation. All those concerned about peace, international justice, sustainable development and protection of human rights need a democratic world order through UN reform.

The UN Parliamentary Assembly, an Old-Fashioned Project

At a distance of approximately ten years from the publication of the booklet *The Case for a United Nations Parliamentary Assembly*, written by Dieter Heinrich, it is necessary to reconsider this proposal, which has become one of most well-known and most cited world federalist programs and has received important acknowledgements from various milieux: the latest and most significant was the 2000 Millennium Forum. It is worth recollecting that the proposal was inspired by the example of the European Parliament, which, at the beginning, was an assembly made up of members of national parliaments and endowed with consultative powers. It was conceived as a preliminary step toward creating a real World Parliament directly elected by the world citizens and endowed with legislative powers. Even though the UNPA has not been established yet, we must ask ourselves whether it is still an adequate relpy to the impetuous growth of globalisation and the parallel increasing influence of the global civil society movements on international politics.

The European federalists started the campaign for the direct election of the European Parliament when the European custom union was achieved (1968) and a new goal the Economic and Monetary Union was put on the European agenda. This objective demanded an increasing intervention of the Council of Ministers, the ultimate decision-making authority in the Community, which was pursued without corresponding parliamentary scrutiny and approval. Hence the sharpening of the democratic deficit of the Community, which paved the way to the claim of the direct election of the European Parliament and the strengthening of its powers.

Now the process of globalisation has reached an analogous turning point. With the creation of the WTO the custom tariffs, which in 1946 amounted to 50% of the value of imported goods, have been reduced to less than 3%. If the present degree of world commercial integration is comparable to that of the six member states of the European Community in 1968, today the world has to face the contradiction between the increasing intervention of international organisations in the field of economy, finance, human rights, environment and so on and the democratic deficit of these organisations.

Since globalisation wipes out the distinction between domestic and international politics, the extension of democracy, which has asserted itself in a vast majority of states, to international relations has become an inescapable imperative. What is more, the growing activism of the global civil society movements proves that there is a popular pressure demanding citizens participation in global decisions that affect individual daily life.

In conclusion, I think that we are faced with a crucial choice. Should we continue to support the UNPA and consider ourselves satisfied with campaigning for an objective which seems too weak with regard to the big changes which are occurring in world politics and in the global civil society? Or should we propose a much more ambitious project aiming to the constitution of a World Parliament that seems a bold reply to the challenge of globalisation and the claims coming from the global civil society?

A World Parliament

I think that we should choose the second alternative. "For a World Parliament" is the simple and strong watchword that identifies the sharpest contradiction of our time, the contradiction between globalisation and the lack of international democracy, and expresses at the same time the deep reasons that inspire the global civil society movements, the need for an assembly representing the general will of mankind. But we must be aware that the objective of a World Parliament is not incompatible with the four projects I have taken into consideration. All of them can be conceived as preliminary steps toward the final goal. The historical role that the WFM can play is to become the reference point and the leading force of a large coalition of NGOs striving for a UN Parliament. In fact, most of global civil society movements are striving for peace, the protection of the environment, international justice and the defence of human rights, but do not yet have a strategy for achieving these goals. The task of the WFM is to make these movements aware of the means (that is to say the institutions) which mankind needs to attain peace and international democracy and justice.

The role that the civil society movements have acquired on the international scene paves the way for new forms of political action, now termed *new diplomacy*. One of the most significant examples is the alliance between reformoriented nations and NGOs, which generated enough critical mass to give rise to the ICC. It is the updated version of an old scheme of action largely experimented by the European federalists. It stems from the experience of the creation of a new power on the area covered by many independent powers. The strategy of state unifications is twofold in nature. It requires the combination of two political sujects: a government-inspired current and a popular-inspired one.

Governments view political unifications in terms of co-operation among sovereign states, while federalists conceive them in terms of the creation of a new power. Governments have the power, but are opposed to use it for objectives that go beyond international co-operation. Spinelli used to say that national governments are at the same time the vehicle and the obstacle on the way towards the European

Federation.The vehicle, because they hold power, the obstacle, because they never spotaneously surrender national sovereignty. On the other hand, the federalists do not have the strength, but have an *initiating capacity*, which can be used during moments of crisis in order to move the governments to transfer their authority to supranational institutions.

The action for the construction of a World Parliament cannot be conceived otherwise. The World Parliament will be the result of the dialectical unity of the two currents mentioned above. According to two American academics, Richard Falk and Andrew Strauss, who published an article in *Foreign Affairs* at the beginning of this year entitled *Toward Global Parliament*, an alliance such as this could give rise a treaty instituting a World Parliament. It could begin to exist after being ratified by a minimun number of states (20, according to the authors). But, if we consider that the European Union member states are 15 and their number will double in the next future, 20 states seem to be few. 50% of the UN members and world population can provide the sufficient basis for the entry into force of the treaty. As Falk and Strauss write, "once the assembly became operational, the task of gaining additional state members would likely become easier. A concerte organisation would then exist that citizens could urge their governments to join. As more states joined, pressure would grow on nonmembers states to participate".

Before the conclusion, I would like to emphasize the difference between Falk and Strauss's project and the federalist one. What the two authors fail to state is that in order to democratize globalisation, a global Parliament is not enough. The experience of democratic regimes teaches us that no parliament can govern a country alone. A government is necessary. So the World Parliament must be seen as a crucial milestone on the way toward forming a democratic government endowed with the necessary powers to enforce the laws passed by the World Parliament.

11

International Relations and World Politics in the Twentieth Century

International Relations has not come out of the Cold war. Many may think the Cold war ended with the demolition of the Berlin Wall or with the decline of the USSR. Nothing could be further from the truth. In fact, the Cold war is a virus-like phenomena. It has changed the outlook from being a tussle between the West and the Communist block to a war between the developing and developed economy.

The Russian President and U.S President all spoke the same language. Whether they spoke different languages in the so called Cold War period is it self to be questioned. Thus in the 21st century only the players change but not the game plan. Its always between the haves and have-nots.The study of International Relations in political science gained strength during the Cold War. Many political scientists feared that the Soviet Union and the United States would launch themselves into a global nuclear war. It was hoped that by studying how countries interact with each other, it would be easier to predict what the reactions of the United States or Soviet Union would be in any given situation, making it easier to avert war. The study of International Relations has been, until very recently, the study of how states interact with other states.

Liberal International Theory vs. International Realism Theory

The two modern major schools of International Relations theory are International Liberal Theory and International Realism Theory.

Liberal theory is often marked by an analysis of an ideal, or utopian, outcome. Realist theory, however, focuses on the ways and means that states interact. An excellent discussion on the differences of the natures of these two theories can be found in Edwards H. Carr's "The Twenty Years' Crisis, 1919-1939" (he uses the term 'utopianism' for 'liberalism') or in Hans Morgenthau's "Politics Among Nations."

Realists often credit Thucydides as the first realist thinker for his desire to leave an account of war as a "possession for all time," his writing style in which he was only concerned with facts from reliable sources, and for his concentration on power in "The History of the Peloponnesian War." The Melian Dialogue is often given extra attention due to the unique use of dialogue, leading many to believe that Thucydides is trying to highlight an important event. From this comes the quote "The strong do what they have the power to do and the weak accept what they must," expressing the realist theme of might-equals-right. However, for an interesting look at the worldview that shaped Thucydides' writing". Realism has traditionally focused on power, and in the Westphalian state system, the state is seen as having the most power. Because it is concerned with power, realism has tended to focus more on high politics than low politics. However, with most wars since the early 1990s being fought within states instead of between states, this is currently being redefined within realism.

Liberalism (also called "Idealism" pejoratively) gained popularity following the end of World War I and the triumph of Wilsonian liberalism. Liberalism in international relations theory is generally associated with internationalism, institutionalism, and socialism. Essentially, they believe human nature is good, war can be avoided, and there is a moral universalism. They do not trace a long history of their theory, like realists do. Key themes include international law, sovereignty, international organisations, and global governance.

Formative thinkers in the liberal tradition include:

- Francisco de Vitoria and the School of Salamanca (De Indis debates) (1)
- Immanuel Kant (Perpetual Peace) (2)
- Vladimir Lenin (Imperialism: The Highest Stage of Capitalism)
- David Held (Democracy and the Global Order)

There are many ways of thinking in international relations theory, including Constructivism, Institutionalism, Marxism, Neo-Gramscianism, and others. However, two schools of thought are predominant: Realism and Liberalism.

Realism

The term Realism is often associated with the German term realpolitik. Realpolitik is a combination of two words: the German "real", meaning "real" or "substantive," as in the German "Realität" (meaning "reality"), and "politik" (meaning "politics" or "policy"). Bismarck used the term after following Metternich's lead in finding ways to balance the power of European empires. Balancing power meant keeping the peace, and careful realpolitik practioners tried to avoid arms races. However, during the early-20th Century, arms races (and alliances) occurred anyway, culminating in World War I.

Realism makes several key assumptions. It assumes that the international system is anarchic, in the sense that there is no authority above states capable of regulating their interactions; states must arrive at relations with other states on their own, rather than it being dictated to them by some higher controlling entity (that is, no true authoritative world government exists). It also assumes that sovereign states, rather than international institutions, non-governmental organisations, or multinational corporations, are the primary actors in international affairs.

According to realism, each state is a rational actor that always acts towards its own self-interest and the primary goal of each state is to ensure its own security. Realism holds that in pursuit of that security, states will attempt to amass resources and that relations between states are determined by their relative level of power. That level of power is in turn determined by the state's capabilities, both military and economic. Moreover, Realists believe that States are inherently aggressive ("offensive realism"), and that territorial expansion is only constrained by opposing powers. The principal Realist theorists are Carr, Morgenthau and Waltz.

There are two sub-schools of realism: maximal realism and minimal realism. The theory of maximal realism holds that the most desirable position to be in is that of the hegemon, the most powerful entity in the world, and that smaller entities will align themselves with the hegemon out of political self-interests. Under maximal realism, the position where there are simultaneously two equally powerful co-hegemons (such as was the case during the Cold War between the United States and the Soviet Union) is an inherently unstable one and that situation will inevitably collapse into a more stable state where one nation is more powerful and one is less powerful.

The theory of minimal realism holds that non-hegemonic states will ally against the hegemon in order to prevent their own interests from being subsumed by the hegemon's interests. Under the minimal-realism theory it is possible to have two equally powerful co-hegemons with whom a smaller entity may ally in turn depending on which hegemon better fits with the smaller entity's policies at the moment (playing both sides against the middle).

Liberalism

Liberalism holds that stssate preferences, rather than state capabilities, are the primary determinant of state behavior. Preferences will vary from state to state, depending on their culture, economic system, or type of government. Many different strands of liberalism have emerged; some include commercial liberalism, liberal institutionalism, idealism and regime theory. Recently, realism and liberalism have evolved into neo-realism and neo-liberalism.

Other Schools of Thought

Other schools, which cannot yet be counted to the established mainstream in the Study of International Relations, include postmodern, feminist and Neo-Marxist approaches, and Neo-Gramscianism. These perspectives differ from both Realism and Liberalism in their epistemological and ontological premises and are postpositivistic in nature.

Different schools of thought in international relations can predict the same events. The theories are differentiated by the assumptions they make in their reasoning toward predictions. For example, both realists and liberals claim that events as disparate as World War I, the Cold War, and the relatively conflict-free post-Cold War Europe were predicted by their theories. The theories differ in the fundamental assumptions they make in predicting state behavior. It is possible that one liberal theorist will predict war while another liberal theorist will predict peace; their disagreement arises from how they interpret events, but their fundamental assumptions are the same. Similarly, it is possible that a realist theorist and a liberal theorist could both predict peace, but their fundamental assumptions as to why that occurs would be different.

History

The history of international relations is widely traced back to the Peace of Westphalia of 1648 where the modern states system as we see it today was developed. It was not until 1919 that the first university department devoted to 'international politics' (and its Woodrow Wilson Chair of International Politics) was founded by David Davies at the University of Aberystwyth in Wales. The first university to found an international relations department was the London School of Economics in 1924.

12

PERESTROIKA MOVEMENT

The Perestroika Movement in political science is a faction that works towards methodological pluralism and to heighten relevance of political science to people outside the discipline. The movement is against what it sees as dominance for quantitative and mathematical methodology in political science. Such dominance breeds academic isolation and poor quality in scholarship, according to the movement (Schram and Caterino 2006).

The Perestroika Movement began in 2000 with an anonymous e-mail message sent by one "Mr. Perestroika" to the editors of the American Political Science Review calling for "a dismantling of the Orwellian system that we have in APSA." The message went to seventeen recipients who quickly forwarded it to others, and within weeks the Perestroika Movement became a force calling for change in the American political science community (Monroe 2005).

In the years that followed, the Perestroika Movement established itself with its own literature, conferences, websites, and blogs. Main books about the movement are Monroe (2005) and Schram and Caterino (2006). Oxford University professor Bent Flyvbjerg's book Making Social Science Matter (2001) has been called a manifesto for the Perestroika Movement. Political science is receiving increased critical scrutiny as a discipline these days, and much of that scrutiny is coming from within its own ranks. A growing number of political scientists have signed on to a movement to challenge the dominance of positivistic research, particularly research that assumes political behavior can be predicted according to theories of rationality and that such predictions underwrite cumulative explanations that constitute the growth of political knowledge. The movement to question such thinking is most dramatically represented in the network of scholars that has developed in response to the eponymous Mr. Perestroika letter that raised this challenge in poignant terms when it first circulated over the Internet back in October of 2000.

A loose collection of political scientists, from graduate students to senior scholars, Perestroikans do not always themselves agree on which features of the dominant approach they want to critique—some focus on the overly abstract nature of much of the research done today, some on the lack of nuance in decontextualised, large sample empirical studies, others on the inhumaneness of thinking about social relations in causal terms, and still others on the ways in which contemporary social science all too often fails to produce the kind of knowledge that can meaningfully inform social life. As a group, the Perestroika movement, however, has championed methodological pluralism, charging that exclusionary practices have made graduate education less hospitable to historical and field research, qualitative case studies, interpretive and critical analysis, and a variety of context-sensitive approaches to the study of politics.

The major journals of the field, Perestroikans argue, have become preoccupied with publishing research that conforms to overly restrictive scientistic assumptions about what constitutes contributions to knowledge of politics. Perestroika is a healthy development for political science and all other social sciences as well, opening for reconsideration these very questionable assumptions about what constitutes political knowledge in particular and social knowledge in general.

From the vantage point of many Perestroikans, the dominant paradigm in the field operates according to the following hierarchy of assmumptions:

(1) Political science exists to help promote understanding of the truth about politics;

(2) Political science research contributes to this quest by adding to the accumulation of an expanding base of objective knowledge about politics;

(3) The growth of this knowledge base is contingent upon the building of theory that offers explanations of politics;

(4) The building of theory is dependent on the development of universal generalisations regarding the behavior of political actors;

(5) The development of a growing body of generalisations occurs by testing falsifiable, causal hypotheses that demonstrate their success in making predictions;

(6) The accumulation of a growing body of predictions about political behavior comes from the study of variables in samples involving large numbers of cases; and

(7) This growing body of objective, causal knowledge can be put in service of society, particularly by influencing public policy makers and the stewards of the state.

This paradigm excludes much valuable research. For instance, it assumes that the study of a single case is "unscientific," provides no basis for generalising, does not build theory, cannot contribute to the growth of political knowledge, and, as a result, is not even to be considered for publication in the leading journals and is to be discouraged as a legitimate doctoral dissertation project. While there have always been dissenters tothe drift toward "largen," quantitative research in service of objective, decontextualised and universally generalizable truth about politics, there is a good case to be made that the dissenters have increasingly been marginalised as the center of gravity of the discipline has drifted more and more towards reflecting these core assumptions about knowledge of politics.

Perestroika in political science has at a minimum provided an opportunity to halt this drift by questioning these assumptions and posing alternatives. At its best, the Perestroikan impulse creates the possibility to question the idea that political science research exists as a unitary enterprise dedicated to the accumulation of an expanding knowledge base of universal, decontextualised generalisations about politics. In its place, Perestroika would put amore pluralistic emphasis on allowing for the blossoming of more contextual, contingent, and multiple political truths that involve a greater tie between theory and practice and a greater connection between thought and action in specific settings. Perestroika lays open the possibility that political science could actually be a very different sort of discipline, one less obsessed with proving it is a "science" and one more connected to providing delimited, contextualised, even local knowledges that might serve people within specific settings.

Such a political science would therefore have very different standards as to what counts as meaningful political knowledge. It would, for instance, be less interested in studying such things as "development" or "modernisation" in the abstract as objects of inquiry on their own, as when economics becomes the study of "the market" as opposed to the examination of the variety of markets. Instead of focusing solely on "development" or "modernisation" per se, political science would be more about studying change in particular countries or using concepts like development or modernisation in contextually sensitive ways to compare change in different countries. This alternative political science would also be less preoccupied with perfecting method or pursuing research strictly for knowledge's own sake. As Rogers Smith has underscored, "knowledge does not have a sake"; all knowledge is tied to serving particular values. Therefore, this new political science would not be one that is dedicated to replacing one method with another. Instead, such a discipline, if that word is still appropriate, would encourage scholars to draw on a wide variety of methods from a diversity of theoretical perspectives, combining theory and empirical work in different and creative ways, all in dialogue with political actors in specific contexts.

Problem driven research would replace method-driven research. My own version of Perestroika would build on this problem-driven, contextually-sensitive approach to enable people on the bottom working in dialogue with social researchers to challenge power. My Perestroikan-inspired political science would be open to allowing ongoing political struggle to serve as the context for deciding what methods will be used in what ways to address which problems. This new dialogic political science would not find its standards for credible scholarship in arcane vocabularies and insular methods that are removed from local contexts and seem objective but are not without their own agendas. Instead, my political science would find its standards of knowledge in asking whether scholarship can demonstrate its contributions to enriching political discourse in contextualised settings.

Such a new political science, however, would at the same time recognize the risks associated with connecting to ongoing politics. It would guard against losing its critical capacity for the sake of achieving relevance. It would retain its critical capacity while in dialogue with ongoing political struggle, providing therefore a powerful "critical connectedness"—what Charles Lemert has called "global methods." It would however be less interested than the old political science in serving the state with objective knowledge.

It would forego the dream of scientific grandeur that aims to produce socially useful, decontextualised, objective knowledge, independent of politics. A political science that forgoes the dream of a science of politics in order todedicate itself toenhancing the critical capacityof people topractice a politics is, for me, an exciting prospect. A political science that does this to enhance the capacity to challenge power from belowis all the more exciting. I would argue that the new political science would not just be more politically efficacious but also more intelligent, offering more robust forms of knowledge about politics. Important philosophical justification for this Perestroikan-inspired alternative to political science can be found in Stephen Toulmin's magisterial book Return to Reason. Tolumin's book builds on his life's work in the philosophy of science, ordinary language philosophy, rhetoric, and the analysis of practical arts. It is written with an erudition rarely seen. Its sweeping panorama places the problem of scientism in the social sciences in a historically rich context.

His primary argument is that since Descartes, and especially since Kant, Western philosophical thought has been increasingly enchanted with the dream of realising universal rationality as the highest form of knowledge and the basis for truth. Yet, Toulmin stresses that it was only relatively recently with the twentieth century that this dream came to be ascendant as the hegemonic ideal for organising knowledge practices in the academy in general and the social sciences in particular. The dream of universal rationality as the gold standard for objective knowledge of truth became ascendant with the rise of modern science and the growing influence of the argument that science, as best represented by particular natural sciences, was the best route toward achieving universal rationality, objective knowledge, and truth with a capital.

In its wake, the modern university was built, and then increasingly compartmentalised into the multiversity, with growing numbers of specialised disciplines, each increasingly preoccupied with perfecting its own methodological prowess as to how to best arrive at truth. Toulmin's main argument is that this derangement was a long time coming involving arduous efforts as part of a campaign that achieved hegemonic status relatively recently only in the twentieth century. For Toulmin, before then, much of the history of modern Western philosophy can be understood in terms of striking a balance between universal rationality and contextual reason. The campaigners had to confront time and again the problem that what is universally rational may not be reasonable in particular situations.

For centuries, the dream of universal rationality was counterbalanced with the practice of everyday reason. Humans experienced their lives and made sense of them between these poles. Yet, the rise of modern science increased the emphasis on the production of objective knowledge in the most abstract and generalizable terms possible. Theory was everything and practice was subordinated to it.

Theory-driven modern science's preferred discourse was mathematics that, since Descartes, was the ideal idiom for expressing in abstract and generalizable terms the objective knowledge of universal rationality. Sciences began to be ranked by the degree to which they could produce universal rationality as expressed in mathematical terms. Physics envy spread. Then again, in the twentieth century, science in general became ascendant as the best way to produce such knowledge. The fact that "science as use" was conflated with "science as truth" helped greatly in vaulting science to the forefront as the supposed superior road to truth as dramatic developments in technology were increasingly showcased as proof positive that science not only could do things but also knew the truth of what it was doing.

The idea that there is a distinctive scientific method that all sciences shared began to gain greater currency, and all other forms of knowledge production came to be seen as inferior to the degree that they failed to conform to the dictates of the scientific method. Physics envy morphed into science envy with the social sciences increasingly miming what was seen as the methods of the natural sciences in order to lay their own claim to scientific legitimacy.

At this point, the precarious balance between emphasising abstract rationality and everyday reason was now seriously upset, and universal rationality in service of abstract generalizable knowledge stated in the mathematical terms was seen as the only real form of truth worth taking seriously. The wisdom of everyday reason was increasingly relegated to folklore or to applied fields and it itself started to become a popular area of study, not so much for the truths it afforded but as an object of inquiry that could be used as data to test various hypotheses about which types of people in what cultures tended to think in what ways and why. The science of wisdom, as it were, whether studied in anthropology or philosophy, was a sure sign that rationality had triumphed over reason.

Toulmin effectively illuminates the rise of universal rationality first in philosophy from Descartes on, then in the sciences, but also in the social sciences and applied fields as well. He highlights how a consistent bias in favour of abstract knowledge of universal rationality continued to work its way across disparate realms of knowledge production. Toulmin is not a social scientist and in the past he has written about almost everything but. Yet, Return to Reason demonstrates a real feel for how the social sciences rose in the shadow of the preoccupation with the abstract knowledge of universal rationality and how that played out in selected fields. This is a wide-ranging book, written in a very inviting conversational style, from an Olympian vantage point; however, this is no mere dilettante rumination on the misguided project John Dewey called the "quest for certainty."

My favourite example in the entire book is Lancelot Brown, the famous nineteenth-century landscaper, who was also popularly known as "Capability" Brown because the designs for his quintessentially British gardens developed out of the available landscape, rather than, as with the French style, imposing an idealised image of a garden on the landscape and forcing it to conform to that ideal. Toulmin uses Capability Brown to demonstrate how British empiricism in contrast to French idealism very pragmatically offers a way to "play it as it lays" and work with what is available within any particular context rather than trying to impose abstract, universal ideals on situations. In Toulmin's hands, Capability Brown effectively illustrates the value in a return to reason as a counterbalance to the excessive emphasis on abstract knowledge of universal rationality. Toulmin is most convincing when he notes that for the social sciences, the scientistic preoccupation with universal rationality was a particularly troubling turn. His primary case in point is the popular one—economics. He calls it the "physics that never was." Toulmin effectively shows that the history of the development of economics as a discipline involved the progressive elimination of historical and social considerations, increasingly decontextualising its subject matter in ever more abstract and mathematical terms to produce its own universal rationality of market-related behavior. The application of abstract economic models to problems of public policy increasingly became the vogue.

Theory dictated to practice in often-ruthless terms, particularly when First World lending institutions prescribed "structural adjustment" or "shock therapy" policies that required nation-states to retrofit their economies to conform to the models' requirements. The central problem here for Toulmin, as for so many others, is that these sorts of applications all too often mistook contextually specific understandings or predictable market behavior as universally applicable, abstracted them from those contexts, and imposed them in social settings, cultures, and political systems where they make very little sense at all, and did so all too often at great cost to the well-being of the people who were supposed to be helped by such "development" schemes.

Toulmin counters these disasters of "top-down" theory-driven economic practice with the example of Muhammad Yunus, who works from the "bottom up" with his Grameen Bank that provides small loans in over 50,000 Bangladeshi villages so that local people can develop "appropriate" enterprises fitted to their communities, values, and local practices. Yunus, a professional economist, is quoted by Toulmin as saying, "If Economics (as it stands) were a social science, economists would have discovered what a powerful socio-economic weapon credit is. . . . If we can re-design economics as a genuine social science, we will be firmly on ourway to creating a poverty-free world" (p. 65). Toulmin ends his tale of the disenchantment of economics by saying, "This message does not, of course, affect Economics alone: similar traditions in the other human sciences have led to similar misunderstandings and errors of practical judgment" (p. 66).

For Toulmin, the antidote to the twentieth-century hegemony of universal rationalism is respect for everyday reason, as practiced in contextualised settings, in ways that can not be legislated by theory from the top down and are open to living with the uncertainty that such situated knowledges must accept as the ineliminable contingency of what Toulmin calls the "clinical arts." The social sciences are, for Toulmin, more akin to "applied sciences," but "applied" mischaracterises the situation, suggesting that theory is applied in practice—an idea most significantly popularised by the reports Abraham Flexner wrote on professional medical education in 1913 and on social work in 1915.

Instead, drawing on the work of Donald Schon and others, Toulmin wants us to learn that social theory is better seen growing out of practice, as an intensification of those meditative moments in social practice. Toulmin sees the need for social sciences, operating ever more beyond disciplinary boundaries, to be more about teaching practical wisdom, *phronesis*, as Aristotle termed it, as something that grows out of an intimate familiarity with the contingencies and uncertainties of various forms of social practice embedded in complex social settings.

We need therefore to revise the standards for acceptable research methodologies, reincorporating context-sensitive research, such as case studies, not to dictate what is to be done but more to inventory infinitely unique cases from which social actors can learn to appreciate the complexities of social relations and practice various social crafts all the more effectively. Social science would be more like bioethics than like moral philosophy, basing itself on the insight that Toulmin provides when he notes that bioethics owes very little to moral philosophy, which, as theory, is incapable of specifying from the top down most bioethical decisions, that instead grow from the bottom up, in unlegislated form, varying with contexts, negotiating ambiguity, living with uncertainty, and still doing the necessary work of determining life and death every day.

Case study research for bioethicists and many others, often conducted in dialogical and collabourative relations with the people being studied, can help enable social actors to use knowledge to address their problems. Such participatory action research would for Toulmin be more fitting of a real social science that better understood its relationship to its contingent, contextual and ever so thoroughly social subjects. For Toulmin, the return to reason will then best be evidenced in the social sciences when wisdom of this sort is taught not as an object for scientific scrutiny, as evidence of cultural variation, but as the very goal of knowledge production itself.

In his introduction, Toulmin cites one book as a sign that some social scientists are tapping into the themes he emphasises. The book is Making Social Science Matter: Why Social Inquiry Fails and How It Can Succeed Again by Bent Flyvbjerg. It too is a remarkable book that adds fuel to the idea that perhaps Perestroikans are part of broader academic currents. Flyvbjerg's book takes us one step further down the road that Toulmin has laid out for us and it does it eloquently with its own impassioned argument that not only demonstrates what is wrong with the social sciences today but provides a detailed list of examples of how a phronetic social science is already possible and already happening here and there among the detritus of contemporary social science.

Flyvbjerg's book is such a breath of fresh air; he creatively uses Aristotle, Nietzsche, Foucault, Bourdieu, and others to make many of the same points as Toulmin, but in his own distinctive way. He fuses an Aristotelian concern for phronesis with a Marxist concern for praxis, adding in a Foucauldian critique of Habermas's preoccupation with consensus to demonstrate that a phronetic social science that can offer a praxis worth pursuing is one that would work within any contextualised setting to challenge power, especially as it is articulated in discourse. Flyvbjerg's phronetic social science would be open to using a plurality of research methods to help people challenge power more effectively.

Flyvbjerg begins where Toulmin left us, in the present with social science hopelessly lost seeking to emulate the natural sciences with a quest for theory-driven abstract knowledge of universal rationality. Flyvbjerg adds a compelling critique that demonstrates convincingly that there is no symmetry between natural and social science in that natural science's interpretive problems are compounded by what Anthony Giddens called the "double hermeneutic" of the social sciences. By virtue of its distinctively human subject matter, the social scientists inevitably are people who offer interpretations of other people's interpretations. And the people being studied always have the potential to include the social scientists' interpretations in theirs, creating an ever-changing subject matter and requiring a dialogic relationship between the people doing the studying and the people being studied. For Flyvbjerg, this situation unavoidably means that there can be no theory for social science in the sense that social science needs to forego the dream that it can create time-tested theories of a static social reality.

As a result, argues Flyvbjerg, the social sciences should not seek to emulate the natural sciences. In such a comparison, the social sciences will always fare very poorly, being seen as inferiors incapable of producing knowledge based on tested theories that can evince prediction of the worlds they study. Instead, Flyvbjerg feels that the social sciences are better equipped to produce a different kind of knowledge—phronesis, practical wisdom—that grows out of intimate familiarity with practice in contextualised settings. Local knowledges, even tacit knowledges, that cannot be taught a priori, grown from the bottom up, emerging out of practice, foregoing the hubris of seeking claims to a decontextualised universal rationality stated in abstract terms of false precision.

Add a sense of praxis, seeking the ability to push for change, leaven it with an appreciation of the ineliminable presence of power, and this phronetic social science can help people in ongoing political struggle question the relationships of knowledge and power and thereby work to change things in ways they might find more agreeable and even satisfying. Such a phronetic social science can contribute to what I have called "radical incrementalism"or the idea that praxis involves promoting change for the least advantaged by exploiting the possibilities in current political arrangements.

Yet, what is most exciting is that Flyvbjerg not only goes beyond critique to offer a positive program; he demonstrates it in detail, pointing to a rich variety of contemporary work from that of Bourdieu, to Robert Bellah, to his ownwork. Flyvbjerg's research spanned fifteen years and focused on a major redevelopment project initiated by the Danish city of Aalborg, where Flyvbjerg continues to teach urban planning. His research on the project evolved over time, quickly becoming more phronetic as he came to appreciate how social science could make real contributions to the ongoing dialogue over the city's redevelopment efforts once his research was retrofitted to the specific context in which the issues of development were being debated.

At first, Flyvbjerg was put off that decision makers rejected the relevance of studies about education elsewhere and he came to be concerned with power. Without saying so, he evidently took to heart the idea that he had to work harder to produce research that, even while it challenged power, demonstrated its sensitivity to the Aalborg context. In the process, power relations got challenged in a very public way, the framing of the development agenda got successfully revised to include more grassroots concerns, an ongoing dialogue with participants in the redevelopment process got richly elabourated, and social science research that gave up an interest in proving grand theories became critical to a very robust discourse on urban planning. As a result, the Aalborg planning project gained increased visibility as a successful project that went out of its way to democratize its decision making in part by allowing social science research to help keep it honest, open, and collabourative.

Phronetic social science such as this would be very different than the social science that predominates today. For Immanuel Wallerstein, that would be a good thing, at least for the most part.Asecond edition of his 1991 work Unthinking Social Science: The Limits of Nineteenth-Century Paradigms was released in 2001. Revised to include a new preface, these essays demonstrate the consistency in Wallerstein's thinking even as he continues to add new concerns, as he did in his 1999 collection, The End of the World As We Know It: Social Science for the 21st Century. For over thirty years, Wallerstein has championed his World-Systems Analysis not just as a critique of global capitalism's 500-year climb to ascendancy but also, as the titles of his more recent books indicate, as a critique of the epistemological assumptions that undergird that system, especially in terms of the implications for social science.

His preoccupation with social science's role in the reproduction of theWorld System is not some idle theoretical point. In 1996, as chair of the Gulbenkian Commission on the Restructuring of the Social Sciences, he issued, with the nine other international committee members, a report, Open the Social Sciences, which has since been published in twenty different languages. For Wallerstein, when the contemporary social sciences began to be formed in the nineteenth century, they were organised to produce specialised knowledges that would be consistent with the World System's need for a universal rationality that would rationalize its dominance across the globe, over a diversity of cultures and wherever capitalism sought hegemony.

Wallerstein places the quest for universal rationality by the social sciences on a very dramatic world-historical stage and in a most critical light. World-Systems Analysis provides, therefore, not just a way of understanding how the capitalist core metropole subjugates the periphery for resource extraction and expansion of commodity exchange relationships. World-Systems Analysis, more profoundly, is for Wallerstein a way of critiquing the knowledge assumptions that inform the World System. World-Systems Analysis is first and foremost a way of unlearning or "unthinking" the social sciences that serve the World System. Such an unthinking involves breaking down disciplinary boundaries, rejoining normative philosophy and empirical research, understanding the production of knowledge in terms of its relationship to the structural imperatives of the World System, and finally, and perhaps most importantly, appreciating that the World System is increasingly in crisis and that its grip on knowledge production is loosening, thereby opening opportunities in our time to contribute to its demise by developing the World-Systems critique.

Waller stein has much to offer the campaign tore vitalize social science and move it in politically protean directions. I am a bit hesitant, however, to endorse what Waller stein calls in a moment of modesty the World System "hypothesis." As historically rich and politically trenchant a critique as is Waller stein's, it still risks merely replacing one paradigm, as he calls it, with another. I have two problems with the Waller stein call for a paradigm shift. First, his World-Systems paradigm tries but fails to resolve its own contradictions regarding the relationship of structure to agency, with structure over determining agency and agency largely becoming the pantomime of structural insistences. Second, I am increasingly convinced that social science is ideally better seen as post paradigmatic rather than as organised by one paradigm or another.

For me, the idea of paradigm has no relevance to social science except as its own form of mimicry. Paradigmatic research is what natural scientists do. Social science for the reasons provided in this essay ideally should not be seen as amenable tobeing organised paradigmatically in any strict sense of the term. The strict sense of the term is of course subject to intense debate starting with its author Thomas Kuhn. Erich von Dietze makes this clear in Paradigms Explained: Rethinking Thomas Kuhn's Philosophy of Science. Dietze provides a very clearly written, extremely systematic and comprehensive recitation of Kuhn's theory of paradigm, the critics' complaints, Kuhn's responses, and finally Dietze's own assessment that suggests that Kuhn's admittedly brilliant and important work failed to shore up paradigm as a sustainable concept for understanding the framing and structuring of knowledge production in the natural sciences. Dietze concludes by suggesting a "coherence theory of evidence" as a replacement for the concept of paradigm.

Paradigm, Dietze notes, started in Kuhn's The Structure of Scientific Revolutions and served as the lynchpin for his theory that in any one field "normal" science was periodically punctuated by "revolutionary" science that induced a conceptual transformation of the subject matter and initiated new ways of studying it. Dietze notes that from the beginning Kuhn struggled to respond to critics by relying in particular on two additional concepts—exemplar and disciplinary matrix. An exemplar is an exemplary example, usually in the form of an innovative experiment or analytical treatment, that by its very success implied a particular way to understand and study the subject in question. To the extent that they are contingent upon exemplars, Kuhn's paradigms are to a great degree therefore implicit in the very act of "learning by doing" in a contextually sensitive fashion, making them in their own way forms of phronetic reasoning, learned and elabourated through situated practice.

The disciplinary matrix is the social, institutional, and organisational side of the process where cohorts of scientists were introduced to the paradigm and encouraged to practice normal science according to how they were socialised by the disciplinary matrix. It therefore is as if paradigms had both material and symbolic dimensions. Through learning to practice exemplars, graduate students became normal scientists. Natural science was its own form of phronesis, if only so as to practice natural scientific reasoning in the context of actually doing it.

Once a new exemplar arises that is seen as providing a preferred understanding of the subject matter in ways that the prevailing paradigm cannot, scientists have to learn the new rules for study implied by the new exemplar. Translation into the old system of study would not work because the paradigms were, in Kuhn's mind, to anineliminable degree, by definition, incommensurable. Each paradigm's evidence is of a nature that it always has to be evaluated by its own standards, in its own context, making it impossible to use evidence to decide if one paradigm was better than another. For Kuhn, knowledge does not grow cumulatively with one paradigm building on another. We should never say that we now know more or better only, that with a paradigm change we know differently. What was most radical then about Kuhn's notion of paradigm is that it unmasks the necessary fiction that the twentieth century metastory of science teaches us about the growth of objective knowledge. This Kuhnian claim led critics to charge him with relativism on the grounds that Kuhn seemed to be implying that one paradigm might be as true or right as another. Kuhn spent much of the rest of his life responding to critics with clarifications that more often than not moved him away from the relativistic implications of his work.

Dietze is of the opinion that Kuhn's responses did not salvage the concept of paradigm successfully. Dietze missteps here by going beyond Kuhn in accepting the charge of relativism as posing a legitimate problem in need of solution. He therefore concludes by trying to make the best of what he sees as an untenable situation by offering an alternative—the coherence theory of evidence. This position builds on the Kuhnian insight that empirical adequacy alone is not sufficient for theory adjudication. Underdetermined by evidence, theories need more than facts to receive affirmation within a field of study. There are "super empirical" considerations, including in particular "coherence virtues" appropriate to all knowledge claims regardless of their theoretical premises.

Beyond evidence, a knowledge claim must fit logically with related claims of a theory in ways that are consistent with the generic standards of how interrelated knowledge claims ought to be seen as fitting logically together. Dietze defends this perspective as one that salvages Kuhn's theory of paradigm from the charges of relativism. Dietze concedes, however, that the super empirical and Transco textual criteria for coherence among interrelated knowledge claims are themselves constraining conditions that need to be examined for their potential to exclude certain understandings as illogical when they are in fact just logical according to a different standard.

Dietze provocatively notes at the end of his book that Kuhn's relativism is really a product of a failure to break more fully with logical positivism. Kuhn took too seriously logical positivism's press clippings and ended up showing that its supposed objective facts were more context dependent, value laden and theory laden than it was prepared to admit. Kuhnwas right about that, but for Dietze, Kuhn makes his case in too aggressive a fashion, sliding into a relativism that he himself was reluctant to endorse.

I leave it to others to decide whether paradigm or coherence theory helps more to understand that science is not objective, does not produce cumulative knowledge, and does not lead to universal rationality or absolute truth. I would suggest however that Dietze prematurely accepts the charges of relativism as pointing toward a legitimate problem. Dietz tries to save Kuhn by standing him on his head and making the issue of relativism the problem it is not. As Richard Rorty has reminded us, when someone calls you a relativist, the better responses include saying thank you for highlighting your well founded commitment to challenging the illegitimacy of the master narrative of science. Yet, Dietze joins others in appropriately leaving to the side whether paradigm has relevance to understanding social sciences. Given the subject matter, there ideally should be no normal science in any one of the social sciences. Regardless of the fact that both natural and social science are forms of learning in context that produce value-laden facts, social life, as opposed to the objects of natural scientific inquiry, involves multiple interpretive lenses offering a cacophony of competing perspectives emanating from its origins in conscious, thinking human beings. Under these conditions, no one form of disciplined study of social life should be organised paradigmatically to exclude the consideration of multiple perspectives.

Ironically, the objectivists in social science themselves most often resist the application of Kuhn's idea of paradigm to their fields since it implies that their scientific work was value laden. I agree with them about resisting its application to social science but for the different reason that multiple perspectives are inherent in the subject matter. It is a sad irony then that even though the objectivists resist paradigm, methodological hegemony by objectivists is the reality today in social sciences such as political science and economics. This is a doleful reminder that paradigms involve the very human power struggles of a disciplinary matrix as much as they do the practices of inquiry demonstrated in exemplars. Paradigms can be imposed socially even where they are most inappropriate intellectually.

Yet, it is one thing to issue a post paradigmatic call for a phronetic social science and it is another to emphasize the idea that social theories should serve as the foundation for practice. The latter is exactly what Joseph Lepgold and Miroslav Nincic do in *Beyond the Ivory Tower: International Relations Theory and the Issue of Policy Relevance*. Lepgold and Nincic know the field of international relations theory inside and out. Their book is well written and their thesis is provocative. They argue that academic scholarship on international relations has become increasingly technocratic and disconnected from the practice of international politics. The authors succinctly overview the field's developments in this regard. Eventually they point to several strands of contemporary scholarship on international relations, which they suggest indicate ways in which academics studying international relations can make their work more relevant to, and even serve as a foundation for, international relations practice.

While I find the critique of the field's increased technicism to be persuasive and consistent with the arguments made by Toulmin and others, their examples of work that is connected to international politics are less so. The authors provide two examples of international relations theory that have usefully connected to international politics— "inter democratic peace" research on how democracies are more peaceful with one another than other political systems, and international institutions research on how institutionalised settings create conditions and incentives for cooperation and conflict.

The analysis provided on global peace never really demonstrates effectively how such theorising provides, any more than any other political ideology, the explicit basis for practicing international relations politics by nation-states or nongovernmental actors. And international institutions research too does not some across as the firm foundation for practice that the authors suggest, though with qualifications, it could be. Both examples are from within the hegemonic camp of objectivist political science and both share the hegemonic camp's insensitivity to context. Yet, more important, the very argument that international relations theory should overcome its alienation from practice by reestablishing itself as a foundation for practice strikes me as misguided.

The solution to overcoming the alienation of international relations scholarship from international politics is not to reinscribe epistemic privilege and the idea that theory is fundamental and should serve as a blueprint for practice, or even more concretely for specific public policies. This foundationalism simply recreates the problem in the first place, encouraging scholars to privilege theory as some legislating and authorising activity that it is not. Such foundationalism reflects a lingering commitment to universal rationality and fails to appreciate the contextualism that Toulmin and Flyvbjerg emphasize as central to understanding and contributing to social and political life.

A better approach would be a phronetic social science that sees theory as growing out of the practices in specific contexts while still working to achieve critical distance on prevailing understandings of those political practices. This would be the beginning of research that could better help ordinary people—nongovernmental actors—challenge power internationally. Phronetic social science already exists; it is just not organised or recognised as such, existing here and there where scholars come to it on their own.

It also has multiple sources of intellectual sustenance. One prominent institution that has at times successfully promoted social research that makes a phronetic approach plausible is the School of Social Science in the Institute for Advanced Study at Princeton, which from its inception in 1973 sought to encourage innovation in the social sciences by promoting interdisciplinary work along interpretive and critical lines. Independent of any university, including Princeton, the

School has survived handsomely, celebrating its twenty-fifth anniversary symposium in 1997 with the publication of *Schools of Thought: Twenty-Five Years of Interpretive Social Science*, edited by Joan Scott and Debra Keates. This collection includes essays by twenty prominent philosophers, theorists, and social scientists, each responding to the symposium's theme toaddress changes in their field of study in the last twenty-five years. As Clifford Geertz, the first appointed professor at the School, notes in his introduction, the School was always meant to be a place that was open to innovation and resisted promoting any one program or paradigm. It did, however, seek to challenge the orthodoxy of scientistic social science and it stressed interdisciplinary work that contributed to what came to be called "interpretive social science."

The essays in this volume are a rich set of diverse pieces. Some, like David Apter's piece on empirical theory in political science, tack more to a historical line over viewing major developments in a field. Others, like William Sewell's piece on the rise and decline of social history, tell interesting stories about significant events that were part of those developments. Still others, like Joan Scott's piece on the changing understanding of "history," illustrate how a particular form of interpretive social science makes an important difference in the practice of social inquiry in specific areas. And still others, like Anna Tsing's piece on globalisation, examine a substantive issue and its implications for a discipline like anthropology.

Together these essays comprise a rewarding collection, suggesting the significance of what several of them refer to as the "interpretive turn," the subsequent linguistic turn, and all the other related turns that followed, once the hegemony of scientistic social science had begun to be seriously challenged. Yet, this collection rarely points to an instance of what I am calling here with Flyvbjerg phronetic social science. The interpretive turn helps provide resources for developing such work; it does not by itself constitute that work. Will the road ahead take more turns? That depends to a large extent on the plays of power, in the academy, the government, the think tanks, and anywhere else knowledge and power are being "disciplined."

13

E-DEMOCRACY

E-democracy, a combination of the words electronic and democracy refers to the use of information technologies and communication technologies and strategies in political and governance processes. Democratic actors and sectors in this context include governments, elected officials, the media, political organisations, and citizens/voters. E-democracy aims for broader and more active citizen participation enabled by the Internet, mobile communications, and other technologies in today's representative democracy, as well as through more participatory or direct forms of citizen involvement in addressing public challenges. E-democracy is a relatively new concept, which has surfaced out of the popularity of the Internet and the need to reinvigorate interest in the democratic process. Access is the key to creating interest in the democratic process. Citizens are more willing to use Web sites to support their candidates and their campaign drives. In the United States, just over 50% of the population votes, and in the United Kingdom, only 69% of citizens vote.

The research indicates that the political process has been alienated from ordinary people, where laws are made by representatives far removed from ordinary people. The goal of e-democracy is to reverse the cynicism citizens have about their government institutions. However, there are doubts about the real impact of electronic and digital tools on citizen participation and democratic governance, and warning against the "rhetoric" of electronic democracy.

TOOLS AND TYPES

There has been a significant growth in the last four years, and implementation rates have topped out in many of the categories. Public-

and private-sector platforms provide an avenue to citizen engagement while offering access to transparent information citizens have come to expect.

To develop these public-sector portals or platforms, governments have the choice to internally develop and manage, outsource or sign a self-funding contract. The self-funding model creates portals that pay for themselves through convenience fees for certain e-government transactions. Early players in this space include govONE Solutions, First Data Government Solutions and Nicusa.com, a company built on the self-funded model.

Social networking is an emerging area for e-democracy, as well as related technological developments, such as argument maps and eventually, the semantic web. Those are seen as important stepping stones in the maturation of the concept of e-democracy. The social networking entry point, for example, is within the citizens' environment, and the engagement is on the citizens' terms. Proponents of e-government perceive government use of social networks as a medium to help government act more like the public it serves.

Government and its agents also have the opportunity to follow citizens to monitor satisfaction with services they receive. Through ListServs, RSS feeds, mobile messaging, micro-blogging services and blogs, government and its agencies can share information to citizens who share common interests and concerns. Some government representatives are also beginning to use Twitter which provides them with an easy medium to inform their followers. In the state of Rhode Island, for instance, Treasurer Frank T. Caprio is offering daily tweets of the state's cash flow.

Practical Issues

A number of practical issues surround e-democracy. In the media, on the Internet, and in popular consciousness, there is a strong and generally unchallenged view that the Internet is the new electronic cradle of democracy. The original source of this view is probably the relatively unfettered speech found in Internet newsgroups, mailing lists, blogs and chat rooms.

The Internet currently does have several attributes that encourage thinking about it as a democratic medium. Part of this can be traced to the design principles that were established early in its evolution. The lack of centralised control suggests to many people that censorship or other attempts at control will be thwarted. Other attributes are a result of social design in the early days, the strongly libertarian support for free speech, the sharing culture that permeated nearly all aspects of Internet use, and the outright prohibition on commercial use by the National Science Foundation, for example. The Internet's most significant contribution was the idea of unmediated many-to-many communication on a large scale, through newsgroups, chat rooms, MUDs, and many other modes. This type of communication ignored the boundaries established with broadcast media, such as newspapers or radio, and with one-to-one media, such as letters or landline telephones. Finally, because Internet is a massive digital network with open standards, universal and inexpensive access to a wide variety of communication media and models could actually be attained.

Some practical issues involving e-democracy include: effective participation; voting equality at decision stage; enlightened understanding; control of the agenda; and inclusiveness.

Citizens' Roles

The Internet provides a distinctive structure of opportunities that has the potential to renew interest in civic engagement and participation. Civic engagement can be understood to include three distinct dimensions: political knowledge (what people learn about public affairs), political trust (the public's orientation of support for the political system), and political participation (conventional activities designed to influence government and the decision-making process).

The information capacity available on the Internet allows citizens to become more knowledgeable about government and political issues, and the interactivity of the medium allows for new forms of communication with government, *i.e.* elected officials and/or public servants. The posting of contact information, legislation, agendas, and policies makes government more transparent, potentially enabling more informed participation both online and offline. For more information, visit transparent-gov.

Internet as a Campaign Tool

The Internet is viewed as a platform and delivery medium for tools that help to eliminate some of the distance constraints in representative democracy. Technical media for e-democracy can be expected to extend to mobile technologies, such as cellphones.

Most importantly, the Internet is a many-to-many communication medium, whereas radio and television, which broadcast few-to-many, and telephones, which broadcast few-to-few, are not. Also, the Internet has a much greater computational capacity, allowing strong encryption and database management, which is important in community information access and sharing, deliberative democracy and electoral fraud prevention. Further, people use the Internet to collabourate or meet in an asynchronous manner—that is, they do not have to be physically gathered at the same moment to get things accomplished.

Using the Internet as a political campaigning tool has become a cheaper and more convenient alternative for many politicians, in comparison to traditional door-to-door knocking or telephone campaigning. Candidates are also beginning to use social networking sites to reach younger audiences, creating potential supporters to campaigns. E-mail chains and political blogs also have had a major impact with online campaigning. Views are expressed by adding comments to political blogs or web pages. Point-and-click advertising (interactive advertising online) also has influenced traditional mail or television campaigning.

The lower cost of information exchange on the Internet, as well as the high level of reach that the content potentially has, makes the Internet an attractive medium for political information, particularly amongst social interest groups and parties with lower budgets.

For example, environmental or social issue groups may find the Internet an easier mechanism to increase awareness of their issues, as compared to traditional media outlets, such as television or newspapers, which require heavy financial investment. Due to all these factors, the Internet has the potential to take over certain traditional media of political communication, such as the telephone, the television, newspapers and the radio. The civil society has gradually moved into the online world.

Another example is openforum.com.au, an Australian non-profit eDemocracy project that invites politicians, senior public servants, academics, business people and other key stakeholders to engage in high-level policy debate.

Novel tools are being developed that are aimed at empowering bloggers, webmasters and owners of other social media, with the effect of moving from a *strictly informational* use of the Internet to using the Internet *as a means of social organisation* not requiring top-down action. Action triggers, for instance, are a novel concept designed to allow webmasters to mobilize their viewers into action without the need for leadership. These tools are also utilised worldwide: for example, India is developing an effective blogosphere that allows internet users to state their thoughts and opinions.

Electronic Support for Local Democratic Groups

Citizens' associations play an important role in the democratic process, providing a place for individuals to learn about public affairs and a source of power outside that of the state, according to theorists like Alexis de Tocqueville. Public-policy researcher Hans Klein at the Georgia Institute of Technology notes that participation in such forums has a number of barriers, such as the need to meet in one place at one time. In a study of a civic association in the northeastern United States, Klein found that electronic communications greatly enhanced the ability of the organisation to fulfill its mission.

There are many forms of association in civic society. The term *interest group* conventionally refers to more formal organisations that either focus on particular social groups and economic sectors, such as trade unions and business and professional associations, or on more specific issues, such as abortion, gun control, or the environment. Other traditional interest groups have well-established organisational structures and formal membership rules, and their primary orientation is toward influencing government and the policy process. Transnational advocacy networks bring together loose coalitions of these organisations under common umbrella organisations that cross national borders. The Internet may serve multiple functions for all of these organisations, including lobbying elected representatives, public officials, and policy elites; networking with related associations and organisations; mobilising organisers, activists, and members using action alerts, newsletters, and emails; raising funds and recruiting supporters; and communicating their message to the public via the traditional news media.

Benefits and Disadvantages

Information and communications technologies are neither democratic nor undemocratic; they are merely means to an end and not normative by their nature. They are tools that may be deployed to achieve certain goals (*e.g.*, contradictory goals, such as coercive control or participation can be fostered by digital technology). However, certain institutional framework conditions may either support or hamper the use of electronic means for the benefit of democratic processes. Risks and opportunities of the digitisation of democratic processes depends therefore to a large extent upon the particular institutional framework conditions of the chosen democratic model (which is mainly set out in the Constitution, including the type of the underlying social contract, specific aspects of the rule of law, representative democracy or direct democracy, *etc*.).

Benefits

Contemporary technologies, such as electronic mailing lists, peer-to-peer networks, collabourative software, wikis, Internet forums and blogs, are clues to and early potential solutions for some aspects of e-democracy.

A number of non-governmental sites have developed cross-jurisdiction, customer-focused applications that extract information from thousands of governmental organisations into a system that brings consistency to data across many dissimilar providers. It is convenient and cost-effective for businesses, and the public benefits by getting easy access to the most current information available without having to expend tax dollars to get it. One example of this is transparent.gov.com, a free resource for citizens to quickly identify the various open government initiatives taking place in their community or in communities across the country.

Another valuable source is USA.gov — the official site of the United States government. The website is directly linked to every federal and state agency. The information provided by the website is valuable to all citizens, and non-citizens, of the current news and regulations of the U.S. government. These are just some examples of e-government's influence in the Internet.

E-democracy leads to a more simplified process and access to government information for public-sector agencies and citizens. Electronic democracy can also carry the benefit of reaching out to youth as a mechanism to increase youth voter turnout in elections and raising awareness amongst youth. With the consistent decline of voter turnout, e-democracy and electronic voting mechanisms can help revert that trend. Youth, in particular, have seen a significant drop in turnout in most industrialised nations, including Canada, the United States and the United Kingdom. The use of electronic political participation mechanisms may appear more familiar to youth and, as a result, garner more participation by youths who would otherwise find it inconvenient to vote using the more traditional methods. Electronic democracy can help improve democratic participation, reduce civic illiteracy and voter apathy and become a useful asset for political discussion, education, debate and participation.

Disadvantages

Equally, these technologies are bellwethers of some of the issues associated with the territory, such as the inability to sustain new initiatives or protect against identity theft, information overload and vandalism. Some traditional objections to direct democracy are argued to apply to e-democracy, such as the potential for governance to tend towards populism and demagoguery. More practical objections exist, not least in terms of the digital divide between those with access to the media of e-democracy (mobile phones and Internet connections) and those without, as well as the opportunity cost of expenditure on e-democracy innovations.

Furthermore, there are still those who are skeptical to the amount of impact that they can make through online participation. Although the government projects supply information, IT illiteracy and the digital divide are grounds to discourage participation. The political advances on the Internet can potentially dishearten non-users to adapt the new technologies.

Electronic Direct Democracy

Electronic direct democracy (EDD) is the strongest form of direct democracy, in which people are involved in the legislative function. Many advocates think that also important to this notion are technological enhancements to the deliberative process. Electronic direct democracy is sometimes referred to by many other names, such as open source governance and collabourative governance.

EDD requires electronic voting or some way to register votes on issues electronically. As in any direct democracy, in an EDD, citizens would have the right to vote on legislation, author new legislation, and recall representatives (if any representatives are preserved). Technology for supporting EDD has been researched and developed at the Florida Institute of Technology, where the technology is used with student organisations. Numerous other software development projects are underway, along with many supporting and related projects. Several of these projects are now collabourating on a cross-platform architecture, under the umbrella of the Metagovernment project.

EDD as a system is not fully implemented in a political government anywhere in the world, although several initiatives are currently forming. Ross Perot was a prominent advocate of EDD when he advocated "electronic town halls" during his 1992 and 1996 Presidential campaigns in the United States. Switzerland, already partially governed by direct democracy, is making progress towards such a system. Senator On-Line, an Australian political party running for the Senate in the 2007 federal elections, proposed to institute an EDD system so that Australians can decide which way the senators vote on each and every bill. A similar initiative was formed 2002 in Sweden where the party Aktivdemokrati, running for the Swedish parliament, offers its members the power to decide the actions of the party over all or some areas of decision, or alternatively to use a proxy with immediate recall for one or several areas.

Liquid democracy, or direct democracy with delegable proxy, would allow citizens to choose a proxy to vote on their behalf while retaining the right to cast their own vote on legislation. The voting and the appointment of proxies could be done electronically. The proxies could even form proxy chains, in which if A appoints B and B appoints C, and neither A nor B vote on a proposed bill but C does, C's vote will count for all three of them. Citizens could also rank their proxies in order of preference, so that if their first choice proxy fails to vote, their vote can be cast by their second-choice proxy.

ICTs and Political Participation

Information and communication technologies (ICTs) play a major role in organising and informing citizens in various forms of civic engagement. ICTs are used to enhance active participation of citizens and to support the collabouration between actors for policy-making purposes within the political processes of all stages of governance. ICTs offer citizens not only the means to organize themselves, but also to produce cultural codes to represent themselves. ICTs can be seen as an important enabler to the empowerment of citizens or e-mancipation of citizens.

Civic Engagement of Youth Through the Internet

There has been much speculation about the Internet's potential to facilitate the engagement of younger citizens in politics. This group of young people, under the age of 35, frequently labelled Generations X and Y, have been noted for their lack of political interest and activity for the last two decades. The younger generation is less likely to have established long-standing habits of media use, and is willing to experiment with new technologies and formats. Young adults view the benefits of new technologies as a means of gaining advantage in education, employment, and in the political realm. Younger people have ease with Internet technology and are more likely than older citizens to use web-based platforms to research and access political information. However, there is no clear consensus about the capacity of new media, including the Internet and social networking websites, to engage young people in the democratic process.

14

POLITICAL EXECUTIVE

Public policy making is the most significant activity of the government as it touches almost every facet of the life of the citizens and the nation as a whole. Policy making is one of the major functions of the political executive. Broadly speaking, the structure of the public policy making involves the entire political system. The ultimate authority in policy making, planning and budgeting rests with those who hold the power to legitimise policy. Legally, this power may be in the hands of a single individual (a king or a dictator), in the hands of a group of persons (a political party or military) or in the hands of the entire citizenry of a country. Policy making is not one person's or one political group's job, the actual formulation of policies is shared by political leaders of different political parties, pressure and interest groups, policy making units and the people as a whole.

The U.N. publication on Development Administration (1975) says, "In view of the magnitude and complexity of various policy questions today, a king or party alone cannot make public policies and must, therefore, establish some central units to assist in policy making. Similarly, the citizenry, who usually exercise their power to legitimise policy through persons elected by them, directly or indirectly, normally require some central units to initiate, examine and formulate policy proposals. Sometimes such units may even take policy decisions explicitly or implicitly in the name of those with the power t o give policies legal authority. Such central units for policy making are mostly located in the executive branch of the government".

In a parliamentary democracy like India, the leadership o f the government is in the hands of the Prime Minister, who is the real executive, the nominal executive being the President.

Through the party system and the authority of patronage which the Prime Minister enjoys, the Prime Minister has usurped the authority of the Parliament, The ever increasing authority or influence of the Prime Minister has changed the Cabinet government into 'Prime Ministerial government'. Before we examine the role o f the executive, let us first understand the meaning of the term 'Executive'. J.W. Garner observes. "In a broad and collective sense, the executive organ embraces the aggregate or totality of all the iunctionaries and agencies which are concerned with the execution of the will of the state as that will has been formulated and expressed in terms of law". In India, it comprises the Prime Minister leaders of the different parties, the ministers of the ruling party and the opposition, the Cabinet, its committees, Cabinet Secretariat and the Prime Minister's Secretariat. Before dealing with their role separately, it would be of relevance to discuss briefly, the broad functions of the executive which are as follows:

- Maintenance of internal peace and order is the major function of the executive but maintaining external relations and saving the country from external aggression is also a n equally important responsibility. In other words, the formulation of the national policy for domestic, as well as, external purposes is the chief concern of the executive. It includes all activities pertaining t o the maintenance and well-being of the State.
- As already mentioned, the initiative for legislative work has also become the responsibility of the executive. The bills are first approved by the Cabinet, and the government does not face any difficulty in getting the approval of the Parliament where, generally, it enjoys a majority. In the present context, though we have a minority government yet its proposals are accepted, with or without modification, by the Parliament as holding elections at short intervals imposes financial and political pressures on the system.
- The executive proposes the budget and decides about the imposition or abolition of taxes. It may increase or decrease the tax rates. The executive also sees that provisions of the budget are implemented after the approval of the Parliament. It is,

therefore, clear that the executive has all pervasive authority over the activities of the State. Now, we shall briefly discuss the role of the political executive in policy making by highlighting the role of the Cabinet, Cabinet Secretanat, Cabinet Committees, Prime Minister and Prime Minister's Secretariat.

THE ROLE OF CABINET IN POLICY MAKING

The Cabinet plays a very important role in policy making a s would be clear from the following :

- It defines the direction which the national policy shall take and decides how each problem a t home o r abroad is to be tackled.
- The Cabinet is responsible for all types of legislation. It gets the proposals prepared from various departments and only after its approval, these are submitted to the Parliament.
- The Cabinet is held responsible for every detail of the administrative work carried on by the ever-growing administrative machinery.
- It is also responsible for the finances o f the State.
- It is the Cabinet which decides as to what business is to be submitted to the Parliament and how much time be allotted for the same.
- Higher appointments at home and abroad are also made by the Cabinet through its Committee on Appointments.

Thus, it is clear that the Cabinet initiates and decides public policy concerning almost every sphere of government's activity. Without its approval no policy proposal can become effective. While examining the role of the Cabinet, S.R. Maheshwari opines, "Policies acquire final approval at various levels of governance depending on their import and nature. Certain proposals are required to be brought before the Cabinet for its decision, and the Cabinet may take them up either directly or may refer them to one or its sub-committees for a more detailed examination.

The Cabinet, functioning on the principle of collective responsibility, is the top policy making body in the government, but only major proposals are taken to it for its decision, other matters get disposed of by the minister at his/her own level. Even otherwise, it functions more as a referral body than an original one, more as a policy satisfactory organ than a policy formulating one. But occasionally, in its meetings some new policy items may get thrown up. Much more systematically powerful as policy making machanisms are its subcommittees, particularly the Political Affairs Committee and the Economic Affairs Committee, both presided over by the Prime Minister and consisting of the key ministers". Role of the Prime Minister's.

The Prime Minister always enjoys a special position in the realm of policy making and other ministers play varying levels of subordinate role. It is said that the crucial policy decisions are taken not in the Cabinet but in the inter-departmental committees, in Cabinet Committees or in conversation between the Prime Minister and the individual minister. Hence, the Prime Minister is the crucial element in the decision-making process. However, it is also pointed out that the Prime Minister's influence on the policy making may be exaggerated, as the spheres of state activity have increased enormously, that no one person is able to survey the whole field. The policy initiatives come from many sources, not just from the Prime Minister but also from the party policy, from the civil servants, from administrative necessity, from sheer pressure of events at home and abroad, and from the demands of public opinion channelled in various ways. Prof: Maheshwari further says that the Prime Minister is not often involved in the germinating stage of a policy. However. The shape that any policy would take does depend on the personality of the Prime Minister.

The Prime Minister along with his/her council of ministers, as we have already mentioned acts as the real executive in the parliamentary system. The council is a very large body, its membership crossing the 60 mark invariably, consisting of Deputy Ministers, Ministers of State and Cabinet Ministers. All its members meet officially very rarely. The effective policy making body is the Cabinet which consists of only the Cabinet Ministers and the Prime Minister-a Minister of the State is invited its meetings when hid her subject matter is to be discussed. It acts as a collective body where the ministers take integrated decisions reflecting the national perspective. For facilitating the work of the cabinet, it makes use of the committee system. According to the Rules of Business, standing committees of the Cabinet can be provided for specific aspects of governmental business. The committees are set up to ensure speedy decisions on vital questions of political and economic significance and other urgent matters. These also help in bringing about effective coordination in well-defined fields of administration. The number and functions for which the cabinet committees are appointed vary from time to time. Sometimes ad hoc committees are set up for dealing with matters of temporary nature but requiring urgent attention of the Government.

The most important of the cabinet committees is the Political Affairs Committee. Some other committees are on Appointments, Economic Planning and Coordination, Parliamentary Affairs, etc. For effective performance, the Cabinet is assisted by the Department of Cabinet Affairs headed by the Cabinet Secretary.

Cabinet Secretariat and Prime Minister's Secretariat : Their Role in Policy Making: The office of the Cabinet Secretary and its functions have evolved over the years. As head of the civil service he presides over the committees of secretaries. These committees examine inter-ministry matters and other issues that concern the government as a whole. As a rule, the Cabinet Secretariat does not prepare papers for the Cabinet or its committees, these functions are performed by the concerned ministries. However, the Cabinet Secretary only oversees the agenda papers. It is only on rare occasions that the Cabinet Secretary prepares a paper for the Cabinet.

He, however, attends all the meetings of the Cabinet and its committees. He is also responsible for preparing the agenda, priority of items and allocation of subjects to cabinet committees on the direction of the Prime Minister. He also prepares minutes of the cabinet meetings and committees t o the concerned ministries. Ishwar Dayal and others opine that "there is no system of briefing the Prime Minister on the agenda items although the Cabinet Secretary may assist him during the meetings.

The process of decision-making in the Cabinet, is a long and complex process and strong differences among the members are often assigned to a committee, or to the Cabinet Secretary to 'inquire and report'. He, therefore plays a very significant role in the policy apparatus but, essentially, in a servicing sense, except in personnel matters where he, as the head of the civil service, has a much greater influence. However, the significance of his position depends upon the style of functioning of the Prime Minister and the amount of confidence he reposes in the Cabinet Secretary, All the same, the Cabinet Secretariat has established itself, over the years, as a significant institution in the policy making process.

The institutional framework for policy making has changed sufficiently since 1965, when Shri Lal Bahadur Shastri, the then Prime Minister, created an independent institution known as the Prime Minister's Secretariat. Over the years, this office has grown in size and importance. The advisors and officials in this secretariat perform a variety of functions. In the words of Ishwar Dayal and others, "They advise the Prime Minister on the matters of importance and follow-up issues as necessary. They must collect all relevant information from varied sources and properly scrutinise it, and while doing so anticipate what is likely to be considered important by him. The secretarial personnel keep tabs on interministerial matters, and have access to data from different sources, and, due to their own study or contacts, they tend to provide information links. In developing integrated policy perspectives. In official matters they work closely with the Cabinet Secretary. By virtue of their positions, the secretariat personnel become an important link between the Prime Minister and others".

It is quite evident that the secretariat staff performs significant Ructions and deals with many delicate and crucial matters which require the attention of the Prime Minister. Another important aspect of this Fine in the words of Pai Panandikar is that "the advice given by him (PM's secretary) is not recorded in the files of the Government. The Prime Minister's secretary's advice is purely for the benefit of the Prime Minister and since it is not recorded in the files, the secretariat truly becomes a kind of Super Ministry".

It is understood that the creation of this office has, to some major extent, circumvented the role of the Cabinet Secretariat in public policy making, and has substantially increased the role of the Prime Minister: Pai Panandikar has observed, "The creation of the Prime Minister's Secretariat has perhaps been the single most important institutional change in the structure of the policy making apparatus in post-independent India. It signifies in many essential terms the changing policy processes in India and the role of the Prime Minister in the cabinet-system". Now, we will familiarize ourselves with the process of policy making. The process of policy making follows a systematic pattern, a well laid down method which is very essential for policy formulation. Policies are not one minute decisions. They are made after thorough discussion and analysis of issues and problems requiring attention.

The policy issues can be brought to the notice of the Government by one or more members of the ruling party, these may come from the different streams of the opposition parties. Various interest groups may throw a number of issues t o the Government. These map also be initiated by the executive. These may even come as recommendations from the civil service, due t o administrative necessity or due to certain sudden developments in the socio-economic system. Public opinion channelised through various sources including the news papers, radio, T.V., etc., also lays stress on certain issues of public importance. These issues may ultimately become policy issues.

The Policy Issues and the Public Opinion: The importance of the public opinion in a democratic society can hardly be underestimated. In fact, the health and vigour of public opinion determines the soundness of the Government. It is, therefore necessary to understand what is meant by public opinion. In simple words, public opinion means the concern of the public regarding certain problems that they might be facing. It may be defined as preference for a course of action expressed by that proportion of the population which is concerned and involved with a particular issue.

Public opinion can influence tile course of the governmental actions including policy formulation. It has also been found that the public opinion is not a unified whole but an aggregate of naive, generally diverse, individual opinions. There is not any agreed view on the amount of influence that public opinion can exercise in getting a problem identified as ; policy issue. Edmund Burke was of the view that the elected representatives in a democratic system are supposed to care for the interests of their electorate but this dims not mean that they should necessarily act in accordance with the wishes of the people so far as policy making is concerned.

Moreover, it is difficult to decide who influences who, whether the public opinion exercises its influence over policy makers or the policy makers mould public opinion to suit their interests. We have scan in India and elsewhere, that the Government always attempts to mould public opinion for preparing a strong support base for all its actions. We have also seen that in case of resonation for 'other backward classes' in India, it was public opinion which compelled tile government to adopt the economic criteria as a basis of reservation.

There is, no doubt that the public opinion does influence the policy makers but, the intensity of its influence is not known. One does not come across qualitative and substantial material to this effect. However, the role of public opinion has always been limited and in today's context, it is much more true because in this materialistic age the common person is busy earning the daily bread and does not have the time, money level of awareness, or the required interest for understanding the issues and voicing an opinion. This is largely true about a vast majority of Indians.

Moreover, how the public opinion can be effective when we forget all the wrongs committed by the Government soon after their occurrence? It is very rarely that one finds consistent) in the thinking of the masses over a given issue. Rather, public opinion is, generally, inconsistent and unstable. Then, should we stop airing our views o r feelings? The answer is no, because a voice unheard by the authorities is much better than a complete mum over an issue. We need to organise the people and make the media more effective for helping the common citizens by informing them about the issues of public concern and seeking their involvement on the issues. The literacy drive will go a long way in solving this problem. The agenda is a list of items for carrying out discussions and arriving at decisions. It Role of Political Executive is important t o know how some items make to the agenda and why others cannot.

We already know that in a Welfare State, the expectations of the people are always on the increase and the pressures on the government are enormous. We also find that citizens face, both individually and collectively, a number of problems, major as well as, minor. The Government machinery selects only a few of such problems or issues causing tension or anxiety among the masses. The demands and issues preferred by the government make the policy agenda. Such an agenda is always brief in relation to policy demands and one can easily make a distinction between the two. Demands or problems are the ones which people want to achieve or get rid of whereas the agenda is the one which the government decides for making policies.

Sometimes the policy agenda is considered as synonymous to the priorities of the party in power. It is felt that the party in power shall put only such items in the agenda as will help it in translating its ideology/manifesto and other promises made vital electorate during the elections. Once the Government has identified the problems/issues, it starts finding and analysing the alternative solutions. As already mentioned, most other issues/problems which are taken on the agenda come from organised apparatus like political parties, interest groups, social orgaaisations, civil services, the leader of the party in power, etc. Sometimes influential individuals are also successful in convincing the government for including a given issue on the agenda. However, the common masses do not get any worthwhile opportunity of even raising the issues.

It is, equally, important to understand the non-inclusion of certain issues in the policy agenda. Usually, the policy makers are compelled by influential individuals or interests not to include an issue in the agenda or not to take a decision on the same if its inclusion is of utmost necessity for the party in power. It is known as 'non-decision'. It happens when an issue is, likely to hamper the interests of the elite if translated into a policy. For the elite it is significant to see that the issue is torpedoed to the best of its liking at the time when the issue raises its head. The political parties, normally, allow a situation of non-decision uh such issues as they get support from the elite in the form of money and manpower at the time of elections, and a decision on the issue may become detrimental to the party in power and its allied interests. Sometimes, the political system, itself, is not interested in solving all the problems just in one go. It tries to benefit by solving some of the issues and prefers to wait for greater rewards by taking a delayed decision in the case of other issues.

It may be noted that the government machinery frames the policy agenda keeping in view the welfare programmes, certain compelling situations, interests of the party in power, and some major demands supported by the mass of the people. The machinery for policy making, usually, takes up only those issues which help the Government in maintaining itself. The mass media play an important role in mobilising mass opinion in favour o r against a given issue.

The problems and issues which, ultimately, find place in the policy agenda are known as policy proposals. However, all these proposals, may, not find the shape of a policy as the political executive still enjoys the choice of accepting or rejecting a particular proposal though, it might have included the same in the agenda under severe pressure. Therefore, it cannot be categorically stated that every policy proposal is going to be converted into a public policy. Converting a policy proposa l into a policy needs a decision by the institution established under the law. The institution (say Cabinet or its committees) has a number of individuals, who at times, may have different or conflicting viewpoints on a given issue. However, even in such a situation where there is a plurality of decision-makers having conflicting parameters, certain decisions are taken as the leader may adopt a style that may clinch the issue for him. The styles which are used in such cases are-bargaining, competition, command, conflict and cooperation. These are also called techniques of converting policy proposals into policies. Let us discuss them briefly.

Bargaining: The policy decision, usually, are the result of active interactions among several individuals and organisations. Objectives and preferences of all these persons are diverse though there may be some commonalities between some of them. The similarity of interests can be brought about in the majority of those involved in the policy making process. Hence, a forum is established where the majority view prevails. *i.e.* a process of give and take operates to an extent that an agreed alternative be conies acceptable to most of the persons. Since the majority has agreed, the minority also gives in, though in the process it might get some other major or minor benefits or promises. The Prime Minister in India, while formulating his/her Coronial of Ministers adopts bargaining as a technique for reaching an acceptable decision. This technique is very common in modern times be it political decision-making or administrative policy making.

Competition: The existence of very strong values and preferences among various individuals and groups lead to situation where more than one party starts competing for a policy decision that will protect their interests the most. This is known as competition, a technique of reaching decisions in policy making. The various political parties try to use their strength for getting the best possible gains. However, in real competition, strength is, generally, equal and, as such, the gains or losses do not vary significantly. In the developing countries, such a stage of competition comes very rarely, as one or a combination of parties enjoy political power for a longer period of time.

Command: It is a technique which refers to the assertive use of the Constitutional/legal and extra-Constitutional authority by the leader. In a controversial or complicated situation the leader issues a command and a decision is, accordingly, reached. This technique is largely used in the authoritarian political systems where the word of the supreme leader is taken a s final and his dictates are reflected in the decisions. It is also used in democracies like U.S.A. and India. The leader of the party in power issues commands, which become quite handy in resolving problems.

In India, we have seen that the order of the central leadership of the party has resulted in the change of Chief Ministers, though it is the prerogative of the concerned legislative party. The concept of 'Issuing Whips' is based on the discussions and consensus reached in the party meetings. However, it has also been used by the leader as a command without going into proper discussions at the relevant party forums. The command establishes a hierarchy which is bound by chain of command. It is the system of establishing superior-subordinate relationship.

Those subordinates who comply with the command are, suitably, rewarded in due course of time and those who oppose or are passive to the command are deprived of some major benefits.

Conflict: It is also a mealis of reaching decisions at the organisational level. A conflict situation is one when the parties concerned are adamant on protecting the interests of the organisation though the perception of interests varies from group to group. Clash of interests is quite visible but all the concerned are very much interested in finding an acceptable solution. Such a situation can be tackled through domination, compromise and integration, as suggested by Mary Parker Follett.

Cooperation: A policy decision is to serve the best interests of the people at large. Therefore, it must take into account the socio-economic environment and the cultural factors. It is due to these factors that it becomes very essential for the decision-makers to cooperate in reaching the ultimate decision. The demands are many and resources are limited. It is through cooperation and proper understanding that priorities are reached and policy decisions are taken accordingly. However, it is not easy to reach such an understanding. It requires all out coordinated efforts on the part of all concerned with the process of the policy making.

It may be mentioned that any one of the above techniques is just no! enough a combination of more than one is, generally, put into operation for recharge on agreed policy decisions. Besides, substantiating policy proposal? by the government become very essential. The government in a democratic system has to have legitimacy for its policies and programmes. In other words, the people, by and large, should not only be appreciative of the Governmental actions but should also extend distinct support for such actions. Such a situation can be attained by substantiating the policy proposals with all the relevant data. For example, if the Government intends to frame a policy with regard to the development of agriculture, it shall have to collect the data and information regarding total availability of the cultivable land, different types of cultivable land available, the crop that can give best yield in a given soil, availability of irrigational facilities, type of fertilisers to be used and their availability, marketing of the produce, and the basic requirements, both for the domestic and exports purposes, of the country. In order to make people aware of the policies, in order to make them understand and support policies, this exercise is a must.

15

POLITICAL EXECUTIVE AND BUREAUCRACY

The working of government rests on two pillars—political and permanent executive. The smooth working of this system depends on the harmonious relationship between the two. In recent years, however, the administrative and political environment has changed which has produced tensions in the mutual relationship of the two groups. So, let us first understand the meaning and role of bureaucracy and then analyse the relationship between the political executive and bureaucracy and finally identify the recommendations of Administrative Reforms Commission for streamlining the relationship between the minister and the civil servants and reflect upon the present scenario in India in this respect.

The term 'Bureaucracy' lacks a definition that is universally accepted. Bureaucracy is sometimes used in a disparaging manner to mean unimaginative, rigid and inefficient government administrators. It is associated with red-tapism, delay and wastefulness. Many social scientists however, describe bureaucracy in a neutral way to mean a specific form.

ADMINISTRATIVE SYSTEM IN INDIA

It is a machine, which is needed to run the government of the day. It is the only tool available to any modern government to administer. We no longer live in simple Greek city-states or tiny Indian republics. Society has become more complex today. Accordingly, the government has become a huge complicated machinery which can be serviced and run only by a distinct group of officials known as bureaucracy. Some scholars have even given bureaucracy the status of "the fourth organ of the government". Therefore, bureaucracy cannot be wished away. Max Weber, the German social scientist who was the first to make a systematic study of bureaucracy, described it as rational and the most efficient form of organisation. He described an ideal-type of bureaucracy as one characterised by:

1. Officials organised in fixed jurisdictional areas,
2. A hierarchical arrangement of offices (organised in a pyramid like structure with each lower office under the control of a higher one),
3. Written documents (files) that contain rules to be applied in every case,
4. Anonymity,
5. Impersonality in applying rules uniformly.
6. Political neutrality.

Bureaucracy with such formal characteristics is considered essential for running any large organisation. To quote Max Weber "the decisive reason for the advance of bureaucratic organisation has always been its purely technical superiority over any other form of organisation...precision, speed, unambiguity, reduction of friction and of material and personal costs – these are raised to the optimum level in the structurally bureaucratic administration".

Bureaucracy has become a universal phenomenon. It is a pre requisite of modernisation of every society. Most developing countries are engaged in the process of nation building and bringing about rapid socio-economic development, *i.e.*, providing social services such as health, education, infrastructure like roads, electricity, productive activities in agriculture, industry etc. The complex of such formidable activities connected with the development enterprise is essentially government's responsibility. Here, public administration becomes the key agency of development. Bureaucracy can immensely contribute to development by serving as an adviser, as an inventor, and a decision-maker. It can vitalize administration by building up a social environment emphasising responsibility by creating incentives, by encouraging healthy competition and self-development, by organising institutional management under competent and progressive leadership and by delegating authority to lower levels for maximising development.

Bureaucracy constitutes the apparatus and mechanism through which the state realises its purposes. It has been rightly said that a country's life is largely shaped by the quality of administration. A plan can succeed only if its administrative implications have been worked out in detail. Hence, a high degree of bureaucratic competence is essential to push through speedy development measures. In most developing countries, the problem is not the inability of the governments to devise rational programmes for development, but their incapacity to carry them out.

Politics/Administration Dichotomy

The conventional view of public administration is based upon the dichotomy of politics and administration *i.e.* administration and politics should be kept separate. Politics or policy making is the proper activity of the legislative bodies and administration is the proper activity of administrators who carry out policies. It is opposed to any political role of the civil servants.

It visualises the relationship between the administrator and the politician in terms of a neat division of labour – the politician formulates the policy and the administrator executes it. The bureaucrat acts as pure adviser to his political master, presents facts of the case, suggests lines of action and implications of alternative policies. It is the prerogative of the political master to decide the policy. The bureaucrat is expected to implement the policy faithfully, whatever the decision. He is to be anonymous and neutral in the discharge of his duty. He is expected to render impartial advice without fear or favour. The doctrine of neutrality and anonymity has been one of the fundamental tenets of the Weberian Administrative System in India.

It insulates the bureaucrat from any politicisation and makes him professional in his outlook. The planners in India too subscribed to the Weberian ideal of neutral civil service. In our country, the Civil Service Conduct Rules prohibit the government employees from active participation in political activities. Except for the limited right of voting in secret, a government employee cannot participate in any way in any political movement or activity including election campaigns. He cannot join a political party even as an inactive member or contribute financially to its funds; he cannot express any opinion on political issues;

and he cannot stand for election to any legislature. An impersonal, strictly rule-bound, neutral bureaucracy was expected not only to provide the necessary administrative objectivity but also enhance the democratic principle of equality and provide protection from arbitrary rule.

Decline of Neutrality Concept

The traditional concept of neutrality, however, has been challenged on many grounds. The earlier concept of separation of politics and administration in watertight compartments is considered no more valid. The role of the Civil Service has been changing from being a mere agent of the political executive to that of collabouration with it. The involvement of bureaucracy in political arena is now widely prevalent.

The breakdown of the theory of neutrality has come about because of a number of reasons. Firstly, the processes of policy making are no longer confined to the political executive. The truth is that the bureaucrats play an important role in policy formulation, perceived to be the exclusive preserve of elected politicians. This has happened because the statutes passed by the parliament are not clear enough. The legislative behaviour follows no consistent pattern. Whereas, some measures are too detailed, some only identify the problem. The minister is rarely an expert in the work of his department or the techniques of public administration. He merely has general ideas in line with the political ideology of his party, but he often is not sure what is the best solution to a particular problem. He is therefore, forced to rely on his permanent staff for facts and advice. In effect then, it is the administrator who has a major role in framing the policy.

Secondly, the decline of neutrality can be attributed to the demands and pressures of coalition politics. In coalition governments, ministers are busy in the power game and maneuvering for their survival, and have neither time nor inclination to guide, direct and control their department or bureaucracy. Also at times, the legislative process is so stormy and full of diverse views that a statute passed incorporates a number of a contradictory policy guidelines. The necessity of reaching a compromise solution to hold the coalition together leads the legislators to use vague language and the administrator has to use his own judgement to interpret the policy. Therefore, bureaucracy has clearly made inroads in policy making and despite the regulations governing the civil servants they have been politicised considerably.

Thirdly, according to some political commentators, the classical theory of civil service neutrality presupposes agreement on principles fundamental to democracy. In other words, neutral, value-free bureaucracy is possible only in a society where consensus exists on values; but in transitional societies like India, where dissent and conflict exist, it is too much to expect anyone to be neutral.

For a developing country like India where speedy socio-economic development has to be steadily pushed through, the nature and character of bureaucracy assume special significance. The involvement of civil servants in numerous decisions be it the location of a steel plant or a school building in a village, makes them partners in development along with the politicians. Their value preferences get inextricably mixed up with technical advice.

In the context of large-scale welfare programmes therefore, neutrality is not possible. In fact a certain commitment to the goals and objectives of the state on the part of bureaucracy is inescapable. Neutrality cannot be allowed to degenerate into disinterestedness. The successful carrying out of developmental tasks requires on the part of administrators not only qualities of initiative and leadership but also a sense of emotional integration with the policies and programmes and identification with the interests of the common man. The idea of bureaucracy as a neutral instrument in the conduct of public affairs thus stands refuted.

Committed Bureaucracy

Weber's model of bureaucracy was found inappropriate to effect the social transformation in many developing countries. In India, it received a good amount of criticism for its failure to meet the growing demands of social legislation. After two decades of independence, Mrs. Indira Gandhi, the then Prime Minister, advocated the concept of committed bureaucracy. Not only did she express her dissatisfaction with the performance of bureaucracy, she expressed doubt about the relevance of the basic assumptions underlying the Indian bureaucracy that of neutrality, impartiality, anonymity etc. and she alleged that the bureaucrats lacked commitment. She disgustingly referred to the administrative machinery as 'the stumbling block in the country's progress' and reiterated the necessity of creating an administrative cadre committed to national objectives and responsive to Indian social needs. She found in 'committed bureaucracy' the answer to the ills of neutrality that crippled the development process in India. She had an earnest belief that only a committed bureaucracy can bring about the desired change.

The concept of 'committed bureaucracy' was much contested in the political and administrative circles. It was alleged that it would permanently damage the fabric of the services. It would create a breed of pliable civil servants who would always say "Yes Minister" and would be ready to crawl when asked to bend by their political masters. It was also alleged that in the name of commitment the ruling party was seeking bureaucracy's alignment with the party's ideology in order to perpetuate its rule. However, it was later clarified by the government that commitment did not mean attachment to the ideology of the party in power, but a commitment to the development of the country and personal involvement of bureaucracy in the tasks as opposed to ostrich like withdrawal and isolation from politics.

Thus, if committed bureaucracy stands for a non-partisan, socially sensitive civil service, which can empathize with the politician who is genuinely, interested in progress and development of the country, then a committed civil service is more appropriate for a developing nation than having an insensitive neutral one.

Sources of Stress

In practice however commitment has assumed the perverted form of politicisation and sycophancy. Commitment to social objectives is one thing and dancing to the tune of a political party is another. Very often it is seen that bureaucracy simply acts according to the dictates of the political executive without any independent examination of issues. This trend can be attributed to the ever-growing political interference in the affairs of administration. Political interference and impartial administration cannot co-exist. While the administrators do not perceive their role in policy making as subservient to the political leaders because of their knowledge and expertise, yet they have to conform to the prerequisites of representative politics.

The political leaders claim to be the true representatives of the people and know what is good for them and because of their superior position succeed in dictating the terms to the bureaucrats. The bureaucrats who are not obliging enough soon find themselves in trouble. The political masters have many means of coercion – both overt and covert. Political interference in all matters including those where the statutory power is vested in the civil servants is a constant phenomenon. There are numerous instances of use of transfer, promotion, supercession and compulsory retirement from service by elected politicians as tools to silence the voice of dissent and expression of difference of opinion.

Well, politicisation works the other way round also. Many administrators use political influence or forge alliance with the politician to brighten their own career prospects. They take advantage of the amateur politician; exploit his weakness particularly in times of a fluid political situation and turn out to be autonomous and irresponsible. This is an equally grim scenario. What emerges out of the analysis is that whether there is collision or collusion between the political executive and the bureaucracy, in both cases it leads to organisational imbalance and ultimately the governance suffers.

Expressing concern over the deteriorating administrative standards, the government appointed the Administrative Reforms Commission (ARC) in 1966 to conduct a comprehensive study of the administrative system and suggest remedies. The two most important areas touched upon by the ARC in its reports were:

(a) Minister— Civil Servants relationship, wherein the ARC emphasised the need for the de-politicisation of the services, and

(b) The creation of a climate and culture of administration that would help assert the growth of unhealthy personal relationship between Civil Servants and Minister.

The ARC took cognizance of the fact that proper relationship between the political executive and bureaucracy is a matter of highest importance to the administrative performance of government. It observed that the existing pattern of relationship was different from what was envisaged. More and more cases of deviation were coming to notice. For instance the extent of bureaucratic involvement in politics was exceptionally high, there was frequent use of transfers and postings to manipulate bureaucracy, there was unholy nexus between politicians and bureaucracy etc. which was taking its toll on administrative efficiency. Therefore, corrective measures were required to restore the health of the system. The ARC stressed the urgency to prevent bureaucracy's aggressive role in politics and also a need to check arbitrary interference of politicians in administrative affairs. It believed that both Minister and Civil Servants must appreciate rather than belittle each other's work and attempt maximum accommodation of one another's views. On the part of the political executive there should be, in the words of the ARC,

(a) A proper understanding of the administrative functions and recognition of its professional nature.

(b) As little interference as possible in service matters, *e.g.* postings, transfers, promotions etc.

(c) No requests for departures from declared and approved policies to suit individual cases.

Similarly, on the part of the civil service it asserts:

(a) There must be a sincere and honest attempt to find out what the political head wants and make the necessary adjustment in policies and procedures to suit his wishes.

(b) Readiness to fall in line with his political chief in all matters, unless strong grounds indicate a different course. In other words, it means an emotional and mental acceptance by the bureaucracy of the ideology of the government policy to be executed by it.

Recent Developments

Inspite of the valuable recommendations made by the ARC to streamline the relationship between the minister and the civil servants, nothing much seems to have changed because of political and administrative apathy. Making the matters worse is the growth in recent times of a nexus between the politicians, criminals, police and the civil servants rooted in the considerations of "mutuality of benefit". An increasing use of money and muscle power by political parties in winning elections is common knowledge. Since the muscle power is mostly provided by the mafia and the criminals, a close nexus has come to prevail between the politicians and the criminals resulting in "criminalisation of politics". This has been the main conclusion of the Vohra Committee Report of 1993 submitted by the then Home Secretary, Mr. N.N. Vohra which was set up to look into the criminalisation of politics. The report observed that the mafia and the criminals enjoyed the patronage of politicians and the protection of government functionaries. It pointed out how the nexus was virtually running a parallel government, pushing the state apparatus into irrelevance. Here the two elites – political and administrative, join hands and become not only thick friends but also grand thieves. Such a nexus is detrimental to public interest.

Therefore, it was felt that corrective steps must be taken to ensure that this evil nexus is curbed. With this objective in mind, the Prime Minister inaugurated a Conference of Chief Secretaries in November 1996 on 'An Agenda for an Effective and Responsive Administration. The Conference emphasised the need for bringing about transformation in public services so as to make them more effective, clean, accountable and citizen friendly. The Conference also highlighted the necessity of adopting the code of ethics for public services which not only regulates the role of the civil servants but also specifies the relationship between the employees in public services and politicians, so that the basic commitment of the civil servants towards the welfare of the public and the principles enshrined in the Constitution is reiterated. We only hope that the implementation of the proposed Action Plan will be effective.

To conclude, a developing nation cannot afford contradictory ethos between the political executive and bureaucracy because it strikes at the root of a progressive administrative culture. The roles of political and administrative elite are complimentary and in the interest of public welfare they must work in harmony with each other. Political executive and bureaucracy are the two pillars of the government. Whereas political executive is temporary and usually represent the party in power, bureaucracy is a permanent fixture. Theoretically they play different roles, for instance, politicians make policies and administrators implement them. But, in practice their roles often conflict and overlap because the line separating development of policy and its implementation is quite blurred and hazy. Bureaucracy is a body of permanent, paid and skilled officials. It aids and advises the government to make plans and carry them out. The role of bureaucracy has changed.

It no longer performs only the regulatory functions but actively engages in development and welfare activities. Conventional image of civil servant has been that of an anonymous servant of the minister who is committed to efficient discharge of his duties and who offers his sincere advice to his master, irrespective of his political ideology. This advice may or may not be accepted by the minister, but once the decision is made, he is duty bound to implement it effectively.

This concept of anonymous and neutral bureaucracy was considered impractical and unsuited to meet the goals of social justice. Therefore, Mrs. Gandhi sought a 'Committed Bureaucracy'. But commitment has degenerated into politicisation of bureaucracy and the relationship between political executive and bureaucracy has deteriorated. The administrators blame the politicians for their irrational, partisan and idealistic approach and for disturbing their service conditions through transfers and promotions. The politicians blame the administrators for their prejudice and flair for creating procedural difficulties. Such irritants have led to deterioration of administrative efficiency. The Administrative Reforms Commission was set up in 1966 to suggest measures to streamline their relationship. The reiationship between the two elite is crucial to the smooth functioning of the government.

16

International Norm Dynamics and Political Change

Normative and ideational concerns have always informed the study of international politics and are a consistent thread running through the life of *International Organisation*. When *IO* was founded, dominant realist views of politics, while rejecting idealism, were very much concerned with issues of legitimacy and ideology. The early Cold War, after all, was not simply a positional convict among anonymous great powers: it was a war for "hearts and minds." The coupling of power with "legitimate social purpose" was central to American foreign policy of this period.

At the same time, international relations scholars were busy studying two of the greatest social construction projects of the age: European integration and decolonisation. Neofunctionalists, like the realists, were consciously trying to distance themselves from "idealist" predecessors (in this case, David Mitrany and his colleagues), but the complex web of technical tasks that they designed aimed at more than promoting material well-being; they aimed ultimately at ideational and social ends. Spillover was supposed to do more than create additional technical tasks; it was supposed to change attitudes, identity, and affect among participants. Likewise, scholars recognised that decolonisation was driven by a profoundly normative agenda and that it explicitly sought to reconstitute the identities of both the new states and their former colonisers, as well as the relationships between them.

Attempts in the 1960s and 1970s to build a science of politics modeled on economics or natural science never displaced these normative and ideational concerns completely. They have surfaced consistently in the stream of critiques of the dominant state-centric paradigms that focused on material power. Scholars of transnational relations in the 1970s called attention to transnational actors who were sometimes in fenced by norms and ideas. The regimes scholarship of the early 1980s similarly emphasised the role of principles and norms in ways that opened the door for a more sweeping "ideational turn" in the late 1980s.

Elsewhere in this issue John Ruggie, James March, and Johan Olsen explore the intellectual history of this recent "turn" and locate its proponents in the more abstract theoretical debates of social science. Building on their contributions, we address theoretical issues facing those of us interested in empirical research on social construction processes and norm in fences in international politics. We are concerned with such questions as How do we know a norm when we see one? How do we know norms make a difference in politics?

Where do norms come from? How do they change? We are particularly interested in the role norms play in political change—both the ways in which norms, themselves, change and the ways in which they change other features of the political landscape. Like other theoretical frameworks in international relations (IR), much of the macro theoretical equipment of constructivism is better at explaining stability than change. Claims that actors conform to "logics of appropriateness" say little about how standards of appropriateness might change.

Such static approaches to IR are particularly unsatisfying during the current era of global transformation when questions about change motivate much of the empirical research we do. Lacking good macrotheoretic guidance, our approach to these questions relies heavily on induction from the extensive and growing body of norms research that has sprung up, not just in political science, but in law, economics, sociology, and psychology. This variety of conceptual and empirical material is useful for our inductive enterprise, but it also raises some important questions for macrotheory that we explore later.

We use our review of scholarship on norms and related ideational phenomena in this discussion to make three arguments. First, the ideational "turn" of recent years is actually a return to some traditional concerns of the discipline, but it has not brought us back to precisely the same place we began. Standards for good empirical research have changed dramatically (and for the better) since the founding of IO, and applying these standards to long-standing normative issues has had real payoffs. Second, we generate some propositions about three aspects of norms—their origins, the mechanisms by which they exercise influence, and the conditions under which norms will be influential in world politics. Specially, we argue that norms evolve in a patterned "life cycle" and that different behavioral logics dominate different segments of the life cycle. Third, we argue that the current tendency to oppose norms against rationality or rational choice is not helpful in explaining many of the most politically salient processes we see in empirical research—processes we call "strategic social construction," in which actors strategize rationally to reconfigure preferences, identities, or social context.

Rationality cannot be separated from any politically significant episode of normative influence or normative change, just as the normative context conditions any episode of rational choice. Norms and rationality are thus intimately connected, but scholars disagree about the precise nature of their relationship. We identify four focal points of debate where the relationship between norms and rationality is least understood and most important, and we show how these debates cross-cut research traditions in potentially fruitful ways.

The Return to Norms

Norms and normative issues have been central to the study of politics for at least two millennia. Students of politics have struggled with questions not only about the meaning of justice and the good society but also about the influence on human behavior of ideas about justice and good. Our conclusions (or our assumptions) about these issues condition every form of political analysis. Aristotle and Plato understood this in the fourth century B.C.E. just as E. H. Carr did in the twentieth century. Carr has become canonised in the discipline as a debunker of Wilsonian idealism, but this simplification misrepresents his message: "Political action must be based on a coordination of morality and power." Realism fails, in Carr's analysis, precisely because it excludes essential features of politics like emotional appeal to a political goal and grounds for moral judgment. This conviction that understanding social purpose and legitimacy was essential to understanding politics continued through the 1950s and 1960s and is evident in the pages of *IO*. In Claude's work on the legitimation function of the United Nations deals precisely with this issue.

Early IR scholarship on certain issues—decolonisation, human rights, education—recognised that much UN activity involved establishing norms, but it often failed to theorize these normative processes. Certainly the work of the integration theorists such as Ernst Haas was implicitly, and often explicitly, about creating shared social purpose. Even realists like Hans Morgenthau wrote extensively about the way in which ideational and normative factors such as nationalism, morality, and international law limit states' exercise of power.

The "turn" away from norms and normative concerns began with the behavioral revolution and its enthusiasm for measurement. Normative and ideational phenomena were difficult to measure and so tended to be pushed aside for methodological reasons. This tendency was reinforced by the emerging infatuation of political scientists with economic methods in the late 1970s and 1980s. Realists began recasting the pursuit of power as "utilitymaximisation" and, following the economists, tended to specify utility functions in material terms only.

Liberals drew on microeconomic analyses of collective action games (Prisoners' Dilemma, Stag Hunt) to reinvigorate their long-standing debate with realists and show that cooperation, welfare improvement, and "progress" were possible even given some of realism's pessimistic assumptions about self-seeking human nature. In fact, these "neos," both realist and liberal, might more appropriately be called "econorealists" and "econoliberals," since what was new in both cases was an injection of microeconomic insights. Although the move to rational choice in no way required a move to a material ontology, its proponents showed little interest in ideational or social phenomena, and study of these issues languished during this period. However, when interest in these matters revived in the 1980s, rest with the regimes project and later with the constructivists led by John Ruggie, Friedrich Kratochwil, Alexander Wendt, and others, the discipline to which norms returned had changed in important ways. Although the behavioral revolution and the "economic turn" of the

1970s and 1980s may have neglected norms, they made important contributions by forcing scholars to think much more rigorously about issues of research design, theoretical clarity, disciplinary cumulation, and parsimony.

As contemporary researchers make their arguments about norms, culture, and ideas, they will need to specify ideational causal claims and mechanisms clearly, think seriously about the micro foundations on which theoretical claims about norms rest, and evaluate those claims in the context of carefully designed historical and empirical research. David Lumsdaine's analysis of the role of morality in international politics, for example, is very different from Carr's. Carr uses evidence anecdotally to illustrate his arguments about the moral character of "the ordinary man" and the political consequences of that morality. The result is a brilliant piece of political thought but one vulnerable to charges of wishful thinking, since Carr provides no systematic evidence that human beings actually *do* behave as his "ordinary man" does and not according to some other conception of human nature. Lumsdaine, by contrast, offers systematic evidence that morality actually does play a significant role in foreign aid by examining predictions from alternative explanations and compiling extensive evidence, both quantitative and qualitative, to arbitrate among explanations.

The same attention to alternative explanations, rigorous standards of evidence, and social theoretic micro foundations has characterised the article-length research on norms in *IO* on such issues as the end of apartheid in South Africa, the end of the Cold War, prohibitions against certain kinds of weapons, the end of slavery, and other prohibition regimes. In a wide variety of issue areas, norms researchers have made inroads precisely because they have been able to provide explanations substantiated by evidence for puzzles in international politics that other approaches had been unable to explain satisfactorily.

Norms are no easier to measure today than they were in the 1930s or 1960s, but conceptual precision is essential for both meaningful theoretical debate and defensible empirical work. In the remainder of this section we take up three issues where conceptual classification seems most pressing and most possible: definitions, the relationship between domestic and international norms, and whether norms are agents of stability or change.

DEFINITIONS

There is general agreement on the definition of a norm as a standard of appropriate behavior for actors with a given identity, but a number of related conceptual issues still cause confusion and debate. First, whereas constructivists in political science talk a language of norms, sociologists talk a language of "institutions" to refer to these same behavioral rules. Thus, elsewhere in this issue March and Olsen define "institution" as "a relatively stable collection of practices and rules defining appropriate behavior for specific groups of actors in specific situations." One difference between "norm" and "institution" (in the sociological sense) is aggregation: the norm definition isolates single standards of behavior, whereas institutions emphasize the way in which behavioral rules are structured together and interrelate (a "collection of practices and rules"). The danger in using the norm language is that it can obscure distinct and interrelated elements of social institutions if not used carefully.

For example, political scientists tend to slip into discussions of "sovereignty" or "slavery" as if they were norms, when in fact they are (or were) collections of norms and the mix of rules and practices that structure these institutions has varied significantly over time. Used carefully, however, norm language can help to steer scholars toward looking inside social institutions and considering the components of social institutions as well as the way these elements are renegotiated into new arrangements over time to create new patterns of politics.

Scholars across disciplines have recognised different types or categories of norms. The most common distinction is between regulative norms, which order and constrain behavior, and constitutive norms, which create new actors, interests, or categories of action. Some scholars have also discussed a category of norms called evaluative or prescriptive norms, but these have received much less attention and, indeed, are often explicitly omitted from analysis. This lack of attention is puzziing, since it is precisely the prescriptive (or evaluative) quality of "oughtness" that sets norms apart from other kinds of rules. Because norms involve standards of "appropriate" or "proper" behavior, both the inter subjective and the evaluative dimensions are inescapable when discussing norms. We only know what is appropriate by reference to the judgments of a community or a society. We recognize norm-breaking behavior because it generates disapproval or stigma and norm conforming behavior either because it produces praise, or, in the case of a highly internalised norm, because it is so taken for granted that it provokes no reaction whatsoever. Thus, James Fearon argues that social norms take the generic form "Good people do (or do not do) X in situations A, B, C . . ." because "we typically do not consider a rule of conduct to be a social norm unless a shared moral assessment is attached to its observance or non-observance."

One logical corollary to the prescriptive quality of norms is that, by definition, there are no bad norms from the vantage point of those who promote the norm. Norms most of us would consider "bad"—norms about racial superiority, divine right, imperialism—were once powerful because some groups believed in the appropriateness (that is, the "goodness") of the norm, and others either accepted it as obvious or inevitable or had no choice but to accept it. Slaveholders and many no slaveholders believed that slavery was appropriate behavior; without that belief, the institution of slavery would not have been possible.

Given this discussion, we can begin to answer the essential research question: how do we know a norm when we see one? We can only have indirect evidence of norms just as we can only have indirect evidence of most other motivations for political action (interests or threats, for example). However, because norms by definition embody a quality of "ought ness" and shared moral assessment, norms prompt justifications for action and leave an extensive trail of communication among actors that we can study. For example, the United States' explanations about why it feels compelled to continue using land mines in South Korea reveal that it recognises the emerging norm against the use of such mines. If not for the norm, there would be no need to mention, explain, or justify the use of mines in Korea at all. Note that we separate norm existence or strength from actual behavioral change in our operationalisation.

Because one central question of norms research is the effect of norms on state behavior, it is important to operationalize a norm in a way that is distinct from the state or non state behavior it is designed to explain. Norms as shared assessments raise the question of how many actors must share the assessment before we call it a norm. In part this is a question of empirical domain.

Norms may be regional, for example, but not global. Even within a community, norms are "continuous, rather than dichotomous, entities. . . . (They) come in varying strengths" with different norms commanding different levels of agreement. We argue that one way to understand the dynamics of this agreement process is by examining what we call the "life cycle" of norms. We show how agreement among a critical mass of actors on some emergent norm can create a tipping point after which agreement becomes widespread in many empirical cases, and we provide some suggestions about common features of "critical mass."

Connecting Domestic and International Norms

Here we are concerned with international or regional norms that set standards for the appropriate behavior of states. Domestic norms, however, are deeply entwined with the workings of international norms. Many international norms began as domestic norms and become international through the efforts of entrepreneurs of various kinds. Women's suffrage, for example, began as a demand for domestic change within a handful of countries and eventually became an international norm. In addition, international norms must always work their influence through the filter of domestic structures and domestic norms, which can produce important variations in compliance and interpretation of these norms.

Even in situations where it might appear at first glance that international norms simply trump domestic norms, what we often see is a process by which domestic "norm entrepreneurs" advocating a minority position use international norms to strengthen their position in domestic debates. In other words, there is a two-level norm game occurring in which the domestic and the international norm tables are increasingly linked. We argue later, however, that all these domestic influences are strongest at the early stage of a norm's life cycle, and domestic influences lessen significantly once a norm has become institutionalised in the international system.

Recent work in U.S. legal circles also suggests that there is more similarity in the way norms and law work domestically and internationally than IR scholars have thought. IR scholars have generally assumed that the existence of a coercive state able to enforce laws made domestic order very different from international order. A prominent group of legal scholars at the University of Chicago, however, now argue that, even within a domestic setting, making successful law and policy requires an understanding of the pervasive influence of social norms of behavior. This is a particularly compelling insight for IR scholars, since the international system is characterised by law and norms operating without direct punitive capacity. The processes through which these legal scholars claim that norms work domestically—involving norm entrepreneurs, imitation, "norm cascades," and "norm bandwagons"—are entirely consistent with the research done on norms by scholars in IR and suggest that IR norms research might also learn from domestic analogies. For example, the normative and legal process through which Southern gentlemen in the United States stopped dueling, examined by Lawrence Lessig, may be relevant for thinking about what kinds of norms and rules could lead to a decrease in conflict in the international system.

Stability Versus Change

Macro-level theorising has provided good explanations of the way norms produce social order and stability. Norms channel and regularize behavior; they often limit the range of choice and constrain actions. From a constructivist perspective, international structure is determined by the international distribution of ideas. Shared ideas, expectations, and beliefs about appropriate behavior are what give the world structure, order, and stability. The problem for constructivists thus becomes the same problem facing realists—explaining change. In an ideational international structure, idea shifts and norm shifts are the main vehicles for system transformation. Norm shifts are to the ideational theorist what changes in the balance of power are to the realist.

John Ruggie argues in this issue that "having identified the possibility of system transformation in the macro level, corresponding micro practices that may have transformative effects must be identified and inventoried." The following section is an attempt to identify these practices.

Evolution and Influence of Norms

In this section we advance some propositions about (1) the origins or emergence of international norms, (2) the processes through which norms influence state and non state behavior, and (3) which norms will matter and under what conditions. We illustrate the arguments with material drawn from two major issue areas: women's rights, especially suffrage, and laws of war. International norms about women's rights often came into direct competition with strongly held domestic norms, and, typically, there was no self-evident state "interest" in the promotion of such norms. Although topics related to gender and women have been absent from the pages of *International Organisation*, the suffrage campaign led to the formal political participation of half of the world's population and therefore seems worthy of study. Laws of war allow us to discuss the impact of norms where we might least expect it—the traditional security field, where such norms limit state discretion in an area perceived as essential to national sovereignty and security.

The Norm Life Cycle

Norm influence may be understood as a three-stage process. The first stage is "norm emergence"; the second stage involves broad norm acceptance, which we term, following Cass Sun stein, a "norm cascade"; and the third stage involves internalisation. The first two stages are divided by a threshold or "tipping" point, at which a critical mass of relevant state actors adopt the norm. This pattern of norm influence has been found independently in work on social norms in U.S. legal theory, quantitative research by sociology's institutionalists or "world polity" theorists, and various scholars of norms in IR. The pattern is important for researchers to understand because different social processes and logics of action may be involved at different stages in a norm's "life cycle." Thus, theoretical debates about the degree to which norm-based behavior is driven by choice or habit, specification issues about the costs of norm-violation or benefits from norm adherence, and related research issues often turn out to hinge on the stage of the norm's evolution one examines. Change at each stage, we argue, is characterised by different actors, motives, and mechanisms of influence.

The characteristic mechanism of the first stage, norm emergence, is persuasion by norm entrepreneurs. Norm entrepreneurs attempt to convince a critical mass of states (norm leaders) to embrace new norms. The second stage is characterised more by a dynamic of imitation as the norm leaders attempt to socialize other states to become norm followers. The exact motivation for this second stage where the norm "cascades" through the rest of the population (in this case, of states) may vary, but we argue that a combination of pressure for conformity, desire to enhance international legitimation, and the desire of state leaders to enhance their self-esteem facilitate norm cascades. At the far end of the norm cascade, norm internalisation occurs; norms acquire a taken-for-granted quality and are no longer a matter of broad public debate.

For example, few people today discuss whether women should be allowed to vote, whether slavery is useful, or whether medical personnel should be granted immunity during war. Completion of the "life cycle" is not an inevitable process.

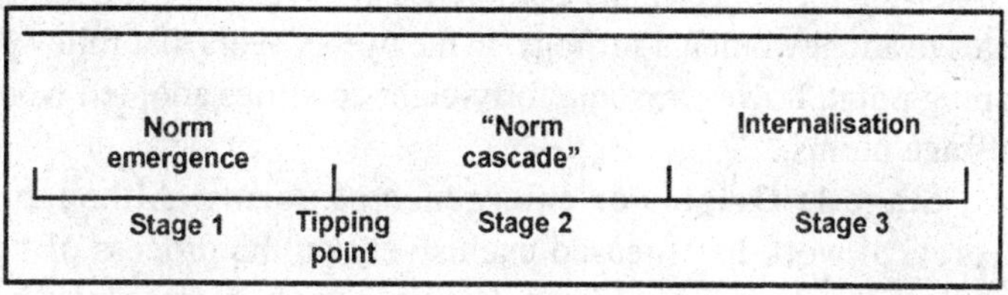

FIG. NORM LIFE CYCLE

Many emergent norms fail to reach a tipping point, and later we offer arguments about which norms are more likely to succeed. Internalised or cascading norms may eventually become the prevailing standard of appropriateness against which new norms emerge and compete for support. Research on women's suffrage globally provides support for the idea of the life cycle of norms and the notion of a "tipping point" or threshold of normative change. Although many domestic suffrage organisations were active in the nineteenth century it was not until 1904, when women's rights advocates founded the

International Women's Suffrage Association (IWSA), that an international campaign for suffrage was launched.

In fact, rather than a single international campaign for women's suffrage, there were three or four overlapping campaigns with different degrees of coordination. A quantitative analysis of the cross-national acquisition of suffrage rights reveals a different dynamic at work for early and late adopters of women's suffrage. Prior to a threshold point in 1930, no country had adopted women's suffrage without strong pressure from domestic suffrage organisations. Between 1890 and 1930, Western countries with strong national women's movements were most likely to grant female suffrage. Although some original norm entrepreneurs came from the United States and the United Kingdom, this was not a case of "hegemonic socialisation," since the first states to grant women the right to vote (New Zealand, Australia, Finland) were not hegemons, and the United States and the United Kingdom lagged ten to twenty years behind. After 1930, international and transnational influences become far more important than domestic pressures for norm adoption, and countries adopted women's suffrage even though they faced no domestic pressures to do so. For women's suffrage, the first stage of norm emergence lasted over eighty years: it took from the Seneca Falls Conference in 1848 until 1930 for twenty states to adopt women's suffrage. In the twenty years that followed the tipping point, however, some forty-eight countries adopted women's suffrage norms.

Stage 1: Origins or emergence of norms: Although little theoretical work has focused exclusively on the process of "norm building," the accounts of norm origins in most studies stress human agency, indeterminacy, chance occurrences, and favourable events, using process tracing or genealogy as a method. Generalising from these accounts, two elements seem common in the successful creation of most new norms: norm entrepreneurs and organisational platforms from which entrepreneurs act.

Norm entrepreneurs: Norms do not appear out of thin air; they are actively built by agents having strong notions about appropriate or desirable behavior in their community. Prevailing norms that medical personnel and those wounded in war be treated as neutrals and noncombatants are clearly traceable to the efforts of one man, a

Genevese Swiss banker named Henry Dunant. Dunant had a transformative personal experience at the battle of Solferino in 1859 and helped found an organisation to promote this cause (what became the International Committee of the Red Cross) through an international treaty (the first Geneva Convention).The international campaign for women's suffrage was similarly indebted to the initial leadership of such norm entrepreneurs as Elizabeth Cady Stanton and Susan B. Anthony in the United States and Millicent Garrett Fawcett and Emmeline Pankhurst in England. Both of these cases are consistent with the description Ethan Nadelmann gives of "transnational moral entrepreneurs" who engage in "moral proselytism."

Legal theorist Lessig uses the term "meaning managers" or "meaning architects" to describe the same kind of agency in the process of creating norms and larger contexts of social meaning. Norm entrepreneurs are critical for norm emergence because they call attention to issues or even "create" issues by using language that names, interprets, and dramatises them. Social movement theorists refer to this reinterpretation or renaming process as "framing." The construction of cognitive frames is an essential component of norm entrepreneurs' political strategies, since, when they are successful, the new frames resonate with broader public understandings and are adopted as new ways of talking about and understanding issues. In constructing their frames, norm entrepreneurs face firmly embedded alternative norms and frames that create alternative perceptions of both appropriateness and interest.

In the case of the Red Cross, Dunant and his colleagues had to persuade military commanders not to treat valuable medical personnel and resources they captured as spoils of war, to be treated as they saw fit. In the case of women's suffrage and later women's rights, norm entrepreneurs encountered alternative norms about women's interests and the appropriate role for women. In other words, new norms never enter a normative vacuum but instead emerge in a highly contested normative space where they must compete with other norms and perceptions of interest.

This normative contestation has important implications for our understandings of the ways in which a "logic of appropriateness" relates to norms. Efforts to promote a new norm take place within the standards of "appropriateness" defined by prior norms. To challenge existing logics of appropriateness, activists may need to be explicitly "inappropriate." Suffragettes chained themselves to fences, went on hunger strikes, broke windows of government buildings, and refused to pay taxes as ways of protesting their exclusion from political participation. Deliberately inappropriate acts (such as organised civil disobedience), especially those entailing social ostracism or legal punishment, can be powerful tools for norm entrepreneurs seeking to send a message and frame an issue. Thus, at this emergent stage of a norm's life cycle, invoking a logic of appropriateness to explain behavior is complicated by the fact that standards of appropriateness are precisely what is being contested.

	Stage 1 Norm emergence	**Stage 2 Norm cascade**	**Stage 3 Internalisation**
Actors	Norm entrepreneurs with organisatinal platforms	States, international organisations, network	Law, professions, bureaucracy
Motives	Altruism empathy, ideational, commitment	Legitimacy, reputation, esteem	Conformity
Dominant mechanism	Persuasion	Socialization, institutionalisation, demonstration	Habit, institutionalisation

Given the costs of inappropriate action and many of the persuasive tools they use, one has to wonder what could possibly motivate norm entrepreneurs. Obviously the answer varies with the norm and the entrepreneur, but for many of the social norms of interest to political scientists, it is very difficult to explain the motivations of norm entrepreneurs without reference to empathy, altruism, and ideational commitment. Empathy exists when actors have the capacity for participating in another's feelings or ideas. Such empathy may lead to empathetic interdependence, where actors "are interested in the welfare of others for its own sake, even if this has no effect on their own material well-being or security."

Altruism exists when actors actually take "action designed to benefit another even at the risk of significant harm to the actor's own well-being.' Kristen Monroe argues that the essence or "heart" of altruism is a "shared perception of common humanity. . . . a very simple but deeply felt recognition that we all share certain characteristics and are entitled to certain rights, merely by virtue of our common humanity." Ideational commitment is the main motivation when entrepreneurs promote norms or ideas because they believe in the ideals and values embodied in the norms, even though the pursuit of the norms may have no effect on their well-being.

Of course, many norm entrepreneurs do not so much act against their interests as they act in accordance with a redefined understanding of their interests. Suffragists, for example, were working on behalf of a coherent conception of women's political interests, but it was not an understanding initially shared by the great majority of women in the world. Women had to be persuaded that it was indeed in their interests to pursue suffrage. Similarly, the Red Cross had to persuade military leaders that protecting the wounded was compatible with their war aims.

Organisational platforms: All norm promoters at the international level need some kind of organisational platform from and through which they promote their norms. Sometimes these platforms are constructed specifically for the purpose of promoting the norm, as are many nongovernmental organisations(NGOs) (such as Greenpeace, the Red Cross, and Transafrica) and the larger transnational advocacy networks of which these NGOs become a part (such as those promoting human rights, environmental norms, and a ban on land mines or those that opposed apartheid in South Africa). Often, however, entrepreneurs work from standing international organisations that have purposes and agendas other than simply promoting one specific norm.

Those other agendas may shape the content of norms promoted by the organisation significantly. The structure of the World Bank has been amply documented to effect the kinds of development norms promulgated from that institution; its organisational structure, the professions from which it recruits, and its relationship with member states and private finance all filter the kinds of norms emerging from it. The UN, similarly, has distinctive structural features that influence the kinds of norms it promulgates about such matters as decolonisation, sovereignty, and humanitarian relief. The tripartite structure of the International Labour Organisation, which includes labour and business as well as states, strongly influences the kinds of norms it promotes and the ways it promotes them. One prominent feature of modern organisations and an important source of influence for international organisations in particular is their use of expertise and information to change the behavior of other actors. Expertise, in turn, usually resides in professionals, and a number of empirical studies document the ways that professional training of bureaucrats in these organisations helps or blocks the promotion of new norms within standing organisations. Peter Haas's study of the cleanup of the Mediterranean shows how ecologists were successful in promoting their norms over others' in part because they were able to persuade governments to create new agencies to deal with the cleanup and to staff those posts with like-minded ecologists.

Studies of the World Bank similarly document a strong role for professional training in filtering the norms that the bank promotes. In this case, the inability to quantify many costs and benefits associated with antipoverty and basic human needs norms created resistance among the many economists staffing the bank, because projects promoting these norms could not be justified on the basis of "good economics.'

Whatever their platform, norm entrepreneurs and the organisations they inhabit usually need to secure the support of state actors to endorse their norms and make norm socialisation a part of their agenda, and different organisational platforms provide different kinds of tools for entrepreneurs to do this. International organisations like the UN and the World Bank, though not tailored to norm promotion, may have the advantage of resources and leverage over weak or developing states they seek to convert to their normative convictions. Networks of NGOs and intergovernmental organisations (IGOs) dealing with powerful states, however, are rarely able to "coerce" agreement to a norm—they must persuade. They must take what is seen as natural or appropriate and convert it into something perceived as wrong or inappropriate.

This process is not necessarily or entirely in the realm of reason, though facts and information may be marshaled to support claims. Affect, empathy, and principled or moral beliefs may also be deeply involved, since the ultimate goal is not to challenge the "truth" of something, but to challenge whether it is good, appropriate, and deserving of praise. In these cases, what the organisational network provides is information and access to important audiences for that information, especially media and decision-makers. In most cases, for an emergent norm to reach a threshold and move toward the second stage, it must become institutionalised in specific sets of international rules and organisations. Since 1948, emergent norms have increasingly become institutionalised in international law, in the rules of multilateral organisations, and in bilateral foreign policies.

Such institutionalisation contributes strongly to the possibility for a norm cascade both by clarifying what, exactly, the norm is and what constitutes violation (often a matter of some disagreement among actors) and by spelling out specific procedures by which norm leaders coordinate disapproval and sanctions for norm breaking. Institutionalisation of norms about biological and chemical weapons, for example, has been essential to coordinating the near universal sanctions on Iraq following the Gulf War and has enabled states to coordinate an invasive inspections regime aimed at securing compliance with those norms.

Institutionalisation is not a necessary condition for a norm cascade, however, and institutionalisation may follow, rather than precede, the initiation of a norm cascade. Women's suffrage was not institutionalised in international rules or organisations prior to the beginning of the norm cascade. The first intergovernmental agency created to deal with women's issues was a regional organisation, the Inter-American Commission of Women (CIM), established in 1928. Although scholars locate the tipping point on women's suffrage around 1930, the norm cascaded in similar ways both in Latin America (where it was institutionalised) and in other places around the world where women's rights were not similarly institutionalised.

Tipping or threshold points: After norm entrepreneurs have persuaded a critical mass of states to become norm leaders and adopt new norms, we can say the norm reaches a threshold or tipping point. Although scholars have provided convincing quantitative empirical support for the idea of a norm tipping point and norm cascades, they have not yet provided a theoretical account for why norm tipping occurs, nor criteria for specifying a priori where, when, and how we would expect it. We propose two tentative hypotheses about what constitutes a "critical mass" and when and where to expect norm tipping. First, although it is not possible to predict exactly how many states must accept a norm to "tip" the process, because states are not equal when it comes to normative weight, empirical studies suggest that norm tipping rarely occurs before one-third of the total states in the system adopt the norm.

In the case of women's suffrage, Francisco Ramirez, Yasemin Soysal, and Suzanne Shanahan place the threshold point in 1930, when twenty states (or approximately one-third of the total states in the system at that time) had accepted women's suffrage. In case of land mines, by May 1997 the number of states supporting the ban on anti-personnel land mines reached 60, or approximately one-third of the total states in the system. After that point, a norm cascade occurred, and 124 states ratified the Ottawa land mine treaty in December 1997.

It also matters which states adopt the norm. Some states are critical to a norm's adoption; others are less so. What constitutes a "critical state" will vary from issue to issue, but one criterion is that critical states are those without which the achievement of the substantive norm goal is compromised. Thus, in the case of land mines, a state that did not produce or use land mines would not have been a critical state. By contrast, the decision in mid-1997 by France and Great Britain, both land mines producers, to support the treaty could well have contributed to the norm cascade that happened in late 1997. Securing support of those same two states was simply essential to producing the norm cascade and near universal acceptance of the first Geneva Convention in Europe 130 years earlier. States may also be "critical" because they have a certain moral stature. For example, the decision of South Africa under Nelson Mandela to support the land mine treaty was very influential, especially with other states in Africa but also globally. Although cascades require support from some critical states, unanimity among them is not essential. For example, after initially supporting the norm of banning land mines, the United States refused to support the treaty, but the norm cascaded nevertheless.

Stage 2: Norm cascades: Up to the tipping point, little normative change occurs without significant domestic movements supporting such change. After the tipping point has been reached, however, a different dynamic begins. More countries begin to adopt new norms more rapidly even without domestic pressure for such change. Empirical studies suggest that, at this point, often an international or regional demonstration effect or "contagion" occurs in which international and transnational norm influences become more important than domestic politics for effecting norm change.

Contagion, however, is too passive a metaphor; we argue that the primary mechanism for promoting norm cascades is an active process of international socialisation intended to induce norm breakers to become norm followers. Kenneth Waltz suggested some of the ways socialisation in occurs: emulation (of heroes), praise (for behavior that conforms to group norms), and ridicule (for deviation). In the context of international politics, socialisation involves diplomatic praise or censure, either bilateral or multilateral, which is reinforced by material sanctions and incentives. States, however, are not the only agents of socialisation. Networks of norm entrepreneurs and international organisations also act as agents of socialisation by pressuring targeted actors to adopt new policies and laws and to ratify treaties and by monitoring compliance with international standards. The International Committee of the Red Cross (ICRC) certainly did not disappear with the signing of the first Geneva Convention.

Instead, the ICRC became its chief socialising agent, helping states to teach the new rules of war to their soldiers, collecting information about violations, and publicising them to pressure violators to conform. Socialisation is thus the dominant mechanism of a norm cascade—themechanism through which norm leaders persuade others to adhere—but what makes socialisation work? What are the motives that induce states opposed to the norm to adhere and adhere quickly? We argue that states comply with norms in stage 2 for reasons that relate to their identities as members of an international society.

Recognition that state identity fundamentally shapes state behavior, and that state identity is, in turn, shaped by the cultural-institutional context within which states act, has been an important contribution of recent norms research. James Fearon similarly argues that one's identity is as a member of a particular social category, and part of the definition of that category is that all members follow certain norms. What happens at the tipping point is that enough states and enough critical states endorse the new norm to redefine appropriate behavior for the identity called "state" or some relevant subset of states (such as a "liberal" state or a European state).

To the degree that states and state elites fashion a political self or identity in relation to the international community, the concept of socialisation suggests that the cumulative effect of many countries in a region adopting new norms "may be analogous to 'peer pressure' among countries." Three possible motivations for responding to such "peer pressure" are legitimation, conformity, and esteem. Scholars have long understood that legitimation is important for states and have recognised the role of international sources of legitimation in shaping state behavior. Claude, for example, described international organisations as "custodians of the seals of international approval and disapproval," and emphasised their crucial role in establishing and assuring adherence to international norms.

Certainly there are costs that come with being labeled a "rogue state" in international interactions, since this entails loss of reputation, trust, and credibility, the presence of which have been amply documented to contribute to Pareto-improving effects from interstate interaction. We argue, though, that states also care about international legitimation because it has become an essential contributor to perceptions of domestic legitimacy held by a state's own citizens. Domestic legitimacy is the belief that existing political institutions are better than other alternatives and therefore deserve obedience.

Increasingly, citizensmake judgments about whether their government is better than alternatives by looking at those alternatives (in the international and regional arena) and by seeing what other people and countries say about their country. Domestic legitimation is obviously important because it promotes compliance with government rules and laws; ruling by force alone is almost impossible. Thus, international legitimation is important insofar as it reflects back on a government's domestic basis of legitimation and consent and thus ultimately on its ability to stay in power. This dynamic was part of the explanation for regime transitions in South Africa, Latin America, and southern Europe.

Conformity and esteem similarly involve evaluative relationships between states and their state "peers." Conformity involves what Robert Axelrod refers to as "social proof"—states comply with norms to demonstrate that they have adapted to the social environment—that they "belong." "By conforming to the actions of those around us, we fulfill a psychological need to be part of a group." Esteem is related to both conformity and legitimacy, but it goes deeper, since it suggests that leaders of states sometimes follow norms because they want others to think well of them, and they want to think well of themselves. Social norms are sustained, in part, by "feelings of embarrassment, anxiety, guilt, and shame that a person suffers at the prospect of violating them."

Fearon has argued that identity is based on those aspects of the self in which an individual has special pride or from which an individual gains self esteem. Thus, the desire to gain or defend one's pride or esteem can explain norm following. In this sense, states care about following norms associated with liberalism because being "liberal states" is part of their identity in the sense of something they take pride in or from which they gain self-esteem. The micro foundations of both the conformity and esteem arguments for individuals are psychological and rest on extensive research on the importance of self-esteem and conformity for individuals. The power of conformity to group norms is so strong in some experimental situations that individuals will make statements that are objectively wrong in order to avoid deviating from group judgments. In situations where the objective reality is ambiguous, individuals are even more likely to turn to "social reality" to form and evaluate their beliefs. Theories of cognitive dissonance may also provide insights into the motivations for norm-conforming behavior. Studies suggest that cognitive dissonance is aroused primarily when people notice that their behavior leads to aversive consequences that cannot be easily rectified. The unpleasant experience of dissonance leads actors to reduce it by changing either their attitudes or their behavior.

We argue that an analog to this exists at the level of the state: state leaders conform to norms in order to avoid the disapproval aroused by norm violation and thus to enhance national esteem (and, as a result, their own self-esteem). It is difficult to generalize to the state level from research on esteem done at the individual level, but norm entrepreneurs frequently target individual state leaders for criticism. Because much norm advocacy involves pointing to discrepancies between words and actions and holding actors personally responsible for averse consequences of their actions, one way to think about norm entrepreneurs is that they provide the information and publicity that provoke cognitive dissonance among norm violators. In the area of human rights a body of empirical research is emerging that suggests that some state leaders care deeply about their international image as human rights violators and make significant policy changes in order to change that image.

Stage 3: Internalisation: At the extreme of a norm cascade, norms may become so widely accepted that they are internalised by actors and achieve a "taken-forgranted" quality that makes conformance with the norm almost automatic. For this reason, internalised norms can be both extremely powerful (because behavior according to the norm is not questioned) and hard to discern (because actors do not seriously consider or discuss whether to conform). Precisely because they are not controversial, however, these norms are often not the centerpiece of political debate and for that reason tend to be ignored by political scientists. Institutionalists in sociology, however, have made many of these most internalised norms the centerpiece of their research program and have done us the service of problematising and "denaturalising" many of the most prominent Western norms that we take for granted—such as those about market exchange, sovereignty, and individualism. Instead of trying to explain variation in state behavior, these scholars are puzzled by the degree of similarity or "isomorphism" among states and societies and how those similarities have increased in recent years. Their explanations for these similarities point to past norm cascades leading to states taking up new responsibilities or endowing individuals with new rights as a matter of course.

Professions often serve as powerful and pervasive agents working to internalize norms among their members. Professional training does more than simply transfer technical knowledge; it actively socialises people to value certain things above others. Doctors are trained to value life above all else. Soldiers are trained to sacrifice life for certain strategic goals. Economists, ecologists, and lawyers all carry different normative biases systematically instilled by their professional training. As state bureaucracies and international organisations have become more and more professionalised over the twentieth century, we should expect to see policy increasingly reflecting the normative biases of the professions that staff decision-making agencies.

A number of empirical studies have already documented a role for highly internalised norms held by professionals determining policy. In addition to the role of economists at the World Bank mentioned earlier, Anne-Marie Burley's work shows a crucial role for legal professional norms in creating the post–World War II political order, and her work with Walter Mattli shows their importance in the European Union. Another powerful and related mechanism contributing to the consolidation and universalisation of norms after a norm cascade may be iterated behavior and habit. Political scientists have understood the power of these mechanisms for years but have not connected them theoretically to norms and social construction debates.

The core of the neofunctionalist argument about integration in Europe, after all, was that frequent interactions among people involving joint work on technical tasks would ultimately create predictability, stability, and habits of trust. As trust became habitual, it would become internalised and internalised trust would, in turn, change affect among the participants. Changed affect meant changed identity and changed norms as empathy and identification with others shifted. Thus, the engine of integration was indirect and evolutionary. Diplomatic tools such as confidence-building measures and track 2 diplomacy may follow a similar logic. Generalised, this argument suggests that routes to normative change may be similarly indirect and evolutionary: procedural changes that create new political processes can lead to gradual and inadvertent normative, ideational, and political convergence.

Which Norms Matter Under What Conditions?

One of the common criticisms of norms research has been that it provides no substantive hypotheses about which norms will be influential in world politics and under what conditions they will be influential. Our review of the literature reveals a number of such hypotheses that could be tested and elabourated in future research.

Legitimation: We argued earlier that an important condition for domestic receptiveness to international norms is a need for international legitimation. If legitimationis a main motivation for normative shifts, we might expect states to endorse international norms during periods of domestic turmoil in which the legitimacy of elites is threatened. If states seek to enhance their reputation or esteem, we would expect states that are insecure about their international status or reputation to embrace new international norms most eagerly and thoroughly. Amy Gurowitz has argued, for example, that Japan has been more open to endorsing international norms about refugees than has Germany because Japan is "insecure" about its international political leadership role. Dana Eyre and Mark Such man similarly argue that developing states may adopt high-tech weaponry out of status concerns rather than from a utilitarian war-fighting calculus.

Prominence: Some domestic norms appear more likely candidates for internationalisation than others. This could be due either to the quality of the norm itself (discussed later) or to the quality of the states promoting the norm. Drawing on natural selection theory, Ann Florini has argued that "prominence" is an important characteristic of norms that are likely to spread through the system. Norms held by states widely viewed as successful and desirable models are thus likely to become prominent and diffuse.

The fact that Western norms are more likely to diffuse internationally would seem to follow from this observation. This fits the pattern of adoption of women's suffrage norms, since almost all the norm leaders were Western states (though the United States and Britain were latecomer norm leaders, not early ones). Jon Elster, however, suggests that prominence should be seen in cultural and economic as well as military terms since there are many examples of countries like Greece and China that were conquered but whose norms were assimilated by their conquerors.

Intrinsic characteristics of the norm: Within norms research, there are several sets of claims that intrinsic qualities of the norm itself determine its influence. We can divide these claims between those stressing the formulation of the norm (its clarity and specificity) and those stressing the substance of the norm and the issues it addresses (its content). Those stressing the form of the norm argue that norms that are clear and specific, rather than ambiguous and complex, and those that have been around for awhile, surviving numerous challenges, are more likely to be effective.

Institutionalisation sociology have also argued that norms making universalistic claims about what is good for all people in all places (such as many Western norms) have more expansive potential than localised and particularistic normative frameworks like those in Bali described by Clifford Geertz. Arguments about which substantive normative claims will be more influential in world politics have varied widely. Work by sociology's institutionalisms suggests that norms about issues congruent with capitalism and liberalism will be particularly powerful, but this formulation is too vague to be useful. Many norms (some of them conflicting) are congruent with liberalism and capitalism, but only a subset of such norms have powerful transnational effects.

John Boli and George Thomas have refined this observation somewhat and argue that five principles are central to world culture: universalism, individualism, voluntaristic authority, rational progress, and world citizenship. By implication they suggest that norms underpinned by these principles will be more successful internationally. Both James Lee Ray and Neta Crawford have argued in a similar vein that there is a long-term trend toward humanising the "other," or "moral progress," that helps to explain both the end of slavery and the end of colonisation and could predict the demise of international war in the future. Margaret Keck and Kathryn Sikkink have advanced more specific claims. They argue that norms involving (1) bodily integrity and prevention of bodily harm for vulnerable or "innocent" groups, especially when a short causal chain exists between cause and effect, and (2) legal equality of opportunity are particularly effective transnationally and cross-culturally. Norm entrepreneurs must speak to aspects of belief systems or life worlds that transcend a specific cultural or political context.

Although notions of bodily harm are culturally interpreted, Keck and Sikkink argue, they also resonate with basic ideas of human dignity common to most cultures. The notion that norms about equality and protecting vulnerable groups from bodily harm will have more transnational resonance than other norms explains why norm campaigns around slavery and women's suffrage succeeded while a similar, powerful temperance campaign organised by many of the same people failed to reach a critical mass or tipping point. It might also explain why norms against drinking or smoking suddenly becamemore powerful when the effects on vulnerable or innocent bystanders of secondhand smoke or fetal alcohol syndrome became more widely known. Arguments that the substantive content of a norm determines whether it will be successful imply that norm evolution has a clear direction if not a final endpoint and suggest that proponents of such arguments support some notion of "historical efficiency."

It moves these norms researchers out of the "history-dependent institutionalism" box that James March and Johan Olsen discuss in this issue into some version of "functional institutionalism." Not all researchers accept functional arguments, however. In his work on the chemical weapons taboo, Richard Price rejects arguments about the intrinsic characteristics of the issue, arguing instead that chemical weapons are not any more terrible than other weapons, and yet they are the only weapons that have been the subject of such a prohibition. Martha Finnemore has also emphasised contradictions among dominant global norms as a barrier to any sort of teleological argument about their effects. Price's recent work on the prohibition of land mines, however, suggests that transnational norm entrepreneurs have successfully used graphic images of bodily harm as a means of mobilising a powerful transnational campaign against these weapons. The speed with which the ban on land mines moved from norm emergence to a norm cascade reinforces the idea that norms prohibiting bodily harm to innocent bystanders are among those most likely to find transnational support.

Adjacency claims or path dependence: The relationship of new normative claims to existing norms may also influence the likeliness of their influence. This is most clearly true for norms within international law, since the power or persuasiveness of a normative claim in law is explicitly tied to the " t" of that claim within existing normative frameworks. Robert Sugden makes a similar argument that "because prominence is largely a matter of common experience . . . the conventions that are best able to spread are those that are most susceptible to analogy. Thus we should find family relationships among conventions.

Political scientists also make arguments about adjacency, precedent, and fit. Price argues that the association of chemical weapons with poison, which had already been prohibited, was important for sustaining the prohibition on chemical weapons. Yet, as Price and others recognize, the meanings of any particular norm and the linkages between existing norms and emergent norms are often not obvious and must be actively constructed by proponents of new norms. Activists work hard to frame their issues in ways that make persuasive connections between existing norms and emergent norms. Opponents of female genital mutilation made little headway, for example, when the practice was called "female circumcision," because male circumcision is often a positively valued practice. However, when they replaced the term *circumcision* with *mutilation* and campaigned under the banner of "violence against women," the issue resonated much more strongly, and the campaign gained adherents. These activists clearly recognised the power of adjacency claims and actively worked to situate their issue in such a way as to make it more difficult to dismiss by tying it to the better-established body of human rights norms.

World time–context: World historical events such as wars or major depressions in the international system can lead to a search for new ideas and norms. Ideas and norms most associated with the losing side of a war or perceived to have caused an economic failure should be at particular risk of being discredited, opening the field for alternatives. This kind of explanation would suggest that the end of the Cold War would be such a period of major normative growth and consolidation, based on the principles of the winning coalition in the "war." Notions of "world time" are also present in the arguments of those who see the current period of globalisations one that promotes dramatic expansion of new norms and creates new opportunities for norm entrepreneurs.

Although norms have always been a part of international life, changes in communication and transportation technologies and increasing global interdependence have led to increased connectedness and, in a way, are leading to the homogenisation of global norms. Although there is still inadequate information to make a conclusive argument, we suggest as an additional hypothesis that the speed of normative change has accelerated substantially in the later part of the twentieth century. If we compare the case of women's suffrage, where norm emergence took eighty years and the norm cascade another forty, to the issue of violence against women, which moved from norm emergence to cascade in less than twenty years, it appears that the speed of normative change is accelerating. The expansion of international organisation (especially with the UN) is contributing to this acceleration process by providing more opportunities to address and negotiate on a broad range of normative issues.

Norms, Rationality, and Strategic Social Construction

The extensive body of empirical research on norms reveals an intimate relationship between norms and rationality. However, there is little good theoretical treatment of this relationship, partly because scholars have tended to counterpose norms to rationality in IR. The opposition of constructivist and "rationalist" arguments that has become widespread in the discipline implies that the issues constructivists study (norms, identities) are not rational and, similarly, that "rationalists" cannot or do not treat norms or identities in their research programs. However, recent theoretical work in rational choice and empirical work on norm entrepreneurs make it abundantlyclear that this fault line is untenableboth empirically and theoretically.

Rational choice theorists have been working on problems related to norm-based behavior for more that two decades now and have begun working on identity problems as well. The fact that rational choice methods have been appropriated in the past by those with a material ontology has tended to obscure the fact that nothing about rational choice requires such an ontology. The utilities of actors could be specified as social or ideational as easily as they can be material. By making different assumptions about social relationships and ideational values, rational choice theorists provide interesting insights into the kinds of normative patterns that may develop and be stable. For example, B. Douglas Bernheim ascribes to actors concern about status and the opinions of others and shows how different patterns of social conformity result, including customs, fads, and subcultures.

Sugden examines the evolution of social conventions and shows how some Nash equilibria are evolutionarily stable in iterated games, whereas others are not, thus yielding certain kinds of social conventions. His analysis, however, finds a large role for "common experience" in determining the "focal points" around which particular conventions will emerge, an argument dovetailing nicely with constructivist arguments about the ways in which social structure and normative context shape the actions of agents and, again, suggesting the need for more theorising about the connection between strategic choice and normative context.

Similarly, empirical research on transnational norm entrepreneurs makes it abundantly clear that these actors are extremely rational and, indeed, very sophisticated in their means–ends calculations about how to achieve their goals. They engage in something we would call "strategic social construction": these actors are making detailed means–ends calculations to maximize their utilities, but the utilities they want to maximize involve changing the other players' utility function in ways that reflect the normative commitments of the norm entrepreneurs. The first half of the process fits nicely in a rational game-theoretic framework. The second half does not.

This suggests that instead of opposing instrumental rationality and social construction we need to find some way to link those processes theoretically. Following Sugden, the editors of this volume make the important observation that what game theorists have called "common knowledge" provides an opening for conversation between rational choice scholars and constructivists, and they further suggest a two-stage division of labour between the frameworks: "Constructivists seek to understand how preferences are formed and knowledge generated, prior to the exercise of instrumental rationality." Although this suggested division of labour captures one possible interaction of the two approaches, it does not exhaust the multiple ways in which norms and rationality interact.

Specifically, this division ignores precisely what the empirical studies reveal—namely, that instrumental rationality and strategic interaction play a significant role in highly politicised social construction of norms, preferences, identities, and common knowledge by norm entrepreneurs in world politics. It ignores the "strategic" character of social construction. One of the consistent features of the empirical research reviewed here is that the common knowledge (or what constructivists would call inter subjective understandings) informing actors' calculations is not static nor is it just "out there" accreted by history and experience in some automatic way like the prominence of Grand Central Station (in Schelling's account) or driving on the left side of the road (in Sugden's account). In many of the most politically salient strategic interactions, it is precisely the changing contours of common knowledge that are the object of the game, at least for some sets of players. Common knowledge about who is a political participant (suffrage), what the rules of war are, and even who is a person (slavery) has been created by strategic actors in highly contested processes that are central to our understanding of politics.

We realize that simply pointing out the complexity of this relationship between norms and rationality is not helpful by itself. We also understand that bracketing segments of a complex process like this one can be a useful way to understand a larger whole. After all, constructivists frequently bracket structure, then agency, to understand their mutual constitution. Our point is simply that processes of social construction and strategic bargaining are deeply intertwined, and pending a better theoretical treatment of this relationship we suggest that, at a minimum, a staged analysis of the relationship between rationality and social context could run either way: one could model rational choice as producing social knowledge as easily as one could model social context as a background for rational choice, depending on the empirical question being researched. Rationality plays a role in virtually all research on norms. Even the institutionalists in sociology, whose work is perhaps most analytically distinct from rational choice, give rationality pride of place in the Weberian world culture that drives behavior and emphasize the ways in which rational action is prescribed and celebrated in that culture.

However, although all these research programs recognize rationality and link norms to rational behavior in important ways, they disagree strongly about the nature of that link. Our point is not that all scholars agree about how to research norms. They do not. Rather, our point is that the fights are not about (or should not be about) whether rationality plays a role in norm-based behavior. The fights are about the nature of the link between rationality and norm-based behavior. By unpacking that connection between rationality and norms we can see more clearly the issues at stake in contemporary research and understand better some of the debates driving it.

Four issues stand out and create broad lines of cleavage and debate among scholars: materialism, utilitarianism, choice, and persuasion. One problem with claims in empirical work that norms are a cause of behavior is that, in fact, such claims do not really tell us very much. There are lots of possible reasons to conform to a norm, and scholars disagree about the motivations they impute to actors in their analyses. One set of disagreements involves the preferences we impute to actors and whether norm-based behavior can be explained by preferences that are entirely material. Certainly, some norm conformance may be driven by material self-interest. Neoliberal institutionalists and regimes scholars have been investigating norms flowing from this type of motivation for many years.

More recently, however, scholars have begun debating the adequacy of an entirely materialist ontology and have emphasised nonmaterial and even other-regarding preferences in their analyses of norm-based behavior. Note, however, that there are no obvious methodological consequences to this particular debate over the specification of preferences, since rational choice can specify a utility function that includes religious, ideological, or altruistic concerns, just as more interpretive accounts could focus on material rather than social facts. Note, too, that frequently heard arguments about whether behavior is norm-based or interest-based miss the point that norm conformance can often be self-interested, depending on how one specifies s interests and the nature of the norm.

Another debate among those studying norms that does, by contrast, have profound methodological and theoretical consequences involves the behavioral logic that scholars believe drives norm-conforming behavior. The behavioral logic underlying the economistic and rational choice approaches to norm analysis is utility maximisation. Actors construct and conform to norms because norms help them get what they want.

An alternative approach to understanding norm conformance is what March and Olsen call the "logic of appropriateness," in which actors internalize roles and rules as scripts to which they conform, not for instrumental reasons—to get what they want—but because they understand the behavior to be good, desirable, and appropriate. Habit, duty, sense of obligation and responsibility as well as principled belief may all be powerful motivators for people and underpin significant episodes of world politics.

The debate over behavioral logics is the focus of both Ruggie's and March and Olsen's articles in this issue and does not require extended treatment here. As those articles make abundantly clear, which logic one invokes to explain behavior has significant methodological and theoretical consequences. Most obviously, the two logics lead one to different sides of the structure-agent debate that has been bubbling through the field for some time. The utilitarian and instrumental approach is entirely agent-driven. It is compatible with rational choice and methodological individualism, which, in turn, have long-standing relationships with realism and liberalism in the field of IR. The logic of appropriateness, however, necessarily has a structure driven component. What channels and directs behavior in this view are components of social structure—norms of behavior, social institutions, and the values, roles, and rules they embody.

Under a logic of appropriateness, notions of duty, responsibility, identity, and obligation (all social constructions) may drive behavior as well as self interest and gain. Theoretically, this logic focuses attention on social construction processes that are not well explained by IR theories in their contemporary incarnations and has led scholars back into political theory writings dealing with the genealogy of morality (Price on Nietzsche), the social construction of rationality (Michael Barnett and Fennimore on Weber), the politics of communication and argumentation (Crawford and Thomas Risse on Aristotle and Habermas), symbolic interaction and the "presentation of self" (Wendt on Meade and Barnett on Goffman), and the origins of individualism and humanitarianism in liberal thought. Methodologically, this group has invoked different kinds of structuration, process tracing, text analysis, and *verstehen.* Unfortunately, debate in the field on this issue has not been over which logic applies to what kinds of actors under what circumstances. Rather, the debate has been over whether a "logic of appropriateness" exists at all or whether one can adequately capture all politically salient normative effects with a utilitarian and instrumental approach. A third issue on which there is disagreement and, we think, some misunderstanding, is the role of choice and its converse, determinism, in norm-based behavior.

For rational choice scholars, actors conform to norms (not surprisingly) out of choice; choices may be constrained, at times highly constrained, but the focus of the analysis is on the choice. Other researchers, however, focus almost exclusively on the way norms are "internalised" in actors, which raises important issues about the locus of causality in norms arguments. When norms become internalised in actors, actors are no longer choosing to conform to them in any meaningful way. For institutionalists in sociology, many norms, including some of the most powerful ones, have been so internalised that we no long think seriously about alternative behaviors. In this view, actors no longer think seriously about whether "the state" is the best or most efficient form of political organisation (it almost certainly is not). They just set up more and more states to the exclusion of other political forms. They no longer think seriously about whether international institutions are the best way to solve international problems (again, a mixed bag). They just set up more and more international institutions.

Institutionalists might argue that "choice" is not a particularly robust analytic tool, since much of the most basic human behavior is not chosen in any meaningful sense. Rather, it is supplied to agents by the larger social and cultural environment. Social structure, not agent choice, institutionalists would argue, is where the real explanatory action lies.

In this understanding, norm conformance driven by a logic of appropriateness starts to look deterministic. Yet, as we survey the norms research that emphasises appropriateness logic in IR, very little of it looks deterministic. Indeed, most of it emphasises the highly contingent and contested nature of normative change and normative influence. We see two reasons for this. First, IR scholars applying a logic of appropriateness in their analysis have never been imperialistic in their claims. The argument has never been that other logics of action do not ever drive behavior; the argument has been that appropriateness is a powerful and important motor of political behavior worthy of investigation. Second, and more important, even within a logic of appropriateness there is often substantial room for agent choice. Actors may face varied and conflicting rules and norms all making claims for different courses of action.

Indeed, most significant political choices are significant and difficult precisely because they involve two or more conflicting claims for action on a decision maker. Actors must choose which rules or norms to follow and which obligations to meet at the expense of others in a given situation, and doing so may involve sophisticated reasoning processes. These processes, however, involve a different kind of reasoning than that of utility maximisation. Actors may ask themselves, "What kind of situation is this?" and "What am I supposed to do now?" rather than "How do I get what I want?" Actors often must choose between very different duties, obligations, rights, and responsibilities with huge social consequences, but understanding the choice depends on an understanding, not of utility maximisation, but of social norms and rules that structure that choice.

A final issue that separates different approaches to norms research is whether and how they treat persuasion. Persuasion is central to most of the empirical case studies about normative influence and change. It is the mission of norm entrepreneurs: they seek to change the utility functions of other players to reflect some new normative commitment. Persuasion is the process by which agent action becomes social structure, ideas become norms, and the subjective becomes the inter subjective.

It is essential to much of the process tracing that scholars are currently doing, yet we have no good way of treating it theoretically. Rational choice can model the ways in which transfers of information may change actor strategies, but changes in underlying preferences cannot be endogenised. Institutionalists in sociology can talk about applying cultural models of action to new situations and the consequent unfolding or elabourating of global culture, but the process by which some models appear compelling and others do not, why some cultural innovations are persuasive and others are not, is not well explained. These approaches thus gloss over this problem in different ways, but persuasion is central to politics of all kinds, and we need a good theoretical apparatus for understanding it.

Looking to other disciplines, we see two types of arguments about persuasion that might be useful in political science: one structural and logical, the other psychological and affective. International legal scholars draw on a complex structure of rules to craft arguments about and adjudicate among competing normative claims. The persuasiveness of a normative claim in law is explicitly tied to the claim within existing normative frameworks; legal arguments are persuasive when they are grounded in precedent, and there are complex rules about the creation of precedent—such as which judgments trump which and how the accretion of judgments is to be aggregated over time. Since normative contestation in law is so explicit and well documented, and since much of contemporary norm politics in the world has a strong legal component, we believe an examination of legal mechanisms for norm selection and dissemination will be instructive for IR scholars.

Approaches in psychology emphasize very different factors in bringing about persuasion. In these arguments both cognition and affect work synergistically to produce changes in attitudes, beliefs, and preferences. Most of this work stresses communicative processes that happen through argumentation, but, unlike the legal approach, logic alone does not dictate the result, since appeals to emotion may well be used to strengthen or undermine logical extensions of norms. German IR scholars, for example, are beginning to apply Habermas's theory of communicative action (which requires empathy) as a means of understanding persuasion, accommodation, and arrival at mutual understandings in international politics.

Debates over these four issues—materialism, utilitarianism, choice, and persuasion —will continue to shape the ways we understand normative influence and normative change in world politics. Our concern here has not been to settle these debates, but to clarify what, exactly, is being debated and what the stakes of the debates are. These are not debates about rationality, although rationality certainly plays a role in all of them. The debates also do not divide norms researchers into two tidy camps. Researchers may marry ideational ontologies with rational choice; they may examine reasoned choice among conflicting "appropriate" behaviors; they may examine highly instrumental and strategic interactions designed to construct new standards of appropriateness, as most studies of norm entrepreneurs do; and they may generally find themselves cross-cut in ways that are refreshing and, we hope, stimulate new kinds of conversations.

Conclusions

The "return" to norms holds immense promise for shaking up the IR research agenda and opening up exciting new avenues for inquiry—and not just because it offers new (or previously forgotten) subject matter to study. More interesting, to our minds, is the way norms research opens up conversations with theoretical traditions that IR scholars have ignored in recent decades. The evaluative and prescriptive character of norms opens the way for a long-overdue conversation with political theory and ethics.

For decades now IR research has been divorced from political theory on the grounds (implicitly, if not explicitly, articulated) that what "is" in the world and what "ought to be" are very different and must be kept separate, both intellectually and in policy. However, contemporary empirical research on norms is aimed precisely at showing how the "ought" becomes the "is." Empirical research documents again and again how people's ideas about what is good and what "should be" in the world become translated into political reality. People with principled commitments have made significant changes in the political landscape: slavery as a legal institution of property rights has been abolished everywhere on the planet for the first time in human history; women, more than half the world's population, have full formal political participation in most states of the world; and though war continues to be a horrible human practice, there is no doubt that it is less horrible as a result of efforts by humanitarians to curb the most awful weapons and practices. At the same time, principled commitments and notions of what "should be" have fueled xenophobic nationalism, fascism, and ethnic cleansing. Understanding where these "oughtness" claims come from, how they are related to one another, which ones will be powerful, and what their implications are for world politics is vital, but it is an inquiry that can only be undertaken at the nexus of political theory and IR.

Similar connections exist between norms research and other fields of study. International law, like philosophy and ethics, has been ignored by IR scholars for decades, yet customary international law *is* norms, and empirical research in IR is, again, demonstrating that these legal norms have powerful behavioral effects. Legal norms are also bound up inextricably with the workings of international institutions, which have been a central focus of virtually all types of IR research in recent years. Further, these legal norms are structured and channel behavior in ways that create precisely the types of patterns political scientists seek to explain. Understanding which norms will become law ("soft" law as well as "hard" law) and how, exactly, compliance with those laws comes about would seem, again, to be a crucial topic of inquiry that lies at the nexus of law and IR.

Micro foundations for norm-based behavior might be improved by paying more attention to studies in psychology, particularly work on the roles of affect, empathy, conformity, and esteem. Like law and philosophy, affect and empathy have been swept under the carpet in recent decades. Ideational phenomena have been treated as "information," which reduces uncertainty or provides new strategies to maximize utilities. The result is politics without passion or principles, which is hardly the politics of the world in which we live. Emotions can be politically dangerous and undesirable in politics; hate, after all, is affect, too. But to pretend that affect and empathy do not exist is to miss fundamental dynamics of political life, and we have tried to suggest how attempts in psychology to wrestle with these issues may be helpful. Finally, we have tried to show how norms research cross-cuts our own discipline in ways that are refreshing and stimulate new conversations.

Scholars are divided, however, about the role that choice plays in norm-based behavior, about what motivates choice, and about the role persuasion plays in normative processes and how to treat it. No school of thought in the discipline is entirely comfortable with its answers to these questions at the moment. We believe this is a good state of affairs, one that will encourage scholars to venture beyond narrow methodological commitments to think more broadly about these issues.

17

Global Environmental Governance: The Post-Johannesburg Agenda

The temptation to draw analogies between domestic and global systems of governance is powerful. The bulk of what we know about effective political decision-making, drawn from daily experience and from the research and analysis of the academic literature, is derived from the national and sub-national level. By contrast, our experience of "effective" global governance decision-making by and for the international community that has a discernable impact on targeted behavior is extremely limited. There is, however, a risk that in seeking to promote effective global governance by replicating at the international level what works well at the domestic level, we will overlook what are fundamental differences between the two systems.

This brief note is in response to a request to explore options for strengthening the "executive" function of global environmental governance. It begins with a quick review of the early philosophical justifications for the executive branch as it has been described in treatises on the role and structure of the state. It then reviews a number of modern constitutions to identify the kinds of functions that have traditionally been assigned to the executive branch in models of domestic governments. A number of basic concepts of governance are extracted from this analysis, including the need to separate, check and balance powers between various branches of government, and the sources of the executive branch's authority and legitimacy. Basic weaknesses in the analogy between domestic and global systems of governance are exposed, focusing, primarily, on the reluctance of sovereign states to cede authority to international institutions. There is, as a result, very little "separation of powers" between states as sovereign rule-makers, and the institutions they create.

The functions and concepts of the executive branch within domestic constitutional frameworks are then compared to the roles and structures of various international organisations, in an effort to identify whether they are necessary, desirable or politically feasible within a system of global environmental governance, and to explore how such a branch could derive both its authority and its legitimacy.

This analysis divides into three brief sections: the first focuses on the use of the term "executive" within global environmental governance to describe operational bodies delegated within treaty regimes to carry out mandates given to them by states parties. These executive committees, councils and bureaus are often appointed by the government delegations, on the basis of constituencies, to represent the Parties as a whole in carrying out the day to day operational functions of the regime. The second section reviews the role of the executive as the administrator of government, in the elabouration, implementation and enforcement of rules established by rule-making bodies. The third section looks at the role of the executive as the head of state, providing overall leadership and policy direction by initiating, validating or overriding rules agreed by the legislative branch.

A number of parallels are found to exist between these executive functions and the roles played, for example, by the international civil service within the secretariats of international environmental agreements, and the implementing agencies that operate the agreements' financial mechanisms. It is stressed, however, that despite this loose functional analogy between domestic and international administrations, their "constitutional" roles are fundamentally different. Rather than checking or balancing the "legislative branch" the role of the executive within the international system is as the servant of the rule makers. Proposals for consolidating these administrative/secretariat functions as part of an effort to improve global environmental governance are briefly reviewed.

Parallels between the domestic system's executive function of "head of state" and positions within the international system are found to be still weaker. International environmental regimes do appoint high-level civil servants who carry titles such as Executive Secretary or

Executive Director. Although these "executives" also serve at the discretion of their "electorate" their appropriate role is to be non-partisan, rather than setting and advancing the agenda of a political majority. Proposals for strengthening the environmental governance by, for example, enhancing the prestige of UNEP Executive Director, or by appointing a High Commissioner for the global environment are briefly reviewed.

Tentative conclusions suggest that the leadership function of the executive, upon which effective domestic governance depends, might best be achieved at the international level by the creation of a position that is separate from the sovereign and bureaucratic constraints of traditional treaty regimes and implementing agencies. Leadership might, for example, be better exercised through the creation of a post of high stature within the international system that would rely upon the independence, expertise and personal character of an individual.

THE ORIGIN AND RATIONALE OF THE EXECUTIVE FUNCTION

The concept of an executive, in terms of the "head of state" is, perhaps, as old as the concept of the state itself. Early "social contract" justifications of the state were based upon on the assumption that without a strong and absolute sovereign, human society would collapse into chaos. The legitimacy of the sovereign, in this early formulation of the modern state, derived from the need of the citizenry for order and safety, rather than divine right. In this sense it provided the earliest articulations of democracy.

The separation and balancing of powers into distinct branches of government arose from a need to check the absolute power granted to the sovereign executive. The division of these powers into three functional branches is, however, a relatively modern concept. Even as the concepts of the executive, legislative and judicial functions emerged they were not necessarily assigned to distinct branches. For example, the key division of powers that followed the English Civil War was only two-fold, between the legislative and the executive branches. The exercise of the judicial function was considered to be an integral part of the executive branch, rather than a third branch. Montesquieu is widely credited for the *trias politica*, proposing a constitutional system that would clearly separate the judicial, executive and legislative powers, institutionalised in distinct branches of government. In this separation, the legislative power lays down general rules of pro-active effect; the executive power executes the rules enacted by the legislature. The judicial power applies and interprets the rules, including by reviewing the constitutionality of actions taken by the other branches. This division of powers has since become the most commonly used in modern constitutional design.

For the purpose of this analysis, States parties to international environmental agreements and similar international organisations will be presumed to perform a function analogous to the legislature, acting through the plenary bodies of these regimes, *e.g.* the "conferences of parties" or the governing bodies of United Nations Environment Programme (UNEP) or the Global Environment Facility (GEF). It must be stressed, again, however, that the analogy is a loose one. The analogy is weak in part because states parties to treaties are themselves sovereign, political units, participating in this system of governance on the basis of a with draw able consent, rather than as officials in an overarching and compulsory constitutional regime. Furthermore, states Parties, unlike legislators, are performing a dual role as both the designers and the main targets of legislation.

In modern domestic constitutions, the functions and powers assigned to the Executive Branch that might be most relevant to this exercise are reflected in these instruments with a remarkable consistency. The Executive is frequently assigned the power to:

- Appoint and dismiss ministers of state
- Initiate some or all kinds of legislation
- Promulgate or veto legislation
- Report annually to the legislature on the state of the nation, and set priorities for the coming year
- Propose and submit to the legislature for approval, an annual budget
- Appoint judges, with the approval of the legislature
- Conduct foreign relations and conclude international treaties

These Executive functions can be divided roughly between those associated with the office of the prime minister, or head of state and those associated with the administration or wider oversight and implementation of the laws. Most constitutions spell out the functions associated with the head of state. Often, but not always, the core executive powers are vested in the office held by an individual. The cabinet, the structure of ministries and the role of the public administration are left to a combination of legislation and executive discretion to design.

EXPLORING THE DETAILS OF THE EXECUTIVE FUNCTION

Before turning to the exercise of comparing the administrative and leadership functions in domestic systems to their potential role in a global system of governance, this analysis looks first at the current use of the term "executive" to describe "delegated functions" in international environmental regimes.

The Delegated Function

Executive committees, governing councils and bureaus created by international environmental agreements and related regimes are established primarily to fill the institutional need to operationalize the will of what can be more than 150 states Parties. In order to enable a large number of Parties to take regular decisions in a more efficient manner, small, representative bodies are elected by and delegated powers from the membership as a whole. For example, the Executive Committee of the Multilateral Fund of the Montreal Protocol was established under that treaty to "develop and monitor the implementation of specific operational policies, guidelines and administrative arrangements".

It performs some functions similar to those identified with the "executive branch" including the development of budgets, and the implementation of policy. But the Executive Committee's membership is composed of "Parties" rather than individuals operating in a function formally distinct from the "legislative" branch of the Conference of Parties. Indeed most executive bodies of this type are formally required to reflect a balanced geographical or developmental representation of the Parties. Their formal legitimacy depends on this representativeness and their formal accountability back to the conference of parties.

Although, in practice, these bodies can develop a degree of functional independence from the plenary bodies that appoint them, it's an independence based on professional and technical discretion, rather than a constitutional separation based on check and balance.

The Administrative Function

In domestic constitutional systems, the executive branch's authority to appoint a cabinet of ministers and its responsibility to ensure that the laws of the land are faithfully executed have given rise to the administrative function, performed by ministers and civil servants. A similar need to support the implementation of agreed rules has led to the establishment of an international civil service that roughly parallels the domestic civil service. In both systems, the civil service derives its legitimacy from its professionalism and its commitment to the underlying legal instruments. Initiatives at civil service reform at both the domestic and the international level have also stressed the need for efficiency and cost effectiveness as an additional standard by which to judge the performance of a public administration.

By contrast, in the international system, the administration function of the "executive" does not check or balance the role of the "legislature" but is, instead, to act as its servant. The chain of command within the international civil service leads to an executive secretary or director, appointed by the parties, rather than to an equivalent of an elected head of state. This function of this executive secretary or director is, in turn, to carry out the duties assigned by the states parties.

The effectiveness of a domestic civil service is greatly enhanced by the role of a coordination mechanism, in the form of a cabinet of ministers. If it were replicable at the international level such a mechanism could be crucial to achieving the kind of "synergies" and "interlinkages" that many have indicated lie at the heart of improving global governance. Much has been written about the institutional and geographical dispersion of the current system of global environmental governance and the need for greater coordination within this system. For example, the split between UNEP administered conventions and those tied more closely to the UNO, or more independent still, continues to frustrate those that would like a more unified administration of these treaties. The pros and cons of these proposals to consolidate treaty secretariats have been well and recently rehearsed as part of the International Environmental Governance process. Institutional distinctiveness is likely to persist as long as the international environmental law continues to be made through autonomous legal instruments made up of different constellations of parties. Geographical dispersion is likely to continue as long as the international institutions continue to rely on the competitive generosity of host countries as a source for infrastructure and other forms of support.

The Leadership Function

Most of the constitutionally assigned functions of the executive branch relevant to this discussion are associated with leadership, in terms of setting agendas, proposing budgets and initiating legislation, and filling positions of importance. In the current, decentralised system of global environmental governance these functions are spread over various regimes in the positions of the heads of secretariats, of agencies and the presiding officers of intergovernmental forums.

As in the administrative function, a strong distinguishing feature between domestic and international executives is the neutrality of the latter. In both parliamentary and presidential constitutional systems, the executive branch serves all its constituents, but specifically advances the policy agenda set by the political majority of the electorate. Heads of international agencies, and heads of diplomatic conferences, by contrast, depend upon a reputation for neutrality and even-handedness for their legitimacy and effectiveness. The primary function of the executive officer, or of a presiding officer of an international environmental institution is to advance and represent the objects and purposes of their constituent instrument. This can sometimes involve the gentle advocacy of positions that run counter to the political majority, and ensuring that the concerns of the politically weak or marginalised are taken into account.

One central characteristic of the head of state function of the Executive Branch, that is key to effective governance at the domestic level, is the authority to convene a cabinet of ministers. A global environmental executive might be placed in a position to convene the administrative heads of the various international bodies with environmental mandates. The executive could represent them within the equivalent of a cabinet convened by a higher executive authority. But as with other initiatives at strengthening global environmental governance, whether it is leadership, rule-making or dispute settlement, the strengthening of environmental governance only answers part of the problem. Strengthening one pillar in the global system (for example, environment) as against another pillar (for example, trade) immediately raises the need for an overarching means of reconciling jurisdictional overlaps and conflicts.

As far back as 1987 there have been calls for the establishment of a new post that voice the concerns of global environment at large that could add to the leadership being provided under existing, individual regimes and institutions. The Experts Group on Environmental Law of the Brundtland Commission recommended the appointment of a UN High Commissioner for Environmental Protection and Sustainable Development. Although the Commission did not itself expressly endorse the proposal it has since been picked up by others. The role of such a High Commissioner differs from proposal to proposal. In some manifestations, the role is more of a quasi-judicial function, an ombudsman for the environment who would receive and seek to address complaints from affected peoples, groups or states, in the manner of an ombudsman. To justify a global profile, a High Commissioner could have special responsibilities for transboundary issues, areas beyond national jurisdiction, as well as for representing the interests of future generations. There are obvious parallels in some of these proposals between an Environmental High Commissioners and the High Commissioners who currently act on behalf of victims of human rights violations and refugees. This suggests a structure that "would allow citizens concerned about environmental protection to circumvent national governments that presently stall on corrective measures." The proposal for a High Commissioner was revived recently, as part of the International Environmental Governance process, and its justification was described by the Norwegian Environment Minister as follows:

> "Overall, environmental questions need to get a higher international profile and I believe that a High Commissioner

for the Environment could help achieving this. This role would in one respect be similar to that of the High Commissioner for Refugees; someone who can cut across bureaucratic and political boundaries when necessary."

The post of the High Commissioner for Human Rights was established by the UN General Assembly in 1993, in order to promote within the system of human rights instruments many of the same goals of systemic reform that have been called for in the area of international environmental law, and that are attributable to the executive function of leadership. The High Commissioner for Human Rights is tasked with, among other things, the coordination of human rights activities in the context of a number of distinct and overlapping legal instruments; engaging in dialogue with governments to remove obstacles to the implementation of human rights laws; and rationalising, adapting, strengthening and streamlining the United Nations machinery in the field of human rights with a view to improving its efficiency and effectiveness.

Such a loose arrangement could provide an opportunity to revive proposals for a leadership position based on the model of the High Commissioner. The GEM's functional model seems to cry out for the kind of catalytic and improvisational role that could be played by an individual who was granted a degree of separation from the formal, statist structures of the treaty-based bodies. While the challenges of negotiating a UNGA resolution along these lines should not be underestimated, it may prove an easier task than maneuvering through the various mandates and institutions of treaty-based bodies. Furthermore a post backed by a direct mandate from the General Assembly may have more freedom to navigate a loosely structured network that includes institutions within and outside the UN system, including those with responsibility for trade, finance and the activities of multinational enterprises. Finally, a High Commissioner might have the ability to respond more directly to the concerns of those most directly affected by pollution and the decline of the natural resource base – the individuals and communities that are still struggling to find an effective voice in global environmental governance.

18

Codification of Law in Modern Continental Europe

Codes and Codifications: An Overview

The legal codes of the modern age served two main functions in civil-law countries. On the one hand, they were the fundamental tool of the trade for legal professionals: Judges, lawyers, public servants, and citizens regarded them as the main source for the cognition of law and as the basic framework of the legal system. This has sometimes led legal scholars to assume, incautiously, that "civil law stands for codification" (Caenegem 1987, 39), even though codes have now lost their central position in contemporary legal systems and no longer characterize the civil-law world.

On the other hand, codes embodied a definite conception of the nature of law and the social function of regulation by law. This is a threefold conception whereby (a) the law consists of a set of general prescriptive sentences forming part of a legal system; (b) a prescriptive sentence is law not by virtue of its content but by virtue of its source, in that the authority of law is identified with the authority of the state's legislative power; and (c) the aim of the law is to guarantee liberty and equality, considered to be necessary conditions of any genuine individual good and of any social justice and welfare.

Once the first modern codifications were completed in the second half of the 18th century this conception began to spread across Europe, and it deeply modified legal methodology and legal knowledge, as well as the way in which officials conceived their own function within the state. This change did not take place all at once, however.

It was the result of a long process that had started at the same time as had the modern natural-law tradition. Moreover, legal scholarship is divided on the course of this change. What conceptual shifts made it possible to understand the law as a codified system of legal provisions, how this assumption modified the general understanding of law, and what its consequences were for the European path to the constitutional state and democracy—all these are still controversial questions.

The ambiguity of the term "code of law" in the "age of codification"—understood here as the period running from the enactment of the Bavarian Civil Code (1756) to the enactment of the Austrian General Civil Code (1811), a period that will be the focus of this chapter—is a first clue to the historical reasons that make modern codification an open question in legal history and legal philosophy. As Diderot and D'Alambert observed in their *Encyclopedie*, the word *code* "means a general presentation of laws; but this name is given to many sorts of presentations that are very different from one another". According to the *Encyclopedie*, this term may refer to (1) collections of Roman law (the Gregorian Code, the Theodosian Code, the Justinianian Code); (2) collections and anthologies of Roman ecclesiastical jurisprudence (the *canons*) and other Church rules and principles (the *Codex canonicum*, the *Codex Gratianiis*, etc.); (3) collections of old and new laws, regulations, writs, edicts, constitutions, ordinances, etc., collected either in a single volume or in a single collection of volumes (the *Code Neron*, the *Corpus Constitutionum Marchicarum*, etc.); (4) collections of statutory provisions that govern an area of the law of the land (the Criminal Code, the Merchant Code, the Civil Code, etc.); (5) treaties of law that include jurisprudential maxims, precedents, regulations, general provisions, principles and other sorts of rules that are relevant to the corresponding legal subject (the *Code de cures*, the *Code des chasses*, etc.).

The boundless variety of codes that were still in effect at the end of the 18th century have often stymied legal scholars looking for a definition of the term code in the modern age. Legal scholars traditionally draw in this regard a distinction between consolidation and codification. Consolidations group existing legal material so as to make it more accessible to professionals; codes strictly understood are bodies of legal rules enforced by authority of the state to replace any preexisting law.

At the same time, codes may have either primary or subsidiary force of law: They include either the law of the land or the law that legal professionals have to apply in only those cases where the law of the land gives no clear answer, under the principle that ius specialis prevails on ius generalis. Both these classifications, however, are surrounded by controversy and show that no definition per genus et differentiam can be assigned to our subject. Codes in a strict sense, such as the French Civil Code of 1804, would typically include preexisting legal material but would do so within a new framework; and subsidiary codes, such as the Prussian General Code of 1794, were in fact promulgated so that they could play a primary role in their respective legal systems, despite their subsidiary status.

It may therefore serve our purposes better if we establish a functional classification of codes of law. From the 18th century to the present day, codes have been designed to present different legal texts and simplify their use, or they have been designed to systematize legal materials so that all legal prescriptions are rationally interconnected, or again they have been designed to set up a new legal system on the basis of a fundamental political decision, so as to support the system's normative authority and the state's cohesion. Modern civil-law codes typically serve all of these purposes. On the contrary, premodern codes serve only the first one, and common-law codes merely aim at simplifying legal information or at rationalising an area of law so as to reduce judicial uncertainty.

Three Discursive Levels

Apart from these definitional problems, it is useful to look at the different discursive levels on which legal codification has traditionally been discussed by legal scholars, since this will help us better clarify the concept of a code in modern legal history.

In particular, legal codification can be considered from the point of view of (1) legislative technique, (2) legal theory, and (3) legal philosophy. It is worth examining these discursive levels separately, even though each of them is closely connected with the others. In fact, if we consider them as a whole, they give us the traditional view of the codification of law in European legal culture, that will come under criticism in this chapter. It is a view still popular among legal scholars as well as among legal practitioners. In particular, legal scholars use this view to emphasize the contrast supposed to exist between common-law systems and civil-law systems, as well as between alternative models on which to base legal training and the administration of justice. Legal practitioners, for their part, typically use it not to describe the structure of statutory legal systems but to justify a solution to a case and to legitimize legal adjudication.

Legislative Technique

As far as discourse on the level of legislative technique is concerned, the age of codification was inspired by three main principles that in the second half of the 18th century were widely upheld by philosophers, legal experts, publicists, civil servants, and "enlightened" sovereigns. Firstly, in keeping with an ancient topos invoked in the Renaissance by T. More, F. Bacon, and T. Campanella, the law ought to be simple: It needs to consist of only a few rules—clear, public, and written—that can be known and understood not only by legal experts but also by its final addressees. Secondly, the law ought to be coherent: It must not admit of alternative solutions to a case and must therefore exclude any legal contradiction. Thirdly, the law ought to be complete: It must regulate all of the cases the courts may be asked to solve and must therefore do away with the need to seek out further sources of law. The code was supposed to be the best means by which to achieve these principles, and so it was supposed to greatly simplify the legal system, guarantee better protection of individual rights, make the outcome of a trial predictable, and subject every person to ordinary law in force within a jurisdiction.

The main argument in favour of codification revolved, in particular, around the problem of the sources of law, a problem that, under the ancient regime, affected both regulation by law and the activity of legal professionals. As concerns the first aspect, the law consisted of a progressive and stratified accumulation of different types of rules drawn from local customs, medieval constitutions, Roman law, canon law, imperial law, royal edicts and ordinances, precedents, expert legal advice, and so on. This variety of sources made it problematic to determine their content and mutual relations, and hence their applicability to the case, which depended on tradition, authority, and territory, and not on deductive reasoning or on any hierarchical relations between legal rules. The criteria for finding the law applicable to the case were not generally fixed: They depended on the subject of the case, the personal status of the parties, the judicial authority that had been asked to decide, and the territory where the case occurred or where the court was located.

As concerns the second aspect, the selection and interpretation of the rules regulating the present case, particularly under Roman law, required forms of non-deductive reasoning that strictly depended on the kind of court, on judicial and doctrinal trends, and on the education of the judges. If one considers, in addition, the lack of unified procedural rules and the central organisation of the judiciary, it follows that the judicial solution of the case "is often felt by its addressees as an arbitrary one" (Svarez 1960, 599).

Franz von Zeiller, the drafter of the Austrian Civil Code of 1811, paradigmatically argued that, If one allows the state's national law to coexist with a foreign law, an old one that in many cases can no longer be applied to current legal matters; if one allows huge amounts of laws to endlessly accumulate, in such a way that even legal experts cannot fully know the law; if judges refer to their own philosophical views in lieu of legal provisions, because they do not know all such provisions or because none of these provisions apply any longer to the case at hand; if a single court and the legal experts confer authority on contradictory statutes, customs, adjudications, doctrinal opinions, and prescriptions (...), then conflict among different laws, doctrinal opinions, and adjudications will enormously increase.

A codified legal system was supposed to overcome all these problems by introducing a new way of drafting and organising legislative provisions, which represented a turning point in the method of regulation by law.

Legal Theory

Where discourse on the level of legal theory is concerned—that is, where the effort is to single out the distinctive features of legal rules, of legal systems, and of legal interpretation—the modern idea of a code is no less revolutionary. According to this idea, the coming into force of a code entails the abrogation of all preexisting law: Codified legal prescriptions become the only source of valid law within the state's territory. In this way, the terms *lex*, *Gesetz*, *loi*, and *legge* (a law or statute) began to merely denote a written legal provision formulated and enforced through the state's legislative authority, in contrast to natural law, Roman law, customary law, precedent, the opinions of legal experts, and so on, which were no longer formally considered autonomous sources of law.

This explains why, in codified legal systems, *all* law is originally considered a system of commands enacted by the sovereign. This gives the sovereign strict control of all legal content and form: Existing legal materials continue as law only if the sovereign *wills* that they still be law. But even where existing materials are so recognised—and hence even when the law's normative *content* seems not to change—such a recognition is not neutral. Existing legal materials assume the *form* of statutory imperatives, and so the various kinds of guidance by law that characterised the ancien regime were drastically reformed. Analogical reasoning, equity (understood as justice or fair dealing), authoritative judicial principles, precedents, jurisprudential maxims, doctrinal opinions, and the like, came to be used as *exceptions* in solving a case. The law was understood to consist only of homogeneous normative entities, *i.e.*, only of prescriptive sentences, and this enables it to be structured as a *legal system*.

This new conception of law and the legal system had important consequences for legal interpretation, too. Legal interpretation was still considered a source of law in 18th-century continental Europe. On the one hand, precedents were assumed by the judiciary to have the force of law (Mohnhaupt 1980, 168). In particular, the courts' constant flow of decisions could acquire a *direct* binding force as customary law, or it would acquire an *indirect* binding force through legal reasoning, in cases where the judge applied the argument from judicial authority in finding the legal source pertinent to the case.

On the other hand, the plurality and indeterminacy of legal sources opened the door to a high degree of discretion in judicial activity, giving rise to the *topos* of "judicial despotism" which characterised Europe's philosophical and political literature in the late 18th century.

The codification of law was considered the means to best suited to overcome these issues. According to the modern codes of the 18th and 19th centuries, precedent has no binding force and so cannot be considered a source of law. Moreover, modern codes would include a detailed regulation of legal interpretation:

They established the way in which to determine their own normative contents. In this way, judicial discretion in legal interpretation was banned by codes. The codes required the judge to interpret codified legal provisions according to their wording understood as the plain expression of the legislator's intent: The judge must *declare* the law, *i.e.*, he is simply required to ascertain its content. In cases of legal indeterminacy, the codes allowed no one other than the legislator to clarify the legislator's own will, even though courts were still allowed to use analogical reasoning to fill legal gaps.

Therefore, the codes seemed to bring into practice two further theoretical *topoi* of the Legal Enlightenment: In the manner of Montesquieu, they reduced the judge to the *bouche de la loi*, that is, to a public official who was strictly obligated to declare the law without interpreting it; and in the manner of Beccaria, they conceived adjudication as the result of a "perfect syllogism" governed by the rules of deductive reasoning. It should be noted, however, that the European science of legislation in the 18th century was perfectly aware that adjudication could not be reduced to deductive reasoning and that modern codification could not eradicate judicial discretion.

In fact, the codification of all areas of law led to an *increased* discretionary power of the judiciary, since general provisions of code law would often replace more detailed forms of regulation. The regulation of legal interpretation introduced by the modern codes simply was aimed at increasing political control on the judiciary by incorporating it in the government of the State.

Legal Philosophy

Where discourse on the level of legal philosophy is concerned—that is, where the problem is to investigate the nature of law and of legal authority—the age of codification is seen as determining the transition from theory to practice in modern natural law. This thesis can be reduced to three main claims as follows.

(1) The three major codes of this era—the Prussian General Code (ALR, 1794), the French Civil Code (or Code Civil, 1804), and the Austrian Civil Code (ABGB, 1811)—positivised the principles of liberty and equality, forming the basis of modern natural law, and drew from them both the rules governing the social and economic activities of citizens.

(2) In this sense, the codification of the natural-law principles at the beginning of the 19th century marked the first step toward the liberal state and toward modern constitutionalism in Europe. Once transformed into a set of positive legal prescriptions, the principles of liberty and equality would govern not only the behaviour of citizens but also the activity of officials and public administrators in general, who would themselves be subject to the law. The next step in this process was to make law subject to legislative power: Once the positive law is understood to bind not only its final addressees but also the judiciary and the public administration, the principles of natural law assume the status of *fundamental rights*, ones that citizens can claim against the state, too. This would set the political system on the road to democracy. On the one hand, in order for citizens to be free and equal, there must be general rules that guide them, and these must be clear, coherent, and public. On the other hand, these rules can ensure freedom and equality only if their content is determined by the citizens themselves, that is, only if they form part of a democratic political system. The codification of law, then, can be considered a fundamental phase in the historical process that led Europe to constitutionalism, democracy, and the rule of law.

(3) The codification phase was a process in its own turn, involving successive evolutionary stages embodied in the three codes previously considered. Thus, on this view, the ALR, the Code Civil, and the ABGB mark the three main stages in the evolution of the European legal systems from the sources pluralism of the ancien regime to the legislative monism of the 19th century (Conrad 1961). The first stage is represented, on this view, by the Prussian General Code, which wrought the sources pluralism

of the Brandenburg-Prussian territories into a unified legal system wholly dependent on the sovereign's will. But this code did not introduce, as the basis of regulation by law, the concept of a "unified legal personality," understood as the basis on which each individual in the state is equally capable of exercising rights and being bound by duties. Instead, the code remained anchored to the personal differences characterising the rank society of the ancien regime. The second stage would then be represented by the French Civil Code, which introduced for the first time the legal device of a unified legal personality. In this way, the French codification radically simplified the structure of the legal system, thereby making possible the development of a modern civil society based on individual autonomy. This code, however, established the primacy of codified legal directives not only over all other legal sources but also over individual rights, which would be legally binding only insofar as they were acknowledged by the legislator through the code. The third and final stage is represented by the Austrian General Civil Code (1811), which recognised in principle the primacy of individual rights over codified legal prescriptions, thus recognising the existence of a private legal sphere that cannot be violated by the state or by any other person.

Natural Law and Codification

This interpretation of the age of codification has been very influential and is worth examining here in greater detail. To begin with, one needs to consider in what sense the code was regarded, in late 18th century Europe, as a way to positivize natural law and turn its principles into directives by which to guide behaviour in society. In fact, the relation between natural law and legislation was the subject of much controversy in the age of codification and can be broken down into three main models, corresponding to alternative conceptions of code law in general.

Bibliography

Adams, G. Legislative Effects of Single-Member vs. Multi-Member, 1996.

Annino, A. ed. *Historia de las elecciones en Iberoamérica*, siglo XIX. Mexico, Fondo de Cultura Económica, 1995.

Applause, At Last, For Desalination Plant, The Tampa Tribune, 2007.

Baker, K. M. ed. *The Old Regime and the French Revolution*. Chicago, University of Chicago Press, 1987.

Benoit, K. District Magnitude, Electoral Formula, and the Number of Parties, *European Journal of Political Research*, 39, 203-224, 2001.

Bernard Gilland "World population and food supply can food production keep pace with population growth in the next half-century?" Food Policy 27, 2002.

Bishop, C. *History of Elections in the American Colonies*. New York, Columbia College, 1983.

Boix, C. Setting the Rules of the Game: the Choice of Electoral Systems in Advanced Democracies, *American Political Science Review* 93, 609-24, 1999.

Brams, S., Fishburn, P. Approval Voting, *American Political Science Review* 72, 3, 831-57, 1978.

Brucker, G. *Renaissance Florence*. Berkeley, University of California Press, 1983.

Cadart, J. *Le régime electoral des États Généraux de 1789 et ses origins (1302-1614)*. Paris, Librairie du Recueil Sirey, 1952.

Calabrese, S. Multi- member District Congressional Elections, *Legislative Studies Quarterly*, 25, 4, 611-643, 2000.

Campbell, P. *French Electoral Systems and Elections Since 1789*. Hamden, CT, Archon Books, 1965.

Colomer, J. M. *Political Institutions*. Oxford, Oxford University Press, 2001.

Ecological Footprint Atlas, Global Footprint Network, 2009.

Feed the world? We are fighting a losing battle, UN admits". The Guardian, 2008.

Flores, N. *A History of One-Winner Districts for Congress*. Thesis at Stanford University, 2000.

Global food crisis looms as climate change and population growth strip fertile land". Guardian.co.uk. August 31, 2007.

Golosov, G. Electoral Systems and Party Formation in Russia: A Cross-Regional Analysis, *Comparative Political Studies*, 36, 8, 912-935, 2003.

Graham, R. *Patronage and Politics in Nineteenth-Century Brazil*. Stanford, Stanford University Press, 1990.

Greene, J. 1993. Colonial Political Culture. In: Cooke, J. (Ed.), *Encyclopedia of the North American Colonies*. New York, Charles Scribbers Sons, vol. 2, 265-286, 1993.

Hoag, C., Hallett, G. *Proportional Representation*. New York, Macmillan, 1936.

Hopfenberg, Russell and Pimentel, David, "Human Population Numbers as a Function of Food Supply", *Environment, Development and Sustainability*, vol. 3, no. 1, 2001.

Hyde, J. K. *Society and Politics in Medieval Italy.* New York, St Martin's., 1973.

J. N. Hays "*The burdens of disease: epidemics and human response in western history.*". p 72, 1998.

Klain, M. A New Look at the Constituencies: The Need for a Recount and a Reappraisal, *American Political Science Review*, 49, 4, 1105-1119, 1955.

LaPalombara, J., Weiner, M. (Eds.), *Political Parties and Political Development*. Princeton, Princeton University Press, 1966.

Leading geneticist Steve Jones says human evolution is over, The Times, October 7, 2008.

Lehoucq, F. Electoral Fraud, Causes, Type, and Consequences, *Annual Review of Political Science*, 6, 233-256, 2003.

Mozaffar, S. Africa: Electoral Systems in Emerging Democracies. In: Colomer, J. (Ed.), *Handbook of Electoral System Choice*. London, Palgrave-Macmillan, 2004.

Mozaffar, S., Vengroff, R. A Whole System Approach to the Choice of Electoral Rules in Democratizing Countries: Senegal in Comparative Perspective, *Electoral Studies* 21, 601-616, 2002.

OGorman, F. *Voters, Patrons, and Parties. The Unreformed Electoral System of Hanoverian England, 1734-1832*. Oxford, Clarendon, 1989.

One sixth of humanity undernourished - more than ever before. Food and Agriculture Organization of the United Nations, 2009.

Phillips, J. *Electoral Behavior in Unreformed England. Plumpers, Splitters, and Straights*. Princeton, Princeton University Press, 1992.

Pole, J. *Political Representation in England and the Origins of the American Republic*. Berkeley, University of California Press, 1971.

Qualified-Majority Rule, *Journal of Interdisciplinary History*, 29, 1, 1- 22.

Ron Nielsen, *The Little Green Handbook: Seven Trends Shaping the Future of Our Planet*, Picador, New York, 2006.

United Nations Population Division Home Page, United Nations Department of Economic and Social Affairs, 1897.

US Census Bureau estimates and news release.of AUG. 14, 2008.

Voting in Practice?, *American Journal of Political Science* 28, 722-738.

Webber C, Wildavsky A. 1986. *A History of Taxation and Expenditure in the Western World*. New York: Simon and Schuster Weber E. 1976. *Peasants into Frenchmen: The Modernization of Rural France 1870–1914*.

Wendt A. *Social Theory of International Politics*. New York: Cambridge Univ. Press Zacher M. The territorial integrity norm: international boundaries and the use of force. *Int. Organ.* 55:215–50, 2001.

Zolberg A. Strategic interactions and the formation of modern states: France and England. *Int. Soc. Sci. J.* 32:687–716, 1980.

Zupko R. 1977. *British Weights and Measures*. Madison: Univ. Wisc. Press, 1977.